BEYOND THE WORLD BANK

BEYOND THE WORLD BANK

The Fight for Universal Social Protection in the Global South

Matthew Greenslade

BLOOMSBURY ACADEMIC
LONDON • NEW YORK • OXFORD • NEW DELHI • SYDNEY

BLOOMSBURY ACADEMIC

Bloomsbury Publishing Plc, 50 Bedford Square, London, WC1B 3DP, UK
Bloomsbury Publishing Inc, 1359 Broadway, New York, NY 10018, USA
Bloomsbury Publishing Ireland, 29 Earlsfort Terrace, Dublin 2, D02 AY28, Ireland

BLOOMSBURY, BLOOMSBURY ACADEMIC and the Diana logo are trademarks of
Bloomsbury Publishing Plc

First published in Great Britain 2026

Copyright © Matthew Greenslade, 2026

Matthew Greenslade has asserted his right under the Copyright, Designs and Patents Act,
1988, to be identified as Author of this work.

For legal purposes the Acknowledgements on p. 239 constitute an extension
of this copyright page.

Cover design by Grace Ridge
Cover images: Zhenia, Victoria Guzeeva and Good Studio via Adobe Stock

This work is published open access subject to a Creative Commons Attribution-
NonCommercial-NoDerivatives 4.0 International licence (CC BY-NC-ND 4.0,
https://creativecommons.org/licenses/by-nc-nd/4.0/). You may re-use, distribute,
and reproduce this work in any medium for non-commercial purposes, provided
you give attribution to the copyright holder and the publisher and provide a link
to the Creative Commons license.

Bloomsbury Publishing Plc does not have any control over, or responsibility for, any third-
party websites referred to or in this book. All internet addresses given in this book were
correct at the time of going to press. The author and publisher regret any inconvenience
caused if addresses have changed or sites have ceased to exist, but can accept no
responsibility for any such changes.

A catalogue record for this book is available from the British Library.

Library of Congress Cataloging-in-Publication Data available

ISBN: HB: 978-1-3505-0881-1
PB: 978-1-3505-0882-8
ePDF: 978-1-3505-0883-5
eBook: 978-1-3505-0884-2

Typeset by Deanta Global Publishing Services, Chennai, India
Printed and bound in Great Britain

For product safety related questions contact productsafety@bloomsbury.com.

To find out more about our authors and books visit www.bloomsbury.com
and sign up for our newsletters.

To all of those who, unnoticed and uncelebrated, are helping to bring universal, rights-based social protection to the world

CONTENTS

Definition of social protection used in this book, also known as 'social security'	ix
Glossary and abbreviations	x
Foreword	xiii

INTRODUCTION	1
Chapter 1 LONDON: LISTENING TO AN ECONOMIST FROM MALAWI	5
Chapter 2 PARAGUAY: LEARNING FROM THE ENXET	17
Chapter 3 FIJI: AN ADDICTION TO SUGAR	29
Chapter 4 CHILE AND THE DEVELOPMENT OF THE PROXY MEANS TEST	37
Chapter 5 INDONESIA: HOW TO HELP A QUARTER OF A BILLION PEOPLE	53
Chapter 6 ISTANBUL: THE WORLD BANK'S LOVE FOR CONDITIONAL CASH TRANSFERS	61
Chapter 7 UGANDA: IN THE HEART OF AFRICA	71
Chapter 8 SUPPORT THE POOR BUT MAKE THEM WORK FOR IT	83
Chapter 9 A MEETING IN GENEVA: THE ADVANCE OF UNIVERSALITY	91
Chapter 10 NEPAL: MAOISM AND THE MYTH OF UNAFFORDABILITY	105
Chapter 11 MAURITIUS, ZANZIBAR AND KENYA: EAST AFRICA TAKES CONTROL	117

Chapter 12
AND THEN THINGS WENT SILLY: SOCIAL REGISTRIES 129

Chapter 13
OTHER ARENAS IN ASIA AND THE ARABIAN PENINSULA 139

Chapter 14
IT'S FULL OF INTELLIGENT PEOPLE, SO WHY DOES THE WORLD BANK DO IT? 149

Chapter 15
WINNING THE BATTLE FOR UNIVERSALITY 163

AFTERWORD 179

Annex 183
Notes 185
Bibliography 221
Acknowledgements 239
Index 241

DEFINITION OF SOCIAL PROTECTION USED IN THIS
BOOK, ALSO KNOWN AS 'SOCIAL SECURITY'

Social Protection System

Tax-financed schemes *Paid for out of government revenue* Tax-financed benefits to specific groups such as children, persons with disabilities, older people, people that are unemployed or 'the poor'. Can be universal or means-tested/poverty-targeted. May also be in-kind transfers e.g. food .	**Contributory schemes** *Paid for by contributions from employees and employers* Social insurance or private account schemes for individuals, linked to illness, injury, disability, unemployment or old age, with usually mandatory contributions. Also, voluntary contributory schemes managed by the private sector.

Social protection is defined in this book as the benefit system, also referred to as 'social security', but note that definitions vary across organizations. For example, social care can be included, as can healthcare and labour market policies such as training. The narrower definition is used here for clarity. Definitions by organization can be found at https://socialprotection.org/learn/glossary/what-is-social-protection. But beware, this may lead to confusion: there are as many definitions of social protection as there are organizations defining it!

GLOSSARY AND ABBREVIATIONS[1]

ADB. Asian Development Bank.

AusAID. Australian Agency for International Development.

Benefitting from social protection including members of recipients' households.

Bilateral donors. Individual country governments providing official development assistance or aid.

Cash transfers. See tax-financed social protection.

Community-based targeting. A method to select eligible households through the assessment of a selected team of community members and leaders. Often used in combination with proxy means testing.

Comprehensive, multi-tiered social protection/social security system. Combination of tax-financed and contributory programmes that, together, enable all individuals in the population to address the risks and shocks experienced across the Lifecycle.

Conditional cash transfers. Transfers of cash to recipients on condition they undertake specific behaviours, for example that children attend school or that parents attend primary health centres.

Contributory social protection. Schemes financed by contributions from employees and employers and paid out in the event of contingencies such as illness, injury, disability, unemployment or most commonly old age.

CSO. Civil society organization.

Development Pathways. The British-Kenyan consultancy company Stephen Kidd set up with Richard Chirchir, Sandra Kidd and others.

DFID. Department for International Development, Government of United Kingdom. DFID merged with the Foreign and Commonwealth Office to form the Foreign Commonwealth and Development Office in 2020.

Donor. Government or international organization, including the World Bank, transferring money or other resources to a government or organization within a low- or middle-income country. Resources from the World Bank are usually in the form of loans rather than grants.

Formal labour market. The regulated part of the labour market where taxes on income and contributions are paid.

GIZ. Deutsche Gesellschaft für Internationale Zusammenarbeit. The German Federal Enterprise for International Cooperation. Acts as a delivery agent for much of Germany's development assistance.

ILO. International Labour Organization. Part of the United Nations system.

IMF. The International Monetary Fund.

Informal labour market. The unregulated part of the labour market where, typically, taxes on income and contributions are not paid.

INGOs. International non-governmental organizations.

Irish Aid. Government of Ireland's development cooperation programme.

Means testing. A mechanism for identifying those eligible for social protection schemes who live below a certain welfare level. Defined here to include poverty targeting.

NGOs. Non-governmental organizations.

OECD. Organisation for Economic Cooperation and Development.

PKH. Program Keluarga Harapan, a conditional cash transfer programme in Indonesia.

Poverty targeting. Targeting programme support below a specified poverty level.

Productive safety net. Social protection programme containing workfare plus unconditional cash transfers for households without labour capacity.

Proxy means testing. A method to identify households eligible for programmes by estimating whether they are living in poverty using non-income, observable household characteristics such as the material a dwelling is made from, whether a household owns livestock or the presence of household utilities such as televisions or refrigerators. Often used in combination with community-based targeting, it is used because a household's welfare level, typically measured by income in higher income countries, can be difficult to measure directly in less formal environments, where there is little documentation.

Public works programmes. Programmes that create employment at the same time as producing or maintaining assets or services that contribute to the public good, typically infrastructure. May have social protection or more general employment creation objectives. Where they have social protection objectives and are poverty-targeted, this is referred to as 'workfare'.

Recipients. Those directly receiving transfers from social protection programmes.

Safety nets. See social safety nets.

SAMS. South American Missionary Society. Part of the Anglican Church.

Single registry. A digital store of information on individuals and families benefitting from social protection programmes.

Social assistance. See tax-financed social protection.

Social insurance. Publicly run contributory schemes providing support in the event of contingencies such as illness, injury, disability, unemployment and old age, which include an element of solidarity.

Social protection. The benefit system, comprising tax-financed benefits and benefits paid for through contributions. As defined in this book, synonymous with social security. Can be defined more broadly to include, for example, social care, healthcare and labour market policies such as training, but defined more narrowly here.

Social registry. Store of information on households used for poverty targeting programmes, usually through proxy means testing.

Social safety nets. Poverty-targeted tax-financed social protection programmes. Often used by the World Bank, though defined by the World Bank to include universal programmes.

Social security. See social protection. Can be defined as, for example, synonymous with social insurance, but defined more broadly here.

Social transfers. See tax-financed social protection.

Tax-financed social protection. Benefit schemes paid for by governments, rather than through contributions. Sometimes referred to as 'non-contributory', though this is misleading as people contribute through taxes. May also be referred to as cash transfers, social assistance or social transfers. Can include in-kind benefits such as food.

UN. United Nations.

UNDP. United Nations Development Programme. Part of the United Nations system.

UNICEF. United Nations Children's Fund. Part of the United Nations system.

Universal lifecycle social protection scheme. Tax-financed social protection scheme providing support to a group in the population, such as children, persons with disabilities or older people, regardless of their level of income.

WFP. World Food Programme. Part of the United Nations system.

Workfare. Poverty-targeted social protection programmes that require recipients to work in return for benefits. A type of public works.

FOREWORD

What do you do when you believe that most of the money that the international community invest through the World Bank in direct poverty reduction does not reach the intended beneficiaries? What if, in some respects, it undermines the long-term objective of reducing poverty and building trust in government actions and cohesive societies? You call for a change in World Bank policies of course. You call loudly.

But the task is not easy, because the issues can sound technical and complicated and only of interest to specialists. And you are challenging the expertise and authority of the World Bank, one of the most influential international institutions in the world, which has strong muscles, far stronger than the more well-known United Nations system.

What is to be done? You can investigate the issue of course, publish research, present reports at webinars and conferences and engage in dialogue with decision-makers. Many of us have done so, and we will continue to do so. You can also do what Matthew Greenslade has done in this book: tell a story.

This is a story about some of the people who have engaged and are continuing to engage in this policy debate: how and why they acted at different points in time and in a range of different places. It takes us to Fiji, Uganda, Indonesia, Nepal and many other places where decisions are being taken on how to design social protection systems delivering benefits to people in the population that need them. The World Bank has been pushing for poverty targeting in social protection programmes while other stakeholders argue for more universal solutions, because poverty targeting comes at a price, as you will see.

The life and work of Stephen Kidd is the common thread, but we also meet other people, including those at the forefront in the Global South. We see how ideas and policies are developed and spread and how the dynamics between government officials and non-state actors, including the World Bank, play out in concrete situations.

It is a fascinating read. I believe the book is relevant to anyone interested in how international development cooperation is carried out in practice. First and foremost, the book conveys a powerful message about the need for the World Bank to change course. And there are successes to inspire us and give us hope. Matthew Greenslade writes that this is a story that needs to be told. I could add, it is a story that needs to be read.

Gunnel Axelsson Nycander
Act Church of Sweden

Act Church of Sweden provided funding for this book to be open access.

INTRODUCTION

This is a story about a man, Stephen Kidd, who has joined with others to take on one of the most powerful institutions in the world, the World Bank. The collaboration he has been a part of includes the United Nations, non-governmental organizations (NGOs), academics and government officials and ministers in low- and middle-income countries. It sits on one side of an argument about the part of government policy known as social protection. The World Bank sits on the other.

Social protection is social security, put in the language of international development. It is the benefit system that catches people 'from the cradle to the grave', as William Beveridge, the father of the welfare state in the UK, described it. Social protection is one of the pillars of the welfare state that higher-income countries take for granted and is regarded by the United Nations as a basic human right.[1]

In the Global North, the benefit system steps in when people are most vulnerable: when they are in their childhood or old or have a disability, or when they lose their job.[2] Governments invest in it because they gain as well: social protection invests in the future labour supply and supports workers as they move from declining industries to new ones. And, done well, it gives everyone a stake in their societies and economies, reducing inequality which can strengthen national unity and economic growth.

Social protection systems do similar things in low- and middle-income countries, albeit in less wealthy contexts. Or they do if they are up and running. They allow people, including those in the workforce, to eat, to survive and develop physically and mentally. They also allow people to start improving their lives, by paying for a bus ride to a health clinic or for a uniform or textbooks for school. And they help women and girls who suffer poverty disproportionately across the world, including by reducing domestic violence.[3] And they can reduce the risk of social discord, even conflict. This is important in low- and middle-income countries, as it is elsewhere, many of which are dealing with the colonial legacy of ethnic and political division.

And there is another benefit, perhaps the most important of all. Social protection helps protect people against another legacy of the Global North, the climate crisis. By providing a basic income, it means people do not have to sell their tools and livestock to buy food after a flood or drought, reducing the need for relatively ineffective humanitarian support. It also reduces dependence on unsustainable practices like overgrazing or forest clearing and protects people as economies transition to lower-carbon jobs. One other impact which is important in the light of recent history: social protection can respond quickly to pandemics.

Social protection does not act alone: it is one part of social policy, which includes health and education, and one part of the wider government. But it is an important part and is often underinvested in. There are 3.8 billion people, just under half the world's population, that have no access to social protection at all, including the vast majority of people in the poorest countries.[4] So, this is an area worthy of our attention.

The World Bank, which currently provides most donor financing for social protection, knows all of this.[5] It has played an active role for decades in advocating for social protection, in compiling evidence of its impact and lending money to governments in low- and middle-income countries to fund social protection programmes. This is not a story about neglect. This is a story about *how* social protection is done. Because the design of social protection programmes is important. It can determine whether they are a poor fit in countries and are short-lived. Or whether programmes are popular and well-funded and contribute to a system that helps millions and supports national unity, stability and growth over the long term. Design can be the difference between the brief blossoming of a donor-funded development programme and real, lasting change.

This is also a story about control, about who decides what happens in our world. There is much heated discussion among people from the Global North, working for organizations in international development, about the right way to do things. But there are thousands – millions – of other, relatively low-paid people in low- and middle-income countries, working for governments, local NGOs and in communities, who are eminently capable – usually far more capable – of choosing ways of doing things that fit with local politics and will last. Where do they fit into these arguments? The truth is their voices are too often drowned out. This is a problem, and the subject of this story.

This is not an argument against international aid, but about it being done in the right way. It is about supporting local populations appropriately and not seeking to apply technical, top-down development models, which can undermine local democracy. Nor is this a book about heroes from the Global North. Where they do exist, heroes tend to be from low- and middle-income countries. They are the people that do not get in the media in the North, those in governments, local NGOs and communities and in academia, that stand up and do the right thing for their fellow citizens. A few of them are highlighted in this story, but there are innumerable others. They are people that, if they are lucky, are supported by allies in the North who stand in solidarity with them. This is a story about someone who is, arguably, one such ally and his collaborators.

I witnessed parts of this story first-hand, working with Stephen Kidd, the focus of this book, in the UK government and outside. Stephen is the focus of this book because he has been at the forefront of global opposition to the World Bank on social protection for a long time, with others and because his is a story I am able to tell. I have known him for twenty years, from when we both joined the UK Department for International Development (DFID) in its heyday in the early 2000s. From our first meeting, I have watched Stephen battle for what he believes in and at times wondered what drives him. Writing this book has been an opportunity to find out.

The World Bank, and Stephen and other's opposition to it, is the subject of this story because the World Bank is an institution that wields significant influence. It is a flagship of the Global North's support to development in low- and middle-income countries and helps to finance social protection programmes covering hundreds of millions of people.[6] Even then, it is not the most important actor in the world of social protection. National governments that represent and look out for the interests of the people will always be that; it is they that build social protection systems for the long term. But the World Bank has significant influence, and those helping to fund it, along with those resident in low- and middle-income countries, need to know what the World Bank is getting wrong.

My hope is that telling Stephen's story, a human story, bringing in parts of his event-filled earlier life and others he has worked with, will do three things: open a world that is far too hidden, bring alive what it takes to challenge a global institution, and provide readers with hope and inspiration. There is a good deal of documentation on the recent history of social protection, but this is not an academic history or a comprehensive record, though such books are starting to emerge.[7] Rather, it is a description of a selection of events in a selection of countries. It is a story then, but one that I believe reveals wider truths. A lot is based on Stephen's memory and my own viewpoint, and a personal diary from countries where I have worked, such as Uganda, Nepal and Kenya. As a result, it is a view from the Global North. But others at the forefront of the battle in low- and middle-income countries have been interviewed and tell their side of things.

Many people, organizations and countries that have done important work on social protection and in challenging the World Bank are not included, to allow this to be a story rather than a long list of names. Importantly, government officials are almost completely absent from those that have been interviewed. They are not at liberty to criticize the World Bank openly due to the resources and power of that organization. Nor have I interviewed World Bank staff, who are all too well represented in countless documents, books and blogs, many of which are in the bibliography at the back of this book. I will leave others to write the book that includes interviews with World Bank staff and not government officials. This book is to correct, not add to, what seems a clear imbalance in exposure of these two groups. Beyond that, any obvious omissions are sincerely apologized for. But my hope, and belief, is that these do not affect the truth of the messages in this book.

I know many will disagree with parts of this story, which is arranged in chapters that are broadly chronological, though they can be read in any order. Some may disagree with all of it. And I know the World Bank has done good things in low- and middle-income countries, including in social protection. But I would assert that it has too often got things wrong by trying to impose a particular social protection model on the world and in doing so may be holding back progress towards comprehensive systems in some countries for years, even decades. Stephen for his part has both opponents and loyal friends and allies, as is the lot of someone with a clear vision. But he has got a significant thing in his favour. He has been on the right side of the argument on social protection for years, as have his collaborators. And he has led from the front, often being the first to put his head above the parapet. And this is confronting a big institution with a lot of power. So, it has taken guts. And it is in an area that affects the lives of many hundreds of millions. So, it is a story that needs to be told.

Chapter 1

LONDON

LISTENING TO AN ECONOMIST FROM MALAWI

Entebbe

The Imperial Botanical Hotel in Entebbe sits on the edge of Lake Victoria. On 31 July 2019, Stephen Kidd sat on one side of a training room in the hotel grounds, checking endless emails. A colleague was talking to the forty or so Ugandan government officials that were sitting around their tables, learning about social protection in the week-long course that a number of us were helping to deliver. We were working for Development Pathways, the British-Kenyan consultancy company of fifty or so staff which Stephen heads. I sat beside Stephen as he showed me an email from the Social Protection Secretariat in the Government of Kenya. It said that the government's universal pension was under attack. The World Bank had released a paper saying that the benefit was wasting money because it was going to those that did not need it. The pension had been deliberately designed as a universal benefit, going to all older people in Kenya, not just to the poorest. But in World Bank language, money was 'leaking' to the non-poor. To make matters worse, the Kenyan press had picked up the story. A headline in the Kenya Standard read, 'Cash for elderly going to the rich, says World Bank.'

The World Bank's line of attack was based on the argument that scarce resources should only go to those most in need. And it sounds reasonable enough, on the face of it. But delivering a pension, or any benefit that only goes to the poor, is hard to do. This is true in *developed* countries, with all the data and information they have at their disposal. It is very hard in Kenya. It is trying to distinguish between a very poor household and a fractionally less poor household, in a context where the vast majority are living on low incomes. Added to this, incomes among the poor, unregulated and diverse as they commonly are, are changing constantly. The whole exercise can become akin to spinning a roulette wheel. So, why did the World Bank in Kenya, comprising intelligent and decent human beings, think otherwise? Because, like the World Bank elsewhere, it was invested in poverty targeting social protection programmes. This is on the tax-financed, as opposed to contributory, side of the social protection system. It was invested in poverty targeting, and still is.

Stephen knew time was limited. With a portfolio of US$29.5 billion in social protection financing, mainly loans, covering 880 million people, and investments in other sectors, the World Bank is big enough to put pressure on governments that need its resources.[1] The Government of Kenya had introduced its universal pension the year before the training course, in 2018, for a million people seventy years of age and over, building on a scheme aimed at the poor that was already in place. It was their first social protection programme with universal coverage, and they were proud of it. They had witnessed the disruption that poverty targeting caused within their communities. But the universal pension went against the poverty targeting model that the World Bank had worked with the government on for a number of years, with other donors such as DFID, and the World Bank was not happy.[2] It did not have as much leverage as it has elsewhere, because the Kenyan government was paying for the pension itself without donor support. But the World Bank had its analytical resources. Hence the paper that the government had forwarded to Stephen and which he went through now at speed.

Within a couple of hours, Stephen had sent an email back to the Kenyan government, observing that much of the analysis in the paper was misleading, even wrong.[3] Stephen also reiterated the point he had made many times before, that poverty targeting made no sense in a country where 80 per cent of the population lived on less than US$2.80 a day, the cost of a single cappuccino in Nairobi. Then he stood up to take the next training session.

The Kenyan government fired back against the World Bank the next day, including Stephen's ammunition in their reply. The World Bank backed off and took the paper down from its website, though not before Stephen had saved it as an example of World Bank work that was both unreasonable in its criticism and below par in its quality. The threat to the pension was over, at least for the time being.

The poverty-targeted programmes in Kenya that had been part-funded by donors, with government financing an increasing share, were not without points in their favour. They were pioneering when they started in the 2000s and continue to reach hundreds of thousands of people. They, most likely, got the Kenyan government used to the idea of investing in social protection. But they also have fundamental problems because of targeting errors. The accuracy of locating those eligible has been described for one of the programmes as 'little better than random', so, akin to a roulette wheel.[4] Another issue is that, because beneficiaries are limited to 'the poor', it can be difficult to gain enough political support to scale the programmes up to proper national coverage, reaching millions rather than hundreds of thousands.[5] Hang on, you may say. Universal benefits have their own issues: they are clearly more expensive because they go to everyone eligible regardless of income. This is true, other things being equal. And governments must weigh arguments against and arguments for, including that universal programmes can promote unity rather than division. And the Kenyan government had done that, but the World Bank was, apparently, not prepared to accept this.

The pros and cons of poverty targeting and universality form the main battleground running through this story. The ultimate goal is the building of comprehensive social protection systems all have access to, comprising tax-financed and contributory programmes. This story focusses on the tax-financed side. There is an important parallel battle, beyond the scope of this book, to expand coverage of social insurance. Though unfortunately contributory programmes are often constrained by high and persistent informality in labour markets in low- and middle-income countries, leaving most workers outside the formal sector where contributions are made. But the two sides complement each other and both are important. The bottom line is that governments, those that represent populations at least, must be free to choose their own direction. For tax-financed benefits, left to their own devices, governments frequently choose a mixture of universal and means-tested schemes.[6] The problem is the World Bank commonly opposes universal schemes at the outset, limiting governments' choice.

Some parts of what I witnessed in that training room in Kenya are unusual, such as the World Bank's analytical errors. But there are a number of things which, in my experience, are not: the immovability of the World Bank's position, its willingness to promote a partial argument to promote its cause and its presumption in opposing the will of a national government. One thing that is hard to forget is the trust the Kenyan government had in Stephen Kidd, and his willingness to drop things and help. Where did Stephen's commitment to social protection come from?

The Department for International Development

Stephen Kidd's interest in social protection began in earnest a decade and a half earlier, in 2004, when he was appointed head of the Social Protection Team in DFID.[7] He knew little about the subject, though a spark of interest had been generated in his previous role, in which he had looked at levels of inequality in Latin America.

The Social Protection Team was located in DFID's headquarters on Buckingham Palace Road in central London. Inside DFID headquarters, behind the seven-storey facade, open plan offices surrounded a high, light atrium where staff talked with others from around the world about international development. From the top floor, staff could, if they wished, see into the back garden of Buckingham Palace where the Queen hosted her summer garden parties. It was a privileged world, and though most of the ideas discussed in that atrium came to nothing, some became programmes that would affect thousands, or hundreds of thousands, of lives overseas.

DFID staff, like their first secretary of state, the charismatic Member of Parliament Clare Short, had minds of their own. When I joined DFID and the Social Protection Team the year before Stephen arrived from elsewhere in the UK government, I drank in their confidence and warmth. It was those qualities that would facilitate the rise of social protection in the organization. But Stephen stood out for me, even against that background, for his drive to get things done and his determination to avoid those ideas that came to nothing. He summed up his philosophy early on at a team away day. When we were all asked to give a statement of what we believed in, Stephen ignored others' light hearted responses and said, 'I believe that working in the area we do is a privilege and I believe we have a duty to do the best we can every day that we're here.'

Claire Short set up DFID when Tony Blair and the Labour Party won the UK general election in 1997. It soon became the hardest place to get into in the UK government. Jobs were often held by people whose parents had worked in international development or in some other job overseas. It was a somewhat entitled world. Celebrities such as Bob Geldof, Aung San Suu Kyi, Bill Gates and Prince Charles, among others, passed through, and DFID had offices in Barbados, Bangkok, Lusaka, Kathmandu and elsewhere, often in ex-British colonies. When I joined, in 2003, Chancellor of the Exchequer Gordon Brown was a strong supporter and DFID's budget grew year to year. Against this background, its future priorities were discussed energetically. And behind windows in one corner of the atrium, Stephen worked with the ten or so members of his new team to find a place among those priorities.

However, the team had an immediate challenge: no one knew what social protection was, in terms of where its limits lay. It included benefits but should it include, for instance, help to households to pay for health and education services, or to generate livelihoods from small businesses? Nowadays, fortunately, there is something of a consensus – if not agreement on every detail – that social protection is broadly synonymous with social security, in other words the benefit system.[8]

Another challenge was indifference and scepticism among many – though not all – of my fellow economists in DFID towards supporting benefit systems in lower-income countries. I recall three main objections.

(1) Social protection will lead to *corruption*, money will go missing;
(2) Social protection is *unaffordable* in lower-income contexts; and,
(3) Social protection, or 'free money', may make people lazy.

I was particularly interested in the 'may make people lazy' claim. It was made less strongly about the far more generous benefit system in the UK in the Department for Work and Pensions, from where I had recently arrived, where staff took it for granted that people had a right to support through different stages of life. Anyway, the message was that overseas aid was better spent on health and education, or on supporting economic growth to help reduce poverty, through infrastructure and agriculture and improving regulatory environments or other areas. A benefit system may be a good thing to have in developing countries, but at some point further down the line.

There is much legitimate debate here, and of course every context is different. But dismissing national social protection schemes entirely, as I felt the most sceptical did, was out of alignment with history and evidence. We will come back to the detail of that evidence as we go. Except perhaps to say, the risk of corruption is something of a red herring. Social protection schemes are frequently less vulnerable than other sectors, because it is relatively easy to check if those eligible for programmes are getting what they are entitled to.[9] It is harder to check, for example, if the subsurface of a road has been built below standard to save money.

The big picture is that global evidence suggests spending on different parts of government, whatever a country's wealth level, should be balanced and should include social protection. It is a sector now recognized by the International

Monetary Fund (IMF) as a fundamental pillar of any nation's social and economic development, with 'a crucial role in protecting households from poverty, promoting inclusive growth, and maintaining social stability'.[10] That is the accepted evidence now but back then, things were less established.

Adjusting course

In late 2004, shortly after he had become Social Protection Team leader, Stephen called a meeting of the team, which was made up mainly of advisers. Advisers were regarded as DFID's beating heart. They had specialisms in social development, livelihoods, economics, governance, health, education and other areas and were invariably supported by highly efficient administrative staff. In the Social Protection Team, as elsewhere, the advisers were bright and committed and had direct experience of working in lower-income countries, and they taught me, the new economist, many of the basics of international development.

In the meeting, Stephen suggested that, to stop the endless debate on how social protection is defined, the team should narrow its attention. He argued that the focus should be on one area unquestionably within the bounds of social protection, 'social transfers'. Social transfers are what we now call tax-financed benefits. They also came to be called 'cash transfers', in the tortuous evolution of international development language. Both terms were just emerging in DFID and elsewhere, but would soon have global resonance.

As a result of the team's new focus and its collective effort, a paper was prepared for DFID senior management and the outside world. This made the case for the UK government supporting social transfers/cash transfers in lower-income countries, which at the time was only happening on a small scale. Stephen was asked to present the paper to a senior management panel, in early 2005. In the meeting, he sat at the board room table and summarized the paper's messages on the positive impact of cash transfers on poverty, health, education and other areas, with his advisers behind him. There were reservations, but a senior manager signalled a change of mood during the meeting by expressing support. They said, something new was needed for vulnerable households which were being left out by traditional development programmes. The meeting approved the paper.

Social Transfers and Chronic Poverty: Emerging Evidence and the Challenge Ahead would be published, and supporting cash transfers was now official DFID policy.[11] The Social Protection Team marketed the paper across DFID, organizing seminars and crafting briefing notes. Stephen liaised with the *Grow Up Free from Poverty Coalition*, a group of UK NGOs and faith groups, to lobby DFID ministers on cash transfers from the outside. And he got cash transfers included in DFID's White Paper, in 2006, with the help of sympathizers inside the White Paper team.[12] Notwithstanding the reservations of many economists, cash transfers, and social protection generally, was named as a fourth 'basic service', along with the established DFID priorities of health, education and water and sanitation. A clear definition of social protection had still not emerged, but no matter. There were specific spending commitments in the White Paper to scale up social protection in country programmes, and the new secretary of state, Hilary Benn, said at a large staff meeting that 'cash, cash, cash', in other words cash transfers, was the way forward.

All of this activity gave the green light to DFID advisers in country offices to support cash transfers in the countries where they worked. DFID was a decentralized organization: each country office decided, within DFID's overall policy, what it was best to spend aid on in its particular context. In DFID offices across Africa and South Asia, social development advisers and livelihoods advisers – in my experience, confident, warm and independent, like their colleagues in headquarters – lobbied their heads of office to support cash transfers. With heads of office getting the same strategic messages from London as they were from their staff, the ground started to move.

Between 2004 and 2010, in the six years following the presentation of the paper to senior management, DFID spending on cash transfers rose more than tenfold, from US$40 million to US$460 million.[13] Assuming a cash transfer of US$10 per month as sufficient to have a major impact on a family, this was enough to support three million recipients.[14] Allowing for other people in the same household as direct recipients, this amounts to fifteen million people benefitting, per year.[15] This is a small figure set against global need, but an important start. And other donors in the world, as well as some lower-income country governments themselves, may have been influenced by DFID's new direction. Evidence of this was that 'social transfers' and 'cash transfers', which according to later research had been used for the first time in the DFID paper as general terms to describe benefits going to vulnerable households, were quickly in common usage.[16] That said, there were many governments, for example in Bolivia, Brazil, China, India, Mexico, Nepal and South Africa, among many others, already implementing cash transfers, oblivious to the debates on language in DFID, just as they were often on a much bigger scale in high-income countries. The paper did not invent anything new, it just made more visible what was already happening.

The wider international development world

Does the shift in DFID spending make Stephen Kidd and others in his team, and the advisers in DFID country offices, the heroes of our story? No, because of how international development works. Donors including DFID do not do their own thing; they support partner governments in their efforts to do *their* thing. It is a partnership, with governments in the lead. As a quick aside, this is what *should* happen, assuming governments have a sufficient level of legitimacy - if they don't, finer judgements have to be made on how to deliver aid. But legitimacy is a tricky thing for donors to judge. Legitimate in whose eyes? In this story, for legitimacy, a measure of democracy for different countries is used developed by the Economist Intelligence Unit.[17] There is a lot more to it than this which I will leave to others better qualified to set out.[18]

Furthermore, any growth in DFID and wider donor spending on social protection was built on the work of researchers who were creating the global evidence base on the impact of cash transfers on households. These were based in universities and research organizations all over the world and included, from my own point of view, people like Fabio Veras, Ashu Handa and Ben Davis, among many others, whose work on programmes in Latin America was highly influential, as was their subsequent work in Africa. It was also built on the work of other organizations including, again in my own experience in the UK, staff at the Overseas Development Institute (ODI) in London and at the Institute of Development Studies (IDS) at Sussex University, where high-profile academics such as Stephen Devereux, Rachel Sabates-Wheeler and Armando Barrientos worked. Armando Barrientos was co-author, with Joseph Hanlon and David Hulme, of the groundbreaking *Just Give Money to the Poor*, which came out in 2010 and was highly influential in DFID.[19] There were also important advocates at international NGOs like HelpAge International, in governments in northern Europe and in international institutions like the International Labour Organization (ILO), which is part of the United Nations and was soon to become the global soul of universal social protection.

And there were staff working in the World Bank itself, which has a significantly longer history than DFID on social protection, as well as much greater resources. Set up with the International Monetary Fund at the end of the Second World War as a response to underdeveloped global capital markets, the World Bank had been advocating for social protection well before the Social Protection Team's paper appeared.[20] And with 120 offices worldwide and over 12,000 employees, it has considerable capacity to draw on.[21] The World Bank's main focus in earlier days was working with the IMF and others on the privatization of state contributory pensions. However, this had, according to the World Bank's own evaluation, 'not always been effective', and it was a course largely abandoned in the mid-2000s.[22] In a new approach, following the East Asian crisis of the late 1990s, the World Bank identified social protection as key to alleviating the risks faced by vulnerable groups in their daily lives.[23] Between 2004 and 2010, it increased its loan commitments for what it called 'social safety nets', from less than US$0.5 billion to US$2.5 billion, and these would rise much further to the point where the World Bank provided the majority of donor financing.[24] The World Bank also put significant resources and effort into pulling much of the critical evidence together in slick text and visuals on its accessible, informative and influential website.

So, the world is complicated and there is a cast of many. Anyone in international development is only one cog in a big wheel, with governments of course at the centre. Nevertheless, in the context of our story, credit where it is perhaps due. Stephen Kidd and his team of which I was one, and advisers in country officers, with others in DFID, in governments and elsewhere, had helped steer DFID to providing much greater support to social protection in low- and middle-income countries.[25] According to subsequent research, 'There was nothing inevitable about the rise of social protection as a commitment within DFID'.[26] Stephen and others had helped make it happen. And the DFID paper itself was described as 'seminal' when academia later came to study the history of donor support for social protection.[27]

Collaborating on the international stage

Stephen and his Social Protection Team in DFID collaborated with many allies in helping to push forward the global social protection agenda. In the UK, this included HelpAge International, which worked with Stephen to organize an influential conference in Livingstone, Zambia, in 2006. This was funded by Stephen's team but hosted by the African Union and resulted in a number of African governments publicly committing to expanding cash transfer spending.[28] More widely, it included the late Michael Cichon at the ILO, then director of the Social Security Department, whose team in the ILO's cavernous building in Geneva had started estimating the cost of introducing high-coverage cash transfer programmes in a range of countries across the globe. Stephen also collaborated with Michael Cichon and others in developing a new global vision for social protection, which we will come back to in Chapter 9. And he collaborated on social protection with, among many others, like-minded officials in the Government of Finland, including Timo Voipio, and GIZ, which delivers much of Germany's international aid, as well as staff in UNICEF and in international NGOs. He also worked, at that time, with the World Bank. Stephen was travelling to Washington DC to meet World Bank staff including Robert Holzmann, then global head of social protection.[29]

This varied international group were collectively and in different ways helping to strengthen the argument for donors and governments supporting social protection. The main forum in which the international allies met was a new group within the Organisation for Economic Co-operation and Development (OECD) bureaucratic structure that had been set up to address 'risk and vulnerability' in low- and middle-income countries.[30] This group's key paper, *Social Protection, Poverty Reduction and Pro-Poor Growth*, makes a comprehensive case for investing in social protection.[31] It argues that it provides immediate relief *and* supports economic growth, which is the main engine for reducing poverty in the long term. It was on solid ground. Because evidence now shows how social protection supports growth by allowing families to eat nutritious meals, helping early childhood cognitive development and helps pay for health and education services, including fees, bus fares, school uniforms and textbooks, and it reduces child labour.[32] Social protection also reduces income stress in households which improves mental health and lessens domestic violence.[33] It gives women and girls greater independence and choice, as it does for persons with disabilities who can work, by helping them meet the extra costs of things like personal care and transport.[34] Collectively, these impacts help to build the adult labour force on which all economies depend. Moreover, as mentioned, social protection helps households invest in things like livestock and farming tools, which are less likely to be sold in a crisis, at the same time as stimulating local and national markets for businesses to sell into.[35] And it supports macroeconomic reforms by protecting those moving from declining industries to new ones as technology changes and economies decarbonize.[36] It also stimulates the economy in downturns and reduces inequality which can help social harmony, vital over the long term for national development.[37] Other sectors in government do a lot of this too of course, but areas such as health, education and infrastructure were more established at the time of the OECD paper, though they still lacked funding. The argument for social protection was new. The fact that it is a critical piece of the national development pie, as high-income countries have known for many decades, has since become common currency, including in the IMF. But at the time of the OECD paper, it was not. Indeed, inequality was regarded as a natural consequence of growth by many economists, including myself. Against this, social development advisers in DFID argued inequality was damaging to development. Those advisers are now backed by IMF staff research which shows that even relatively low inequality can damage growth.[38]

Discovering Thandika Mkandawire

Despite all this international collaboration and pulling in the same direction, cracks had started to appear between Stephen and his closest collaborators on one side and the World Bank on the other. These were on two points of tax-financed social protection programme design. The first was whether to make schemes 'conditional' or not. 'Conditional cash transfers' are benefits that are paid to recipients, provided they do certain things such as attending health clinics or sending their children to school. This model was already being implemented in Latin America and was being heavily researched, though Stephen and his collaborators had started to challenge the evidence supporting it, as we will see in Chapter 6. The second area of contention was whether to provide social protection only for the poorest members of society, in other words whether to poverty target, as we have seen in Kenya. Here Stephen's views had in fact evolved over time.

Stephen was initially a supporter of poverty targeting, of the argument that finite resources should go to those most in need. His team organized two well-attended seminars in DFID promoting this approach. The first was by Brazilian government staff on the poverty-targeted Bolsa Familia programme, the second was by Bernd Schubert, a well-known supporter of poverty targeting, on a cash transfer pilot in Kalomo, Zambia. But Stephen was starting to develop reservations about whether poverty targeting was what governments in low- and middle-income countries wanted to do, and whether it was practical in any case.

Stephen came across a paper called *Targeting and Universalism in Poverty Reduction*, by the late economist Thandika Mkandawire.[39] Mkandawire grew up in one of the poorest countries in the world, Malawi, and went on to hold various prestigious positions including Director of the United Nations Research Institute for Social Development.[40] He was highly influential until his death in 2020. Mkandawire lived in Sweden for a long time, a country that had given him exile and citizenship following activism in his younger days in support of Malawian independence and against authoritarian rule.[41] Sweden is a champion of universality and appears to have had a significant impact on Mkandawire's thinking.[42]

Mkandawire's paper, published in 2005, goes through the history of poverty targeting. It explains that there were 'ideological shifts in the North' in the 1980s and 1990s away from universality and towards means testing, partly driven by the increasing welfare costs in developed countries arising from demographic changes and mass unemployment. There were 'similar shifts in the South' for countries that were aid-dependent and effectively importers of much northern political thinking. The shift towards poverty targeting was given a further push by the growing 'centrality of poverty in policy discourse' among donors, who were moving away from aiming at 'development' to promoting 'poverty reduction'. The objective became to help the 'deserving poor'. Mkandawire's paper argues there were also forces *within* low- and middle-income countries pushing them away from universality. These included the need to manage macroeconomic instability and debt crises, encouraged by IMF and World Bank-promoted 'structural adjustment', a set of market-orientated policies aimed at balancing governments' books and encouraging growth, to be implemented in exchange for loans.[43]

The largest international donor, the World Bank, went on to argue during this period that the poor were missing out during structural adjustment and needed to be helped through poverty-targeted programmes including social protection. Other donors fell into line. But, Mkandawire argues, there are problems with this increased focus on poverty targeting. History shows *universal* government services and social solidarity have underpinned 'a broad agenda of economic development and social transformation'. In contrast, the poverty-targeted programmes promoted by donors work against solidarity and nation-building. 'Targeting . . . almost by definition leads to segmentation . . . [It] leads to the creation of a dual structure – one aimed at the poor and funded by the state, and one aimed at the well-to-do and provided by the private sector.' Mkandawire quotes Amartya Sen: 'Benefits meant exclusively for the poor often end up being poor benefits.' Amartya Sen may be the most respected development economist of recent times, so Mkandawire was not flying alone.

Mkandawire goes on to argue in his paper that poverty targeting is extremely difficult in environments where 'most people's source of livelihood is in the informal sector, people's "visibility" to the state is low, and the state's overall capacity is low'. Targeting errors are always high, and so are administrative costs during the process of identifying the 'deserving poor'. This begins to undermine the 'cost effectiveness' argument for poverty targeting, which is that aiming at the most deserving gives a greater reduction in poverty per dollar spent.

But, it may be argued, surely poverty targeting is still the best way to redistribute limited resources? Mkandawire points out that, in fact, historically, universal approaches tend to go with progressive taxation and lower inequality as 'non-redistribution in transfers is more than compensated for redistribution in taxation'.[44] He mentions the 'paradox of redistribution', originally set out by Korpi and Palme: 'The more we target benefits at the poor only . . . the less likely we are to reduce poverty and inequality.'[45] This depends, in part, on the assumption that government systems that are more dependent on poverty targeting tend to be smaller and, as a result, less redistributive.[46] If the assumption holds – and we will come back to this – the debate on poverty targeting is really a debate about the size of the state and levels of taxation.

Mkandawire does not dismiss poverty targeting out of hand. 'Policy regimes are hardly ever purely universal or purely based on targeting . . . they tend to lie somewhere between the two extremes.' But he was arguing that universality must be brought back into international development dialogue. And the sooner the better, because 'where [countries] lie on this continuum can be decisive in spelling out individuals' life chances and in characterizing the social order'. Instead of poverty targeting dominating, as in World Bank thinking, it should sit within an overall framework of universality. 'In the more successful countries, overall social policy . . . has been universalistic.'[47]

Stephen took all of this in and his world view shifted. Soon after reading Mkandawire's paper, he visited the poverty-targeted pilot Social Cash Transfer Scheme in Kalomo, Zambia, advertised by Bernd Schubert and funded by the German Development Agency GIZ. He saw an older female recipient hurrying home from the programme's pay point. When Stephen asked her what was wrong, she said that she had lost all her friends who were jealous of her being in the pilot. Here, on a small scale, was Stephen's first real-world example of poverty targeting causing social division.

Leaving DFID

As Stephen's views against poverty targeting took shape, along with his scepticism of conditional cash transfers, he and his team started to work with DFID country offices and with the ILO to oppose World Bank advice to governments across sub-Saharan Africa. The objective was to remind governments that there was a different way of doing things, and that if they wanted to take a different path they should have the confidence to do so. This did not have to exclude means testing, where it is properly done and sits within a comprehensive system supporting the population, but Stephen and his collaborators opposed the World Bank's common dismissal of universal social protection programmes in country after country. To support this effort, Michael Samson, from the Economic Policy Research Institute (EPRI) in South Africa, who had worked on South Africa's wide-coverage social protection programmes, was tasked by Stephen's team to provide training and guidance on social protection for government officials in low- and middle-income countries.[48] This rivalled existing World Bank training. As subsequent research put it, 'DFID started to see itself as an alternative to the World Bank.'[49]

But then things changed. DFID staff are generally required to move on every few years. Stephen was asked to take charge of a much larger team in DFID, a merger of the Social Protection Team and another working on gender and social inclusion. This was more of a management role. Stephen found it dull and in 2007, at forty-seven years of age, he left DFID to join HelpAge International as Director of Policy and Communications. He wanted to work on social protection permanently, as a technical specialist, and moving on would enable this.

Stephen departed DFID with professional allies and a record of achievement. He would go on to collaborate with DFID in future on social protection in a number of different settings. But Stephen also left with professional opponents. Some of these were within DFID, and they were increasingly at the World Bank, with which he had sown the seeds of confrontations to come. Stephen had certainly not kept his head down and chosen the easy road in DFID. But nor had he chosen the easy road in his earlier life, a period which throws light on the values that would be visible later.

Chapter 2

PARAGUAY

LEARNING FROM THE ENXET

Newcastle

Stephen Kidd was born in 1960, in Byker, east Newcastle in the north-east of England. Byker was one of the poorest areas in Britain, and the house where Stephen first lived was demolished in the slum clearances not long after his family moved out, in 1961. Stephen's dad was also born in Byker, into what Stephen describes as extreme poverty. 'He was a foot shorter than me', he says talking to me in his home in Maidstone in England, a house full of books and papers. 'It was the usual effects of malnutrition. *His* mum was four foot eight.'[1] Stephen's own mum was born in nearby Hebburn, next door to Jarrow, famous for the 1936 Jarrow March to London, which protested against poverty and unemployment.

Stephen's dad had left school at fourteen years of age but had educated himself and got a job as a legal executive, and his mother had become a teacher. This meant that the family could move to better housing on the other side of the city before Stephen's brother was born. At eleven years of age, Stephen got his lucky break when, having attended a local primary school with forty-five to a class, his parents put him in for the entrance exam to Dame Allan's direct grant school.[2] He passed and came out several years later with good 'A' levels. Most of his friends from primary school that went to the nearby state schools came out with nothing.

Both of Stephen's parents were evangelical Christians. His dad was motivated by his own father being an abusive alcoholic. Alcohol was banned by Stephen's parents, as was pop music and all activity on a Sunday bar church attendance. The Pope was the anti-Christ for them, and the Church of England 'no better than the Catholics'. Summer vacations were usually in holiday camps hosted by missionary organizations that worked overseas. Stephen absorbed the missionaries' stories about far-off places like the Amazon. By their mid-teens, Stephen and his younger brother Andrew cooked and cleaned at the camps through the summer. At home, Stephen and Andrew attended church twice on Sundays, along with Sunday school and Bible club during the week. Stephen said to his parents when he was seven, 'I really believe.' He described for them his 'conversion experience', as was expected of all members of their evangelical church. Looking back, he says he never really understood what a conversion to Christianity really was, and found church services boring. 'I had no idea you didn't have to be a Christian.' But he admits the good bits of Christianity, the sense of right and wrong and helping others, penetrated deeply into his consciousness.

Along with the evangelical church, Stephen's uncle David, his mum's brother, was a major influence on Stephen's life and a mythical figure to him in his youth. David Young was in the British Royal Navy, in Hong Kong, in 1949. He got into an argument defending a fellow sailor who had expressed support for China, following a firefight between the Chinese People's Liberation Army under Mao Tse-tung and a British warship. David was classed as a troublemaker and a transfer away from Hong Kong was arranged for him. A self-confessed 'red', David had also grown up in the north-east of England and resented the lives he had seen workers leading in the local coal mines. He was politicized by a book *his* uncle had given him, 'Red Star Over China' by Edgar Snow, about the birth of Chinese communism. When David had arrived in Hong Kong with the navy, his interest in China led him to develop local contacts. When his transfer away was imminent, he used those contacts to escape from the navy base and into China. There he linked up with the People's Liberation Army as they moved into Guangzhou, formerly Canton, just north of Hong Kong, and after that he disappeared into Chinese society. David learned Cantonese, lived in a commune and worked as a fitter in a sugar mill, writing to his family in the UK to say he was okay.

Trouble followed later, during the Cultural Revolution of the 1960s and 1970s, when David was suspected of being a Western spy. He was eventually released from solitary confinement thanks to the efforts of Communist Party friends. Stephen remembers a card eventually arriving at Christmas time in 1976, after ten years of silence. Stephen's mum and sister visited David in 1978 and met a journalist from *The Guardian* in the UK, Ian Black, who wanted to write a book about one of the few Westerners living in communist China. But embarrassed by potential fame, David eschewed contact with Westerners. In 1980, Stephen and his brother travelled to China for two months and taught English in a heavy machinery factory in Guangzhou, where David was settled. They were the first white people the locals that they mixed with had seen. Stephen says, 'It was a formative experience.' In the early 1980s, David agreed to the UK television station ITV making a documentary about him, *The Chinese Geordie*, Geordie being a term for people from Tyneside in the north-east of England. David talked about communal life in China and being 'part of a group where everyone tries to do their best for each other'. The programme showed David returning to the UK with his Chinese wife and family. He returned to China and died there in 2005.

Paraguay

In 1978, Stephen began studying geography at Aberdeen University. He had a good time for three years, then worked hard in his fourth year to gain a first. Stephen met Sandra his future wife there. 'We were literally the only mixed-race couple in Aberdeen,' Stephen says. Sandra's parents were from Sri Lanka. Stephen and Sandra started a local branch of the Tearfund, an international Christian charity. Afterwards Stephen went to the National College of Engineering at Cranfield University to study for a Master's degree in Agricultural Engineering, though the actual course was in rural planning and management. His relationship with Sandra, who worked as a biochemist in London, continued remotely.

With his Master's degree, Stephen applied for a couple of jobs with missionary organizations, motivated by those earlier missionary tales of the Amazon and by a desire to help others. He got a job with the South American Missionary Society (SAMS) in Paraguay. The SAMS was a British organization, set up in the nineteenth century, that had played a key role in facilitating the colonization of land within the Chaco region of Paraguay during the late nineteenth and early twentieth centuries. The Chaco is a hot, sparsely populated wilderness that reaches into Paraguay, Bolivia and Argentina. By the early 1980s, recognizing that its actions had resulted in the indigenous inhabitants of the Chaco losing their land and living in extreme poverty, the SAMS began to buy land to help resettle indigenous people, who had been displaced a century earlier by ranch owners.

In late 1984, aged twenty-four, after learning Spanish in Spain and attending the funeral of his father, Stephen left for Paraguay where he would stay for the next three years. His job was to help the Enxet, a Paraguayan indigenous group of around ten thousand people, grow crops on the small plots of land they had been allocated, and to be a missionary for the Anglican Church. Today, we might characterize this as a 'white saviour' complex. Though we can perhaps spare Stephen and his family this label because they were to go on to live with the Enxet, take on their cause and become adopted as one of their own. But Stephen's family had not yet formed. Indeed, from Paraguay Stephen wrote a letter to Sandra, who was doing teacher training in the UK, to say they were splitting up. In their house where Stephen and I are talking, Sandra calls merrily through from the kitchen. 'He didn't have the courage to tell me before he left.' Stephen argues that he only made the decision after he had been living in Paraguay for a few months.

Makthlawaiya, the SAMS main mission station, was three hundred kilometres north of the Paraguayan capital Asuncion, in the Chaco. 'The tarmac road ran out around fifty kilometres from Makthlawaiya,' Stephen says. The mission was on a 60-hectare island in the middle of a swamp, with a mosquito population 'which could turn your arm black'. It had a church lifted straight from rural England and some low adobe mission buildings including a health clinic, where Stephen lived in one of the rooms, and accommodation for the other British and American missionaries and the Paraguayan employees. It was run as a small ranch, employing the Enxet who also lived in Makthlawaiya, around the missionary compound. They were better paid than those employed in surrounding ranches and also able to continue their hunting, fishing and gathering lifestyle.

As well as carrying out services for the Anglican Church, Stephen taught the Enxet how to farm. 'I knew nothing about agriculture, and it wasn't part of my Master's course,' Stephen says. 'I'd almost never planted a thing in my life. Soon after I got there, I had to help weed a field of pumpkins, and in the process, I killed every single one.' The watching Enxet did not say a word. 'But after that I read some books on agriculture and got by', he adds. In 1985, the church bought ten thousand hectares at El Estribo as a place for more than a thousand Enxet to live. Stephen, then twenty-five, was given the job of coordinating the new settlement, moving between there and Makthlawaiya, living with the Enxet and communicating in their language. He dug water holes and generally made things work. 'I was making it up as I went along.'

The El Estribo settlement work and the mission in Makthlawaiya, which were part of a broader integrated rural development project called *La Herencia* (The Inheritance), were evaluated by British anthropologists and an Argentinian who had worked for many years with indigenous people. With Stephen, they came up with a revolutionary idea. Throw out the old colonial way of operating, stop Westerners being 'white saviours' and live humbly among the indigenous people, who should make all decisions for themselves. Stephen was appointed as one of the coordinators of *La Herencia* and spent more and more time with the Enxet, living and sharing with them every day. His appreciation of Enxet culture deepened. Stephen encountered shaman rituals in El Estribo and came to view the Anglican Church in Paraguay as paternalistic, even racist, in its banning of the customs of the Enxet and trying to turn them into Westerners. He began to participate in Enxet traditions and started smoking a pipe so that he could share it with the shamans. 'My world view changed. I rethought everything.'

Stephen would eventually write up what he had learned in a PhD in anthropology, published in 2021.[3] 'For the Enxet, economic relations are not concerned with gaining material wealth but [are] about living well with other people.' He describes how the Enxet community is an environment of social consciousness, of sharing, and that this state of being opens the hearts of community members, strengthening their relations and truly connecting them to one another. 'Economic transactions such as pooling and sharing have tranquillity as their ultimate goal.' But, given their challenging living conditions, it is a process about survival as much as sentiment. 'Theirs is a love born of necessity.' It may not be too much of a stretch to say the Enxet code resonates with the world's major religions, when they are at their best, including the Christian faith. But it contrasted sharply with the manifestation Stephen saw at work in the Chaco. Stephen also recognized, in an echo of his uncle's encounter with the Chinese, how much the indigenous culture before him contrasted with the Global North, which Stephen describes as an 'encroaching society where the value of difference and hierarchy rather than sameness is emphasised and where competition and greed displace equality and generosity'. Stephen learned greater humility and respect for the Enxet culture, but still found his own behaviour and forthrightness contrasted with the Enxet's goal of person-to-person tranquillity.

At the end of his second year in post, Stephen wrote a letter to Sandra asking that they get back together. Stephen looks thoughtful. 'I probably wasn't the best boyfriend.' Luckily for him, Sandra came out to Paraguay for a two-week holiday. Stephen proposed to her and, in 1987, Stephen went back to the UK to get married. The SAMS was worried about Sandra's religious credentials, despite her being an evangelical Christian herself, and asked that she and Stephen attend Bible College, at Selly Oak College in Birmingham. The church didn't like Stephen's growing interest in Enxet traditions which had come to include dancing and with the support of two Enxet, Anibal and Ramirez, shamanistic rituals. Stephen's attachment to Christianity was starting to fade, though it didn't happen passively. 'I went through a very rigorous process', Stephen says. As well as his experience with the Enxet, his eyes were opened in meeting a Brazilian liberation theologian in Paraguay and reading books on liberation theology and Christian socialism. During their six months at Selly Oak, Stephen met more liberation theologians and people from other denominations, with their own take on things. Sandra did too, and they talked and collaborated as they gradually lost their faith together.

Stephen found in the Bible a parable, that of the sheep and the goats (Matthew 25: 31–46). 'That was the clincher.' In the parable, at the gates of heaven, people are sorted into those worthy of entering and those not, like separating sheep from goats. The sheep are steered to the right, to enter heaven. They are allowed in because in life they had helped to clothe the unclothed, feed the hungry and house the homeless, even though they had not been religious. The goats are steered in the other direction, despite their protests that they had worshipped God all their lives. As Jesus describes it, they may have spent their lives worshipping God, but they had not helped others, and in the end, it is deeds not faith that really matters. 'The penny dropped', Stephen says. With great relief, he knew that what was important was doing good for others, and he was free from the stress of having to believe. 'Not that I believed in the Bible and heaven anymore, but it really helped.'

A new approach to the Enxet: land rights

After Bible College, in 1988, Stephen and Sandra returned to Makthlawaiya. Stephen continued to conduct church services but by this time was 'a confirmed agnostic'. He had not told the SAMS for fear of losing his job. Stephen's objective now was 'not to spread the Christian faith but to fight for justice'. And in fighting for justice, to support the Enxet. Wider changes were on his side. Soon after their return, the right-wing Paraguayan dictator Alfredo Stroessner, host of Nazi war criminals such as *Angel of Death* Josef Mengele, to whom he granted full citizenship, was overthrown in a coup d'état. The politics of Paraguay was changing, and the Anglican Church there became exposed, having allied itself with Stroessner: Stroessner's grandchildren attended Anglican schools. The Church was under pressure to change.

Stephen led *La Herencia* with an ever more radical agenda, including handing over the land title of Makthlawaiya to the Enxet and closing the mission station. Completed in 1990, this meant removing all the non-indigenous people, around fifty in total, until only Stephen and Sandra, and in time their new young daughter Sarina, were left. Stephen promoted traditional dancing on the lands of the Anglican Church and encouraged shamans to practise openly. He discovered that many of the Enxet Anglican clergy were shamans and had hidden it from the Church, which watched on but did not intervene. At first the Enxet did not believe that open shamanic rituals and traditional dancing *were* officially allowed, despite Stephen's encouragement. They had been made to fear the power and authority of the missionaries. Then the Archbishop of Canterbury, Robert Runcie, head of the global Anglican Communion, visited Makthlawaiya to hand over the land title to the Enxet. Stephen encouraged the Enxet to dance for him, and when the archbishop joined in, clapping his hands and saying, 'Lovely, lovely', a century-long ban on Enxet dancing was ended.

Stephen and Sandra continued to support the Enxet in having pride in their culture and way of life. Sandra, a qualified teacher now, encouraged them to begin to write in their own language, and Stephen encouraged writing their history. The objective was to remove the shame and alienation involved in trying to live like white society, only to be looked down upon by the people they emulated. Stephen and Sandra regarded this as a causal factor in a recent spate of Enxet suicides.

Then Stephen switched his focus to perhaps the biggest challenge for Enxet survival, the need for more land. He started travelling around the wilderness of the Chaco on horseback with an indigenous guide. He talked to communities about historic land rights and learned the legal side of things and started to put together land claims. In the meantime, the Bishop of Paraguay, a British evangelical, and others in the Church hierarchy who continued to travel to Makthlawaiya to carry out services, refused to stay at the settlement as they had done before. They viewed what was going on there, the dancing and shamanic ceremonies, as the work of the devil. As Sandra puts it, 'They thought the place was possessed.' The Anglican Church withdrew all support to Makthlawaiya. 'Our radio didn't work and we had no transport when the roads were closed', Stephen says. 'They just deserted us. And by then we had Sarina.'

Sandra had gone to the capital, Asuncion, to have their daughter just before Robert Runcie's visit. Sandra says, 'Back in Makthlawaiya with a young baby, Stephen and I didn't have a clue. And the nearest medical facility was back in Asuncion. The Anglicans didn't seem to care that, if Sarina got ill, we had no way of getting her to hospital when the waters in the swamp rose.' But they had friends among the Enxet. 'Every time Sarina cried someone would come in and take her away and tell us off for letting her cry', Sandra says. Stephen adds, 'Sarina would be picked up at eight every morning and taken away for the whole morning, sometimes the whole day. One day I looked for her and found one of the Enxet breast feeding her. It turns out she was being passed around Makthlawaiya being breast fed by all the women with milk.'

Things were hard as Sandra and Stephen battled with the heat and caring for a baby. They made mistakes, and Sarina once got badly dehydrated when their car got stuck in the mud. There were also the endless mosquitoes, and Stephen was hospitalized with bouts of dengue and hepatitis. When he was laid up with the latter, Stephen says that he read books on the Enxet and decided to do a PhD in anthropology. Sandra chips in. 'You're rewriting history. You didn't know what to do with your life. It was me that told you, the best thing to do is a PhD.' When he was well enough again, Stephen returned to his trips by horse to remote Enxet communities, travelling for up to six days at a time and continuing to build community support for land claims. Sandra was accepted by the Enxet as one of their own having learned enough Enxet to get by. And the Anglican Church continued to stay away, until the Bishop of Paraguay finally confronted Stephen on the management of *La Herencia*, in Stephen and Sandra's house. There was a standoff, but Stephen refused to follow the bishop's orders. After this he knew the power dynamic had changed, whether through wider political shifts or his own defiance. His radical agenda for *La Herencia* could stay in place.

In 1991, seven years after Stephen first arrived, he and his family left Paraguay for the UK. Stephen was signed up to do a Master's in anthropology at Durham University, a first step towards his PhD. But Stephen still had six months left on his missionary contract so, as part of a swansong with the Church, he travelled around the UK leading services. 'This time the sermons were full on about the fight for justice', Stephen says. 'I did draw on some biblical teachings but also what I'd learned from the Enxet. It wasn't to everyone's taste. Congregations would shuffle with discomfort. On one occasion, I was talking to a group of children when the local vicar came over to me and said, "Stop talking."'

Doing his Master's, Stephen became enthused with the work of Joanna Overing, an American anthropologist at the London School of Economics who would become his PhD supervisor. Joanna Overing believed in understanding people's day-to-day living, including their emotional life, rather than applying traditional anthropological frameworks. She had pioneered the study of the 'aesthetics of everyday life'. Her work in the Amazon demonstrated 'how the western distinction between ethics and aesthetics is irrelevant in a world where people strive for beauty in their social relations with others'.[4] She was in tune with what Stephen had seen in the Enxet.

Stephen completed his Master's and in his dissertation about the Enxet acknowledged how Sandra 'has shown great tolerance as our spare time and holidays have been surrendered to ... anthropological study'. After Joanna Overing agreed to take him on, he signed on to do his PhD, on the Enxet, in London. Stephen and Sandra had a second daughter, Rebecca, who has Down's syndrome, and lived in a flat near Sandra's parents, in Harrow in north London. They had few savings and survived on the UK benefit system.[5]

Stepping up the land rights campaign

After his first year at the London School of Economics, in 1993, Stephen and his family returned to Paraguay for Stephen to do field work for his PhD and get involved again in the campaign for Enxet land rights, this time based in Asuncion. Stephen worked for the German organization *Dienste in Ubersee*, with which he had made contact in London, and collaborated with the Anglican Church on land claims

- it still supported land redistribution. The Anglicans paid for a lawyer, Modesto Elizeche, to help. Stephen would go back and forth from Asuncion, where the family lived, to the Chaco, supporting Enxet communities in their claims. But the Anglican Church became uncomfortable with the political nature of the land campaign and stopped funding Modesto. So, Stephen and Modesto joined with other sympathetic Paraguayans to start an NGO, *Tierraviva* (Living Earth), to provide legal support to indigenous communities in both land and labour claims. *Tierraviva* was funded by the German organization Bread for the World and recruited young Paraguayans committed to justice for indigenous people, including a lawyer Oscar Ayala, a coordinator Pilar Royg and a young caseworker Rodrigo Villagra.

Tierraviva got indigenous land issues into the Paraguayan media and in late 1993 arranged for one hundred Enxet to come to Asuncion to lobby the Paraguayan Congress, the first land protest by indigenous people in Paraguay. After a speech in the House of Deputies, the lower house of Congress, which was met by spontaneous applause, the Enxet leaders were interviewed by television, radio and the press. They also met the Attorney General, among others, who remarked to Stephen that he had never met someone who was so loved and so hated by so many people. By this point, Stephen had made a lot of enemies among the large landowners in the Chaco, who had been pressing the Attorney General to have him expelled from the country.

A constant stream of Enxet stayed at Stephen and Sandra's house in Asuncion and took part in lobbying and protests in the following months as the campaign continued. There were challenges, including having to dismiss one young lawyer for taking bribes from landowners. But undeterred, *Tierraviva* raised their level of ambition when Stephen and his colleagues successfully lobbied for $40 million to be put in the Government of Paraguay's budget to settle the Enxet's land claims.

However, unhappy landowners continued to campaign against Stephen, accusing him and *Tierraviva* of manipulating indigenous people. One of those involved in one of the Enxet land claims was Heriberto Roedel, who had bought his land from the proceeds of a major fraud committed against pensioners in Germany. Roedel had kicked the Enxet off his ranch, forcing many of them to live on the main road from Asuncion. He took the step of putting a $2,000 bounty on Stephen's head, which was reported in the press. 'Stephen was well known by this point', Sandra calls over from her chair. 'He used to be in the newspapers a lot.' A French mercenary accepted the contract, and Stephen had the misfortune of running into his would-be assassin. 'He was tall, French, a big beard, rude, aggressive – quite frightening', Stephen says. They were in Concepcion, near the Chaco, buying bus tickets. The mercenary was at the other end of the ticket counter and luckily did not recognize Stephen who kept his head down. Nothing happened on that occasion, though when Stephen's mum visited Paraguay, she brought with her a heavy bulletproof vest she had purchased in the UK. 'But it was impossible for me to wear for any length of time because of the heat', Stephen says.

Fortunately, time passed. 'I think I was protected by it all being in the newspapers', Stephen adds, 'although we took precautions.' He had continued to visit the Enxet communities, but he and Sandra were careful where they went, as they would be for the rest of their time in the country. I express shock at the whole episode, but Stephen says, 'I thought I'd be worth more than $2,000. I was quite insulted.' Sandra says, 'I was a nervous wreck. He'd go out and I wouldn't know if he was coming back.' 'It was getting a bit dangerous', Stephen concedes. 'But you need to explain how things worked there', Sandra responds. 'Paraguayans, high-class ones, they controlled everything. Many were cowboys and they were trigger happy.'

Stephen knew that in the long term the Enxet and other indigenous people in Paraguay would never win most of their land claims within the Paraguayan legal system, as it was too corrupt. On the other hand, the Inter-American Court of Human Rights (IACHR) in Costa Rica could make determinations against governments in Latin America and oblige them to act. Stephen and *Tierraviva* focused their efforts there. Collaborating with Oscar Ayala, Rodrigo Villagra and the rest of the *Tierraviva* team, Stephen familiarized himself with international and national legislation and used it to put together a case for the IACHR. This showed that, despite land having passed through four or five hands since it was first appropriated from the indigenous Paraguayan population in the nineteenth century, the land claims were still current as the indigenous land title had never been extinguished. The case was strong, but it would take time to go through the system.

Stephen left *Tierraviva* in 1995, as planned, to live with the Enxet in the Chaco and undertake his PhD field work, while Sandra, Sarina and Rebecca moved back to the UK. Stephen and Sandra had wanted to stay permanently in Paraguay and, at one point, purchased some land in the Chaco to build a house, but there was insufficient support for Rebecca in Asuncion and they made the decision to relocate permanently back to the UK. Stephen stayed on for nine months, living in El Estribo with an Enxet family and focusing on his research. And he had fun, partying and dancing and playing football. He would even journey to Asuncion to watch his beloved Newcastle United on television, a 15-kilometre walk, often along flooded tracks, to the main road and then a 370-kilometre bus ride.

Academia and joining the Department for International Development

Stephen returned to the UK in 1996 to complete his PhD. I ask him if he has any regrets from his time in Paraguay. He says he left too early into the land claims, but that he had no choice due to the needs of Rebecca. He also recognizes that he was regarded by the Enxet as their 'war leader' and he somewhat unwittingly played this role. With more time, he would have put greater effort into strengthening the Enxet so that they were better able to defend themselves against the landowners and the state, although *Tierraviva* did continue this work. It was an important lesson to remember: how to support change that is sustainable. After Stephen left, new organizations were created among the Enxet, but often with support from outsiders who Stephen believes did not always have the best interests of the Enxet at heart.

In 1997, Stephen published a chapter in a book on the working conditions of indigenous people in the Chaco which drew him to the attention of the United Nations Permanent Forum on Indigenous Issues.[6] The Forum was looking into land rights in the Chaco in Paraguay and Bolivia, at the invitation of the national governments, and in turn received their own death threats from landowners. By coincidence, the team from the Forum included Isabel Ortiz, later to be an ally of Stephen's as Director of Social Protection at the International Labour Organization. Isabel Ortiz says when I speak to her, 'One of the best pieces of written evidence we read for Bolivia and Paraguay was that work by Stephen Kidd, this young man who had gone to live in the Chaco in his early twenties and observed the very difficult situation of indigenous people.' The report of the Forum's mission to Paraguay would refer to the 'pioneering work of Stephen Kidd'.[7]

Stephen was also invited back to Paraguay by *Tierraviva* in 1997 to undertake research into what had happened with the $40 million that the government had committed to Enxet land purchases. He found that much of the money had been lost in high-level corruption. Inflated prices were paid to landlords to settle land claims – often for worthless, uninhabitable land, with the large profits paid back into the coffers of the ruling Colorado Party, to be used in its election campaigns. Stephen wrote a detailed report which was reported in the press. Paraguay was a growing democracy, and there was an appetite for accountability. The Minister of Finance was implicated in the report as was the then president of the Paraguayan Institute for Indigenous Affairs (INDI), other government officials and members of NGOs. One arrest was made, that of the president of INDI who spent two years in jail. Stephen says, 'I needed to keep clear of him.'

Stephen moved from the London School of Economics to St Andrews in Scotland to continue his studies, as Joanna Overing had moved there. He took a lectureship in social anthropology at Edinburgh University in 1999 to help fund the completion of his PhD, which he achieved the following year. Stephen also did consultancy work in international development and applied to join DFID in 2000 as a social development adviser. He was not accepted due to his inexperience, notwithstanding his land rights work, but he did well on a critical thinking test and a DFID member of staff helped him prepare for the next recruitment drive with further consultancy work, contracted through Edinburgh University.

Stephen's main role was to support DFID's Overseas Territories Unit, which resulted in trips to St Helena, an island in the South Atlantic with a population of 4,500, to evaluate a DFID development programme. On his second trip, Stephen discovered what he calls 'a non-functioning democracy in which there were serious human rights issues, sexual abuse of children that was not being addressed and people living in fear of the governor'. The governor, in common with other British Overseas Territories, was an ex-UK Foreign Office official. Stephen did a radio interview before he left the island describing St Helena as 'more of a dictatorship than China'. When he was on the boat home, the governor complained to the Foreign Office in London. Stephen's report became classified as top secret and the Foreign Office called for Stephen to be sacked, which would end any potential career in DFID. The head of the Overseas Territories team decided to back Stephen, though he wanted some of the language in the report moderated. The Foreign Office eventually accepted the report and the governor committed to implementing all its recommendations. As in Paraguay, Stephen was willing to call out right and wrong. As a result of his work and that of a colleague, Sue Phillips, who was also temporarily working in the Overseas Territories Unit, the Foreign Office and DFID set up a new programme on human rights across the UK's overseas territories.[8]

When DFID had another recruitment drive, in 2001, Stephen applied and got in. His first task was to collaborate with the World Bank on providing support to China. 'It was an eye opener', he says. He worked with World Bank team leaders who were 'all powerful' and got his first exposure to a culture where programme disbursements, 'getting money out of the door', was often more important than programme effectiveness. Stephen was then put to work on Latin America, shortly before becoming head of the Social Protection Team, where learning about high levels of inequality there sparked his interest in social protection.

Not long after Stephen joined the Social Protection Team and a decade after he and his family had returned to the UK, in 2005, the first Paraguayan indigenous group land claim case was finally heard by the IACHR.[9] Stephen took leave from DFID to travel to Costa Rica as an expert witness. In 2005, 2006 and 2010, in three separate land claim cases brought by Stephen and *Tierraviva*, the IACHR found Paraguay guilty of violating the human rights of their indigenous communities, including their right to the communal property of their ancestral territory.[10] When the land claim campaign had started in the early 1990s, the Enxet held eighty thousand of the estimated three million hectares that they had owned until the late nineteenth century. As a result of the land campaign, an additional fifty-five thousand hectares were handed over. Two other indigenous groups, the Sanapana and Angaite, were supported by the land campaign and have been handed an additional forty-five thousand hectares. All three groups have more cases pending. In a fitting ending, eleven years after the first IACHR ruling, when Stephen and Sandra's daughter Sarina was doing her own Master's dissertation on indigenous rights, she came across the IACHR judgements with which her father had been involved that were now written up in the jurisprudence on indigenous peoples' land rights in Latin America.[11]

Chapter 3

FIJI

AN ADDICTION TO SUGAR

Joining the World Bank team

In 2009, two years after he left DFID, Stephen arrived in Fiji where the government wanted to reform its social protection system. I learn from a local United Nations source, talking to me over a link to Suva, the capital, that Fiji's unelected military government at the time wanted change.

> The government was determined to undertake civil service reform, privatisation of state owned entities, to introduce digital government and to develop a new constitution that provided every Fijian equal citizenry, and they wanted to protect people through inclusive socio-economic development for all Fijians. Lots was changing, there were a lot of young people engaging with government after the December 2006 event [the military coup]. And it was relatively easy for the interim government to get things moving because there was no parliament in place at that time.

The government wanted to reform the government-funded side of the social protection system, and the World Bank was brought in as the global experts. The Australian government was funding the World Bank team and brought in Stephen to work with them, knowing he would bring an alternative view for the Fiji government to consider and help keep the World Bank in check. 'The World Bank team were a bit wary when I arrived', Stephen says. 'I had a bit of a reputation at this point, though I hadn't actually published much yet.'

On joining HelpAge International as Director of Policy and Communications in 2007, Stephen's aim was to increase its focus on social protection. But despite some success, after eighteen months he left. 'Corporate management wasn't my interest or my strength', Stephen says. While at HelpAge, he met Charles Knox-Vydmanov and Steve Barrett, who would be important collaborators in the years to come. Stephen applied to be on the international 'expert panel' for social protection set up by AusAID, the Australian Agency for International Development, joining Michael Samson, Nicholas Freeland, Frank Ellis and Rachel Slater, all well known in the social protection world.

Stephen's assignment in Fiji followed. And, despite him and the World Bank team being in opposite corners ideologically, the encounter would be unusually collaborative. 'But the World Bank team straight away recommended their normal menu for Fiji', Stephen says. Their 'normal menu' included introducing a poverty-targeted benefit that used a technique called proxy means testing to identify recipients. The World Bank was supporting the use of this approach across a large number of low- and middle-income countries, including Kenya where it had attacked the universal pension.

Proxy means testing is complicated-sounding but simple in principle. It is a method to identify who should receive services including social protection by estimating, rather than measuring directly, whether a household is living in poverty. It does this by looking at non-income, observable household characteristics such as the material a dwelling is made from, whether a household owns livestock or the presence of utilities such as televisions or refrigerators.[1] Proxy means testing is used because a household's welfare level, typically measured by income in higher-income countries, can be difficult to measure directly in less formal environments, where there is little documentation. A challenge with proxy means testing is that it often gets things wrong and is associated with significant targeting errors: in most cases, over *half* of properly eligible households are excluded.[2] So it is like a roulette wheel. Why is this? As mentioned, in low- and middle-income contexts, especially in rural areas, it is common for a large majority of households to have similar incomes, so how do you distinguish one household from another? And to make it harder, incomes can change quickly over time.

The 'normal menu' also meant conditional cash transfers and workfare, the latter being poverty-targeted public works where cash or an in-kind payment is exchanged for labour. Workfare was not proposed by the World Bank in Fiji, but proxy means testing and conditional cash transfers were.

A craving for sugar

Taking a step back, from where did the need for social protection in Fiji arise? Like all countries, it faces a mixture of challenges that are particular to its history and those that are common across nations. Fiji comprises three hundred islands in the South Pacific and, like so many low- and middle-income countries, it is in part the product of its colonial past. The population is made up of two main ethic groups, indigenous Fijians, the majority, and Indo-Fijians.[3] Indo-Fijians owe their presence to workers from India being brought in by the British as indentured labour in the second half of the nineteenth century. Fiji was a British colony from 1874 to 1970. Indentured labour schemes were used, after the abolition of slavery, to put workers under contract for years at a time, labouring in harsh conditions for low wages. Globally, fifty million Asians and Africans were relocated across the globe as indentured labour during the nineteenth century, often to support the production of sugar, one of the many stimulants, along with tea, coffee, cocoa, tobacco, rum and opium, which the Global North could not get enough of.[4] Britain's consumption of sugar was an extraordinary 41 kg per person per year in

1901.[5] In line with wider global movements, the workers in Fiji were intended for the new sugar plantations.

The practice of indentured labour ended in Fiji in the early twentieth century. But the legacy of an ethnic divide, between the mainly Hindu Indo-Fijians and mainly Christian ethnic Fijians, remained. Christianity had been introduced, in part, by the Wesleyan Missionary Society from Australia, which began converting local chiefs after arriving in 1835.[6] The connection with Australia continues today, including in the funding of the World Bank team to support the government, despite two thousand miles separating Fiji from Canberra. Fiji has suffered in recent years from regular military coups which have been primarily driven by the battle for rights between the two ethnic groups.[7] The latest in 2006, when Commodore Frank Bainimarama took over to promote the rights of Indo-Fijians, was the fourth military coup since Fiji gained independence in 1970. When the Fiji Court of Appeal ruled that coup illegal, in 2009, there was a constitutional crisis that resulted in the new military government, the one that welcomed the World Bank team and that sought socio-economic development for all Fijians.[8]

Apart from historic ethnic divisions, Fiji has the challenges of poverty and vulnerability. It is not the poorest country in our story. If all the countries in the world are ranked richest to poorest by annual income per person, with Liechtenstein at the top and Somalia at the bottom, it is halfway down.[9] Just under a quarter of the population is below the national poverty line, or 12 per cent using an international poverty line of US$3.65 per day, which in real terms is US$1.70 per day.[10] The international poverty line is set in terms of buying goods in the USA, and in poorer countries goods are generally much cheaper. Also, all Fijians, like the global population, face lifecycle challenges that include having children, losing a job, becoming disabled and getting old. In addition, when Stephen worked there, a full one-tenth of the population of Fiji were living in squatter settlements, hidden from the tourist resorts along the coast, many among them looking for food on a giant rubbish tip in Lautoka.[11]

Another source of vulnerability is the climate crisis. Fijian incomes come largely from agriculture, where the main crop is still sugar, as well as fishing and tourism, and each area is vulnerable. In 2009, cyclones and flooding decimated the sugar crop, and many local families had to choose between sending their children to school and eating proper meals.[12] In 2016, one of the most powerful cyclones ever recorded in the Southern Hemisphere left more than 30,000 homes damaged or destroyed; forty-four people were killed.[13] The surrounding coral reef system, the largest in the Southwest Pacific, was smashed. The reef has partially recovered since, but it suffers ongoing bleaching from warmer seas which in turn reduces fish supplies.[14]

Recommending reforms

Deciding on how to reform any social protection system usually starts with looking at what is already in place. In Fiji, the poverty-targeted Family Assistance Programme was introduced in 1975 and at the time was worth F$60, or US$27, per household per month.[15] It was the largest programme run by Fiji's Department of Social Welfare and had 25,000 direct recipients. Taking account of others living in the same household, 13 per cent of the population of just under a million people benefitted.[16] The World Bank argued that the scheme's targeting was 'quite good', with 56% of recipients in the poorest 20% of the population, but that it could be improved.[17] It also said that it was largely for older people and persons with disabilities, rather than poor households in general.

The World Bank argued that an issue with targeting in the Family Assistance Programme was the use of social workers' assessments, but Stephen contended that the targeting was no worse than you would get with a proxy means test. He proposed having a closer look at the accuracy of social worker assessments. Stephen describes how the World Bank commissioned research which found that, of the fifty recipient households sampled, forty-nine were clearly eligible by the rules of the benefit and living in extreme poverty, and that the last one was borderline. The social workers assessments appeared to be sound.[18] These contrasting takes are possible if incomes change over time, up and down, which social workers can take account of but which a survey snapshot, used by the World Bank, misses. Stephen argued the programme should be left as it was.[19]

Stephen also contributed to World Bank analysis which showed higher poverty levels for older people and families with children, particularly large families.[20] He argued for universal tax-financed programmes aimed at different stages of the lifecycle, focusing on child, old age and disability benefits. Drawing on Mkandawire's landmark paper, Stephen made the point that, although universal programmes cost more, they are also likely to be more popular with taxpayers and attract more funding in the long term.[21] Mkandawire argues in his paper, 'The experience in developed and middle-income countries is that universal access is one of the most effective ways to ensure political support by the middle class of taxes to finance welfare programmes.'

We need to pause for a moment on a couple of points. Firstly, universal lifecycle social protection schemes, providing support to *individuals* in families with children, older people and persons with disabilities, as well as more targeted support to those of working age suffering from unemployment or incapacity, would come to lie at the heart of Stephen and his allies approach to social protection. Drawing on the evolution of social protection in wealthier countries, they came to refer to 'comprehensive, multi-tiered social security systems that enable all individuals to address the risks and shocks experienced across the lifecycle'.[22] The multi-tiered part is because schemes can be tax-financed or contributory, and when contributory, mandatory or voluntary, and people can get more than one benefit.

Secondly, one important reason for Stephen and his collaborators proposing universal lifecycle social protection schemes for *individuals*, instead of poverty-targeted benefits to *households*, is the need to address gender equality. Poverty-targeted benefits often go straight to a male head, based on the false assumption that men and women have equal bargaining power in families, which can lead to women being denied access to benefits. Ensuring individuals have entitlement can help to address this and increase women's bargaining power. Poverty-targeted household benefits can be paid to women of course, but this may not be enough to address any power imbalance. Individual entitlements draw a clearer line.[23] Power dynamics may need addressing in other ways of course, but this is one way.

It should be said, social protection has a track record of helping to address lifecycle vulnerabilities that are particular to women and girls, including early marriage and caring for children.[24] According to the UK Overseas Development Institute, 'the evidence . . . points to cash transfers having a positive impact on women's choices as to fertility and engagement in sexual activity'.[25] In different ways, it can improve gender equality in education, health, nutrition, economic empowerment and protect against exploitation, neglect and violence, which kills more women globally than road-traffic accidents and malaria combined.[26] But only a quarter of women in the world have a legal entitlement to comprehensive social protection.[27] This compares to around a third of men, with the gap explained, in part, by women's caring responsibilities. The United Nations argues that 'Social protection measures should . . . take into account the disproportionate burden of unpaid care work that society places on women [which] obstructs their ability to access formal employment and therefore contributory social security or decent wages'.[28] Tax-financed social protection therefore has a key role in reaching women who are not in the formal labour market, as well as men in a similar position, and in recognizing women's unpaid contribution to households. And schemes for individuals can reach them more directly.

The near-universal pension

Returning to Fiji, despite Stephen's efforts, the World Bank team did not shift in its view and continued to argue that the Family Assistance Programme should be abolished and replaced by a new benefit for all poor households, using proxy means testing. A different World Bank team arrived with the task of finalizing recommendations for the reform of tax-financed social protection in Fiji and getting government approval. The idea of conditional cash transfers was dropped.

Stephen persisted in trying to persuade the new World Bank team leader to propose a universal pension to go alongside the poverty benefit, to address challenges faced by older people. And there was a breakthrough. Stephen says the new World Bank team leader accepted his proposal and agreed to recommend a universal pension to the government.[29] How does he account for this?

> It was down to one-on-one meetings, it was all pretty collaborative. We were all staying in the same guest house and had meals together. The team leader had no problem with recommending the pension. His main interest was getting the proxy means test approved but he came from Eastern Europe where pensions were the norm, so he understood the rationale.

The fact that Fiji is halfway up the scale of richest to poorest countries, not at the lower end, no doubt played a part. But we will come back to the issue of affordability. And the World Bank's role was purely advisory: there was no World Bank loan at stake, as there so often is, and so no need to get approval from the World Bank Board.[30] The World Bank is not in the business of giving loans for national-scale universal pensions.

Most importantly of all, as the local UN source says, support for a universal pension was already strong, things were already in train. The pension recommendation was aligned with political processes already afoot in the Fijian government. In 2009, the cabinet had set up a committee of government and NGOs to work on policy for older people, which held a national consultation in 2010 with ministries, NGOs, academic institutions, corporate agencies, UN agencies, Faith-based and Civil-based organizations. It then held local consultations. The policy produced in 2011 recommended consideration of a tax-financed social pension. The Minister for Social Welfare, Women and Poverty Alleviation thanked 'UNFPA for its technical assistance and the three consultants: Mr Geoffrey Hayes, Dr Bhakta Gubhaju and Alastair Wilkinson, along with Fiji Council for Social Services (FCOSS), for their valuable support and advice'.[31] The government agreed to the World Bank proposal on a new poverty-targeted benefit and also decided, following the 2011 policy, to introduce a tax-financed pension.

In 2013, the Family Assistance Programme was replaced by the new Poverty Benefit Scheme, targeted using a proxy means test, and a new government-funded pension for those 70 years old or over was introduced. It was decided to poverty target the pension for the first two years.[32] 'Lots of people were kicked off the Family Assistance Programme and didn't get on the new programme, so ended up without any support at all', Stephen says. 'There was one island where there were fifty households that had been on the Family Assistance Programme and only one was targeted by the proxy means test.' The local UN source says there were also issues with implementing the pension. They say,

> The age limit started at 70 and gradually came down. Now it is 65, but though poverty targeting stopped in 2015 and it was designed to then become universal, you still only get the pension if you have no other source of income. Also, eligibility depends on your wealth in addition to income. For instance, if someone does not have any other source of income but lives in or owns a good house they may get excluded by the assessors. It's tricky. So, it's not really universal, more near-universal.

That said, taking account of the contributory provident fund in Fiji and civil service pensions, overall coverage of the pension system is approaching, or has already achieved, universality.[33] Though some other issues with the tax-financed pension remain. 'There are instances where people who should be included in the programme are not and those who should not be eligible are in the list of beneficiaries', the local UN source says. But they also see significant potential benefits. 'There is little evidence as yet that the near-universal pension is helping with social cohesion and ethnic tension. But Fiji needs social dialogue and social programmes, including universal social protection. That helps to acknowledge us all as human beings and equal citizenry with human rights, self-respect and dignity.'

Rising spending on tax-financed universal social protection schemes

Charles Knox-Vydmanov, who Stephen had worked with at HelpAge International, now works on the South Pacific with Stephen and the small British-Kenyan consultancy company of which he is CEO, Development Pathways. He and I meet in a café in south London and Charles swings his laptop around to show me what has happened to tax-financed social protection programmes in Fiji following the reforms. Since the government-funded pension was introduced in 2013, with poverty targeting stopped in 2015 to make the pension near-universal, coverage has grown to the point that it now reaches 85 per cent of pensioners. The pension age was reduced to sixty-five in 2017, as the local UN source mentioned, and the value of the benefit increased, from F$30 to F$100 (US$45) in 2017.[34] In terms of trends in spending, government expenditure on the new poverty-targeted benefit has been mostly flat since 2013, starting at 0.27 per cent of GDP and finishing at 0.35 per cent of GDP in 2022. But spending on the pension has increased, from 0.04 to 0.54 per cent of GDP in 2022.[35] This increase, only partly a result of removing poverty targeting, endorses the argument, set out by Mkandawire and taken up by Stephen, that universal programmes can be politically popular and attract increased funding, relative to poverty-targeted programmes.[36]

Since the reforms, in 2017, a universal disability benefit has been introduced worth F$90, or US$41 per month.[37] Spending is currently 0.11 per cent of GDP.[38] This was also recommended by the World Bank and like the near-universal pension, supported by local organisations.[39] The local UN source says, 'Organizations for persons with a disability had a big role in this along with the Fijian Council for Disabled People which helped to set the level of benefit.' A child benefit, for those without other sources of income and conditional on school enrolment and attendance, is in the early stages of development.[40] Since 2023, Stephen's company Development Pathways has been working with the government of Fiji, through an Australian government-funded programme, to build the case for a universal child benefit.[41] Spending on all tax-financed social protection is 1.1 per cent of GDP, and a comprehensive system is emerging.[42] According to a UN study, 'Fiji has taken early steps towards establishing a lifecycle framework for benefits provision.'[43] That framework is, arguably, a mid-point between Stephen's vision and the World Bank's original menu, reflecting the unusually collaborative approach, in contrast to battles elsewhere. Most importantly, it appears to be well-aligned to local political processes and dialogue.

The wider Pacific

Interestingly, the local UN source thinks the government and World Bank probably did the best they could in the circumstances in Fiji with the new poverty-targeted programme, despite likely targeting errors, given the government wanted a programme aimed at the poor. However, they believe the World Bank has taken proxy means testing too far in island states in the Pacific, especially small ones with populations of less than 100 thousand people. 'Proxy means testing is not generally cost-effective. It takes a while to trawl between people when you have got small numbers of households dotted around remote locations. It's much better to have universal programmes. The cost of identifying recipients and collecting data, including the drain on limited ministry capacity, is higher than just transferring cash on a universal basis.'

I ask Stephen what other countries do in the region. 'Across most of the Pacific Island countries, they have mainly universal or near-universal schemes, introduced by governments themselves, not donors', Stephen says. The list of other countries and island states that have introduced universal or near-universal schemes includes the Cook Islands, Kiribati, Nauru, Niue, Palau, Samoa, Tonga and Tuvalu.[44] 'Governments understand the importance of cohesion, treating everybody equally and not being divided', Stephen adds. The local UN source says the two most common tax-financed social protection programmes across Pacific Island countries, where they exist, are pensions and disability benefits. They are not all universal, but those that are not are usually near-universal. The source believes the World Bank is gradually coming around to lifecycle universal programmes and systems, seeing them being supported by governments. So, glimmers of hope, in this region at least.

Chapter 4

CHILE AND THE DEVELOPMENT OF THE PROXY MEANS TEST

In Fiji, Stephen saw the World Bank promoting poverty targeting through proxy means testing, as it has in many countries, despite the risk of high targeting errors. This is, as mentioned, the use of observable non-income characteristics of a household, such as the material as dwelling is made of, to estimate whether it is in poverty. Used when it is not possible to look at household's welfare directly, for example in documentation on income, it is obscure sounding but has an important role in this story. Where did the World Bank's commitment to proxy means testing come from? And where its common opposition to universal schemes, notwithstanding events in Fiji, which we will see more of? How had all of this found its place at the centre of the World Bank's approach to tax-financed social protection?

World Bank headquarters

The centre of Washington DC is organized logically. North to south streets are numbered and east to west they are lettered. At 1818 H Street Northwest is a shimmering glass structure, the World Bank's headquarters. Opposite it, on the other side of 19th Street, is the concrete building of IMF headquarters. To complete the concentration of power, half a mile away, down G Street Northwest, is the White House.

I visited the World Bank in Washington DC in 2004 as a DFID member of staff. I was attending the World Bank's two-week social protection course, *Design and Implementation of Social Safety Nets*, with other attendees from governments all over the developing world. On a quick point of language, for the World Bank, the term 'safety net' is synonymous with 'social assistance' and is assumed to include universal schemes. But 'safety net' and 'social assistance' are red flags to Stephen and his allies, who say they have connotations of 'charity' or 'handouts for the poor'.[1] They argue their use should be restricted to poverty-targeted programmes.

On the first morning of the course, I and two colleagues from the Social Protection Team in DFID passed the police outside the World Bank building, showed our photo identification and walked into the cavernous space inside. Above us, high and in big lettering, was a statement,

Our goal is to end world poverty.

Looking at the big picture, that statement – which has been changed now to *'Our dream is a world free of poverty on a liveable planet'* – is the driver of this story. The focus on the poor was motivated at least in part, as Mkandawire wrote, by observing how the poor had missed out during structural adjustment in the 1980s and 1990s, and it continues today.

The World Bank's website further refines the organization's current goal: 'Our mission is to end extreme poverty and boost shared prosperity on a liveable planet'.[2] So what resources does the World Bank have for achieving this goal? The World Bank Group is made up of five institutions set up after the Second World War. The largest and most well-known are the International Bank for Reconstruction and Development (IBRD) which makes loans to middle-income countries and disbursed US$33 billion in 2024 and the International Development Association (IDA) which provides concessional loans and grants to lower-income countries and disbursed US$28 billion in 2024.[3] This is not enough to solve all the world's challenges – resources from governments must do the heavy lifting – but sufficient to get a lot of things moving in the right direction. World Bank *income* comes from lending its own capital, whether paid in by member countries or accumulated over time.[4] And money disbursed to lower-income countries through IDA comes from forty donor countries which contribute funds every three years.[5] The top three donors are currently the USA, Japan and the UK.[6]

For social protection specifically, the World Bank has, as mentioned, a portfolio of almost US$29.5 billion in financing, covering an estimated 880 million people.[7] It provides support through lending and analytical work to at least 118 countries. Recent global disbursements outweighed all other donors combined, as also mentioned, and its annual commitments have been increasing.[8] As the World Bank itself describes it, commitments rose from US$3 billion annually between 2015 and 2018 to US$9.6 billion by 2021, driven 'by the urgent needs created by the pandemic but also reflecting the broad global dialogue'.[9]

The start and expansion

The course we had arrived for took place in a vast, low-ceilinged basement room full of circular tables fitted with microphones. Margaret Grosh of the World Bank was at the front as one of the principal teachers. In 1995, she had co-authored a seminal paper about the use of proxy means testing in Chile.[10] The World Bank's focus on poverty obviously encourages ideas on how to address it directly, and proxy means testing was one such idea. The paper describes how the approach had been used in Chile from around 1980, to target benefits to poorer households.[11] Chile was then under the dictatorship of Augusto Pinochet, raising the question immediately of whether the top-down nature of proxy means testing, and its arguable lack of respect for individuals given its roulette wheel nature, would have started in a strong democracy. Anyway, the 1995 paper is open in describing how between a quarter and a third of benefits were going to the *non*-poor, meaning there were significant targeting errors.[12] The conclusion is careful but positive: 'household characteristics can serve as reasonable proxies for information on income in assessing eligibility for social programs'. Proxy means testing was being given a qualified green light. So began a difference in perception between the World Bank and Stephen and his allies that would run and run.

In the same year as the training course, Margaret Grosh co-authored another important paper.[13] This was a 2004 review of how proxy means testing, and other targeting approaches, were performing in countries beyond Chile. By 2004, proxy means testing had started in four more countries, Armenia, Colombia, Indonesia and Mexico, and was being set up in another six, Argentina, Costa Rica, Ecuador, Jamaica, Honduras and Nicaragua. It was also being piloted in Egypt, Sri Lanka and Zimbabwe. The bandwagon was moving.

The 2004 paper argues that proxy means testing performs as effectively, in terms of targeting accuracy, as, for example, universal benefits for the young and *better* than universal benefits for the elderly. But how can this be? Universal benefits focus on recording, for example, someone's age, not on a complicated estimation of a household's level of welfare using observable characteristics, as proxy means testing does. The explanation lies in how the authors measure performance. This is from the perspective of how much is going to the poor rather than the non-poor. The annex at the end of the book gives more detail, for those interested. But the implicit assumption is that it is only benefits going to the poor that matter. Benefits going to wealthier households, even those just above the poverty line, are classified as 'leakage'.

This is a highly questionable assumption. It is common for a high proportion of the population to be poor in low- and middle-income countries by any reasonable measure. For example, 78 per cent of the population of Rwanda is below the international poverty line of US$3.65 per day, which in real terms is US$1.30, enough to buy *one-third* of a latte in Kigali.[14] Poverty lines are often somewhat arbitrary. Guidance on measuring value for money in tax-financed social protection programmes published by the UK government in 2013 also makes the point mentioned earlier, that proxy means tests 'are inevitably somewhat blunt instruments, particularly in poor countries where differences in income, assets and other household characteristics are very small, making it difficult to identify which households are above or below an eligibility cut-off point'.[15] And, as also mentioned, incomes can change quickly, which can cause significant churning as people move in and out of poverty from one year to the next. An example of this is in Uganda, where only 46 per cent of households that were in the poorest 20 per cent of the population in 2013 had been in the poorest 20 per cent in 2011.[16] All of this means benefits going to the 'non-poor' *are* of value.

I spoke to the late Philip White, who was the main author of that UK government guidance along with Anthony Hodges. Philip repeated an argument I have seen Stephen present to governments in many countries.

When you realise the poor are not a consistent, definable group, that takes you to the lifecycle approach to social protection, including universal schemes. Their income levels and identity change far more rapidly than household surveys carried out every three or five years allow for. The World Bank are aiming at a group that does not exist as a definable group of people.

Universal programmes, on the other hand, are specifically designed to reach everyone in the eligible group, regardless of income. Surely any estimate of targeting errors should take account of that. But the 2004 review does not.

Like the 1995 paper, the 2004 review is careful in its conclusion: 'targeting can work but... it does not always work everywhere'. And that caution is also repeated in 2008 in a 600-page World Bank social protection textbook, *For Protection and Promotion: The Design and Implementation of Effective Safety Nets*.[17] The book summarizes the 2004 performance index results:

> Proxy means testing, community-based selection of individuals [targeting by 'a group of community members or a community leader'] and demographic targeting of children [targeting by age] showed good results on average, but with considerable variation ... demographic targeting of the elderly and self-selection [which encourages 'the poorest to use the program and the nonpoor not to do so' e.g. by setting wages for public works at a low level] ... showed limited potential for good targeting.

But careful conclusions or not, as in the 1995 paper, proxy means testing was being given official approval.[18]

The debate is joined

In 2011, Stephen and a colleague, Emily Wylde, published a paper, funded by AusAID, which estimated targeting errors arising from the design of programmes using proxy means testing in Bangladesh, Indonesia, Rwanda and Sri Lanka.[19] They found that the proportion of the intended target group excluded in error was around half in each case, sometimes less, sometimes a lot more.[20] The size of the error means, if you are within the target group of say the poorest 10 per cent, you have an even chance of *not* being selected for support. As already stated, you are betting on red or black in roulette. In Stephen's view, the 2011 paper is the first example of proxy means testing being properly challenged. 'Until then, papers on proxy means testing had been World Bank advocacy pieces.'

After that, the World Bank published two papers, in 2014 and 2015, which asserted that proxy means testing 'can accurately and cost-effectively target the chronic poor'.[21] Earlier caution had apparently gone. Then a new voice joined the fray. Martin Ravallion was head of research at the World Bank until 2012 and a major name in international development until his untimely death in 2022. He met

Stephen at AusAID headquarters in Canberra Australia in 2012, where Stephen took the opportunity to communicate his views on proxy means testing, including his recent experience in Fiji. In 2016, by coincidence or not, Martin Ravallion, who had by now left the World Bank, published a paper with Caitlin Brown and his partner Dominique Van de Walle which appeared in 2018 in the *Journal of Development Economics*.[22] Simulating results using data from nine African countries and referring to Stephen and Emily Wylde's work, the paper concludes that universal programmes may well be better than those using proxy means testing *even for poverty-targeted programmes' primary objective, reducing poverty*. The reason for this is high targeting errors, a lack of transparency in terms of who is and is not eligible, the potential to undermine political support for programmes and relatively high administrative costs. We will come back to this list. Martin Ravallion said in another paper in 2016 that the World Bank's 'Social-protection policy advocacy turned "targeting" (avoiding leakage to the "non-poor") into a fetish – oddly confusing the ends and means of social protection'.[23] In other words, the World Bank has mistakenly taken the aim of reaching the poor and reducing poverty to imply support must be targeted only at the poor.

Stephen co-authored two more papers on proxy means testing. The first, an International Labour Organization paper written in 2017 with Bjorn Gelders and Diloá Athias, says, '[proxy means testing] suffers from high in-built design errors, additional errors introduced during implementation, and infrequent surveys, meaning that it cannot respond to the dynamic nature of household incomes.'[24] The World Bank had acknowledged this last point itself in 2015, though apparently without moderating its promotion of proxy means testing.[25] Stephen's second paper, in 2020, another collaboration with Diloá Athias, looks at errors deriving from both programme design and implementation and finds that the proportion of the intended target group excluded in nineteen schemes using proxy means testing varied 'between 29 per cent for Uruguay's Asignaciones Familiares scheme and 96 per cent for Guatemala's Mi Bono Seguro programme.'[26] The paper also looked at four universal programmes which they said 'performed well, with exclusion errors below 10 per cent'.

The full costs of proxy means testing

In 2022, the World Bank published the 539-page book *Revisiting Targeting in Social Assistance: A New Look at Old Dilemmas*.[27] Here the tone is more reasonable. The book says that all targeting options should be considered and trade-offs weighed, because every country is different. It concedes that the often rapid fluctuation of incomes means we must get away from the idea of a static 'poor' population to be targeted. It includes references to papers that Stephen co-authored. And in a positive development, it also acknowledges the potential cost to individuals and communities of poverty targeting, saying, 'there may be stigma or social discord as a result of making distinctions between people of different welfare levels.' The book says, 'Programme recipients may have to identify themselves publicly or semipublicly as in need of help. This may entail . . . being cross-questioned on income and expenditures . . . These experiences can feel demeaning.'

Stephen and his collaborators have long argued that untransparent and error-strewn proxy means testing is not consistent with human rights. The issue of stigma had already been addressed in the World Bank's 2008 social protection textbook, but the 2022 book deepens the acknowledgement of human rights, saying they ensure 'accessibility, dignity and autonomy, non-discrimination and equality, inclusion of vulnerable groups, gender sensitivity, and transparency and accountability'. It adds, 'the litany of criticisms from the human rights perspective of . . . proxy methods of selection can seem almost preclusive of their use . . . there is much in targeting practice to improve upon.' I speak about the tone in the 2022 book with an official in the ILO, a long-standing supporter of universal social protection. They welcome the fact the World Bank 'has finally recognised human rights and international standards'.

But despite these positive signs, the book reverts to type, saying, 'To reduce poverty, it is usually more cost-effective to ensure that a greater share of benefits accrue to the poor than to expand coverage broadly.' In other words, if you want to address poverty, use poverty targeting. The book concedes proxy means testing has 'inbuilt statistical error' and that demographic – that is, universal – targeting is 'possibly pragmatic' in some circumstances. But proxy means testing is described as 'imperfect but realistic'. In 'high informality' contexts, the book says, proxy means testing and community-based targeting – where community members or a community leader select recipients – or some combination of the two, 'becomes the common option'. The message is strengthened by another World Bank publication the same year, *Charting a Course towards Universal Social Protection*: 'it is important to adhere to the principle of prioritizing the poorest and most vulnerable for support . . . it will be critical for countries to build their capacity to accurately identify those most in need'.[28] And again in a 2024 336-page World Bank review of social protection in South Asia, which asks 'countries to initially prioritize the poor and vulnerable when using their limited public resources'.[29] And once more in 2025 when the World Bank's *State of Social Protection Report 2025* says, 'social assistance should be focussed on those in the poorer quintiles, especially in LICs (low-income countries) and MICs (middle-income countries) where fiscal resources are limited and needs are high.'[30]

The World Bank also argues in its 2022 book, resonating with the 2004 paper, that proxy means testing has in fact *lower* targeting errors than universal programmes. It repeats the method of looking only at benefits reaching 'the poor' and treating benefits going to the rest of the population as 'leakage' and of no value, despite its concession on the dynamic nature of incomes.[31] The problems with this approach have been mentioned. One curious feature of the approach is that a programme using proxy means testing in which, roulette wheel-style, only *half* of the beneficiaries are among the poor, can score better than, for example, a universal programme with near perfect targeting for which only 40 per cent of beneficiaries are poor, a result that simply reflects the prevalence of poverty in the population.[32]

Targeting errors are not the only issue, as we have seen. Martin Ravallion and colleagues talk in their 2018 article about relatively high administrative costs, a lack of transparency in terms of who is and is not eligible and the risk of undermining political support for programmes, each of which will be mentioned briefly.

High administrative costs

Relatively complicated proxy means testing will inevitably be more expensive to operate, other things being equal, than universal targeting. Administrative costs from proxy means testing, perhaps in combination with community-based targeting, are likely to be a greater share of the programme budget. This is because of all the data collection and processing required to estimate whether households are eligible for poverty-targeted programmes, as opposed to, say, recording a person's age to test their eligibility for universal programmes aimed at children or older people.[33] In its 2008 book on social protection, the World Bank states, 'proxy means testing will clearly have many of the highest costs.'[34] DFID's guidance on value for money in tax-financed social protection programmes concurs. 'On the cost side, [proxy means tests] are quite "heavy" on data collection and processing requirements to determine eligibility.'[35] The World Bank's 2022 book argues, not unreasonably, that accurate administrative cost information is hard to obtain.[36] But it also says, 'In most cases, administrative costs represent a small portion of the total program budget, even for programs that differentiate eligibility . . . by welfare level.' And, 'The various costs of targeting selected groups, families, or individuals are usually low or within an acceptable range.' It appears to argue costs are barely worth worrying about, even for proxy means testing. This may, at a stretch, be true for existing programmes with high errors. But it is unlikely to be true for poverty-targeted schemes with targeting errors brought down to a more acceptable level, for example through regular data gathering. Such schemes will surely be significantly more expensive to administer than relatively simple universal schemes for children or older people, by any reasonable assumption.

Lack of transparency and social conflict

Proxy means testing may incur social costs because of the lack of transparency of decisions on who is eligible, as Stephen observed in Zambia. The World Bank's 2022 book accepts proxy means tests are 'Difficult for people to understand'.[37] This has consequences. Researchers have found, for a poverty-targeted conditional cash transfer in Nicaragua, 'the targeting process . . . is poorly understood at the community level . . . When asked why some households were beneficiaries and others not, informants offered a range of explanations, from divine intervention to a random lottery.'[38] The UK government's value for money guidance gives other examples and highlights social costs, raising again the issue of compatibility with human rights. 'Supposedly more objective proxy means tests were perceived by communities in Ghana as an unaccountable "black box" process undertaken by some far-off computer, more resembling a lottery than a reflection of actual need. Similar perceptions of [proxy mean tests] among non-beneficiaries in Mexico, Nicaragua, Indonesia and Lebanon led to tensions, unrest and even conflict.'[39] There are other examples. A poverty-targeted programme in Peru was found to generate negative feelings from beneficiaries to non-beneficiaries.[40] The World Bank's 2022 book also describes local tensions for a poverty-targeted programme in Lesotho and in Chad where 'communities [demanded] a share [of benefits] from beneficiaries'.[41] A 2023 review of social protection programmes aimed at improving health outcomes in twenty-four countries finds, 'in settings where some received the cash and others did not, the lack of an equal approach caused tension, suspicion and conflict.'[42] One of the programmes reported on in that review is the poverty-targeted PROSPERA, a conditional cash transfer in Mexico. In a blog, Stephen quotes the anger of a Mexican community doctor at the scheme's targeting:[43]

> Frankly, I don't know how they got the data for [PROSPERA] ... because there are families here in this community who are poor, poor. There are large families that do not have support from [PROSPERA] ... and we have proof. I have been here eight years and know the entire community inside out ... and I've found that there are many poor people who do not have [PROSPERA] ... and we do not know why they have been left outside the program.

The 2023 review reports that the upshot of PROSPERA's targeting has been, as in Lesotho and Chad, a guilt-driven sharing of resources between recipient and non-recipient households.[44] This is behaviour repeated elsewhere, including in Indonesia, as we will see.

Political support for programmes – choices at the design stage

Political support for programmes is obviously critical to their sustainability and is worth a slightly longer look. Perhaps the best test of political support for different programme designs is to see what exists at the moment. Do governments, some of whom will have been influenced by donors, choose means-tested tax-financed benefits – including poverty targeting through proxy means testing or some other method – or do they choose universal or near-universal programmes? As mentioned, they frequently choose a mix. But in terms of the balance for the world as a whole, including countries at all income levels, figures from the ILO suggest that there are more means-tested schemes for pensions and disability benefits, and an equal split between means-tested and universal or near-universal schemes for family and child benefits.[45] But we must be careful in our interpretation. Universal schemes are regularly much larger in terms of spending, as we would expect. To take one example, in the UK, spending on the near-universal state pension is ten times as large as spending on means-tested pension benefits.[46] Shahra Razavi, Director of Social Protection at the ILO, points to evidence 'from a wide range of countries' on inclusive schemes receiving greater funding.[47] In any case, the high number of means-tested benefits globally should not be a surprise, or a problem, per se. The ultimate target is universal *systems*, not programmes. These will be a combination of contributory and tax-financed benefits, and the latter can be universal or means tested. Tax-financed programmes do not all have to be universal, so long as all programmes in combination provide universality. But representative governments, in broadening coverage, should have the choice. For his part, Stephen concurs with Mkandawire's 2005 paper which argues, as we have seen, *not* that there should be no means testing at all, but that means testing, where it exists, should sit within a wider framework of universal provision.[48] This view is supported by a recent paper by Dimitri Gugushvilia and Tijs Laenen in the *Journal of International and Comparative Social Policy* which says, 'targeting ... seems to work best when embedded within the overall framework of universalism.'[49]

That said, in low- and middle-income countries specifically, given the commonly high and persistent informality in labour markets which limits the reach of contributory schemes, and the practical difficulty of targeting by welfare level without very high errors and other costs, as we have seen, there is likely to be a need for tax-financed universal or near-universal schemes to do a lot more of the heavy lifting.

Yet we see poverty-targeted programmes *are* being implemented in large numbers in low- and middle-income countries. I mention to Stephen national poverty-targeted social protection programmes that come to mind. These include schemes that governments have funded, sometimes with donor support, in Brazil, Indonesia, Mexico, Pakistan, the Philippines and Chile. Are these not evidence of the popularity of poverty targeting within governments? He concedes Chile.

> But the rest were started by donors or donors have been all over them. The World Bank and Inter-American Development Bank (IDB) were all over Bolsa Familia in Brazil and PROGRESA [later PROSPERA] in Mexico, giving them loans and doing the evaluation and propaganda. The same people move backwards and forwards between Latin American governments and the World Bank and IDB.

He goes on, 'The Indonesian government are close to, and influenced by, the World Bank. The World Bank and DFID influenced the setting up of and part-funded the Benazir Income Support Programme (Pakistan). In the Philippines, the Pantawid Pamilyang Pilipino Programme is mainly government funded, but receives technical support from the Asian Development Bank and the World Bank.'

We must be careful here not to deny the agency of governments, which may have chosen poverty targeting regardless of World Bank involvement. But we must also acknowledge donors have influence, especially given they control much-needed resources. A recent research paper on the development of the Pantawid Pamilyang Pilipino Programme in the Philippines says, 'Some of our informants (within government) were ... uncomfortable with [the] ... evident role of external influence in the policy process.'[50] In Kenya concerns have been raised by senior members of government that donors have had more influence over social protection policy than the government itself.[51]

I try to think of examples of governments supporting poverty-targeted programmes in larger countries in the world, which are relatively free of donor influence because of their size. I mention the government-funded Mahatma Gandhi National Rural Employment Guarantee Scheme (MGNREGS) in India. 'That's a universal national employment guarantee, it's not poverty-targeted', Stephen says. What about government-funded and poverty-targeted Food for Work in Bangladesh? 'That's just a way of government getting rid of rice surpluses which the government maintains for historic reasons, to avoid famine, which occurred in the 1970s after independence from Pakistan in 1971. Bangladesh has a policy of keeping massive rice reserves, which need clearing out every year. Without Food for Work they'd throw the rice into the sea.' What about China's government-funded and poverty-targeted Dibao programme, introduced to support the population and reduce social unrest when state-owned enterprises were being reformed? 'It's a national poverty-targeted programme, yes, okay, but it's low budget – you'll probably find the pension schemes in China spend way more. And China is an authoritarian state where the government doesn't have to worry about what wins votes, so you'd expect more poverty targeting.' Stephen mentions Uzbekistan as another authoritarian state in which government-funded, poverty-targeted support exists, with very small budgets, and also universal or near-universal schemes with much larger funding. And of course, Chile was an authoritarian state when the proxy means test was introduced there by Pinochet's government.

We go through other countries, Georgia, Ethiopia, Ghana, Tanzania. Generally, poverty-targeted programmes appear to be either donor-influenced - and often funded by donors, at least in part - or on a relatively small scale, or both. 'Okay, there are other poverty-targeted schemes out there, including in Latin America with conditional cash transfers', Stephen says. 'But they are small, less effective, less popular. It is 19th century social protection. You often find them where governments are minimising costs to elites in those societies by minimising taxation but, as I say, they are often influenced by donors.' There may be other schemes in low- and middle-income countries, but, outside of the ex-Soviet bloc where systems are commonly more developed, a long list of relatively large national-scale poverty-targeted programmes which governments have set up and are funding on their own, without donor influence, is not jumping out at us.

What about government-funded universal social protection programmes in low- and middle-income countries? Daisy Sibun and Holly Seglah, a current and former colleague of Stephen at Development Pathways, have constructed a list of governments that have funded universal or benefit-tested social protection programmes. Benefit-tested schemes are available to those in the population not receiving support from elsewhere, such as a contributory pension, typically the vast majority. Their list includes:[52]

Albania
Argentina
Armenia
Azerbaijan

Belarus
Bolivia
Botswana
Brazil
Brunei
China
Cook Islands
Eswatini
Fiji
Georgia
Guyana
Iran
Iraq
Kazakhstan
Kenya
Kiribati
Kosovo
Kyrgyzstan
Lesotho
Libya
Maldives
Mauritius
Mexico
Moldova
Mongolia
Montenegro
Myanmar
Namibia
Nauru
Nepal
Niue
Palau
Papua New Guinea (New Ireland only)
Russia
Samoa
Seychelles
Suriname
Tajikistan
Tanzania (Zanzibar)
Thailand
Timor-Leste
Tonga
Turkmenistan
Tuvalu
Uganda

Ukraine
Uzbekistan
Vietnam

That is fifty-two low- and middle-income country governments which have chosen a total of eighty-eight tax-financed universal or benefit-tested schemes for children, persons living with disabilities and older people. Fourteen of these are ex-Soviet bloc, but fifty-two countries is more than a third of the 152 low- and middle-income countries in the world.[53] How could we not be impressed that fifty-two governments are delivering universal or near-universal schemes? Especially as this is almost entirely without donor support, indeed often in the face of direct opposition from the World Bank, sometimes with the support of the IMF which it works with closely. In this story, we have seen opposition for an existing universal government scheme in Kenya, and we will see it again in Uganda, Nepal, Mauritius, Zanzibar, Mongolia, Kyrgyzstan and Iran. And that is just this particular story. Donor support for universal programmes is rare. Almost all national universal schemes have been introduced by governments without financial support from donors. Stephen cites a universal pension under development in Uganda which DFID has helped to finance, discussed in Chapter 7, and one or two other examples we will come back to. But the list appears to be very short. There are also small pension schemes designed by the World Bank in Kosovo and the Maldives, and the near-universal pension in Fiji which we have seen the World Bank supported, but these are all government funded. In contrast, there is the World Bank and other donors' widespread support, including financing, for poverty targeting. The latest manifestation is the World Bank and other donors' promotion of something called social registries across developing countries. These are data bases designed to poverty target across a whole range of programmes, not just one, which are discussed further in Chapter 12.

Political support for programmes – the evolution of tax-financed programmes

It is also interesting to look beyond programmes' original design, at how they evolve over time. Changes in funding can indicate an increase or decrease in political support, because programme budgets are not fixed. This last point is obvious, but poverty targeting implies that budgets *are* fixed. Lant Pritchett, a well-known former World Bank economist has referred to 'the naïve assumption of fixed budgets' for tax-financed social protection schemes.[54] The potential cost of poverty targeting in undermining political support and funding for programmes is mentioned by the World Bank in its 2004 paper on targeting. 'Excluding the middle classes may remove broad-based support for such programs.'[55] However, the World Bank goes the other way in its 2022 book, arguing that there is a lack of clear evidence of more inclusive programmes getting more support. It refers to a summary of academic writings on what is called median voter theory, the hypothesis related to the idea that voters will support programmes that benefit them directly. 'Empirical research has not found strong support for the median voter theory and its central implication about redistribution.'[56] But Shahra Razavi at the ILO calls this 'a selective review of the literature'.[57]

I am not aware of a comprehensive cross-country study on how tax-financed social protection programmes of different designs evolve over time, and so we are left with a limited but interesting selection of examples of wider coverage schemes attracting more support. We have seen in Fiji the relatively strong political support for the near-universal pension, reflected in the rising budget. For Zambia, Stephen's long-term collaborator Nicholas Freeland describes how the Social Cash Transfer scheme was poverty-targeted and nearly all donor-funded until, around 2012, government money helped to finance an expansion. 'In the five years since 2012, it has become . . . a near-universal old-age and disability pension and it has expanded exponentially: to nearly 600,000 households in all 108 districts of the country.'[58] Then there is the popularity and expansion of universal programmes in countries such as Bolivia, Mongolia, Mauritius and Nepal, among many others.

In contrast, the ILO says, 'Mexico's much-lauded PROSPERA [conditional cash transfer] programme was abolished in 2019, illustrating the particular vulnerability of [poverty] targeted programmes to discontinuation.'[59] PROSPERA, previously known as PROGRESA and then Oportunidades, was no ordinary programme. The scheme that so angered that community doctor with its targeting was the first 'national conditional cash transfer program targeting poor and extremely poor households', and hailed by the World Bank in 2014 as 'A Model from Mexico for the World'.[60] In 2018, Andrés Manuel López Obrador was elected as the first progressive president of Mexico in three decades. He abolished PROSPERA the following year.[61] Going forward, according to the IMF 'The government's social programs since 2019 have focused on universal coverage'. This includes a universal pension.[62] In 2022, the Los Angeles Times labelled López Obrador 'one of the most popular leaders on earth'.[63]

Stephen also argues, in a 2018 paper, that well as tending to have smaller budgets, poverty-targeted programmes commonly have a lower level of benefits.[64] He points out how, in Brazil, 'the slow increase in the size of the [donor-influenced and poverty-targeted] Bolsa Familia benefit is [an] . . . indication of the higher political priority given to Previdencia Social, the near universal and part contributory, part non-contributory pension in Brazil'.[65] In addition, research from Development Pathways, shows that, for countries with a reasonable level of democracy where systems of accountability are functioning, tax-financed pensions in systems with wider coverage are worth more. It shows:[66]

- In countries with a pension system with 70 per cent coverage of older people or more, the value of tax-financed pensions averages 18 per cent of GDP per capita.
- In countries with a pension system with less than 40 per cent coverage of older people, the value of tax-financed pensions averages 11 per cent of GDP per capita.

Stephen concludes, 'Poverty-targeted programmes are programmes for the rich, because they save money and result in lower taxes for the rich, and universal programmes are programmes for the poor, because they have bigger support, bigger transfer values and have a bigger impact, but it's often presented as the other way around.' The ILO agrees, saying as well as receiving more funding, 'inclusive social security transfers... offer higher value transfers to recipients... enjoy much higher quality implementation... [and] are also much more effective in their impacts on poverty and inequality'.[67] This supports the 'paradox of redistribution' mentioned in Chapter 1, that the more we target benefits at the poor, the less likely we are to reduce poverty and inequality.

Letting countries make their own choices

Much of this is selected examples of course, rather than comprehensive evidence. And there will be examples of strong government support for poverty targeting, such as the massive expansion of a conditional cash transfer scheme in Indonesia, albeit in part using World Bank resources, which is discussed in the next chapter. But the fact that inclusive schemes *can* generate greater support and, according to the ILO, receive greater funding 'in a wide range of countries', means it is not defensible to dismiss the case for universal schemes out of hand, as the World Bank too often does. Every context will have its own unique characteristics. We should not forget the costs incurred by universal programmes. It is clearly more expensive in terms of the total cost of benefits to provide them to a wider group of people.[68] But it is for countries to weigh the pros and cons. Donors should be led by what populations and representative governments want, within obvious constraints such as an acceptable level of government legitimacy.[69] It is beholden on them to not pre-judge programme design.

But it is not just the World Bank at fault. Other donors including DFID, for which I worked for many years, suffer from a strong bias towards poverty targeting in terms of the schemes they support, despite attempts to redress the balance. So I am as culpable, within the limits of my role, as anyone in this story. This bias is damagingly dismissive of the role of universality and solidarity in national development. And it can be worryingly insensitive to local political processes. As a result, the important dynamic between choice of programme design and political support can be cut across by donors encouraging governments in a particular direction.

But these are donors with their own internal targets to reduce poverty and whose own budgets *are* fixed in their three-to-five-year programmes of support, a point we will come back to in Chapter 14.[70] Philip White summarized how the logic for donor-supported poverty-targeted programmes can dissipate outside donor offices, in the real world, reflecting the messages from Thandika Mkandawire and Martin Ravallion.

Universal programmes have different objectives over a different time frame and in a much more political context, so they work to a different logic. Cost-effectiveness is about achieving desired outcomes at minimum costs. Poverty-targeted programmes tend to be about cost-effectiveness in the short term, starting with a limited notion of what is affordable, often financed through a World Bank loan agreement over a specified period, and seeking to maximise effectiveness by concentrating those resources on households identified as the poorest of the extreme poor. Universal programmes tend to be about cost-effectiveness in the long term, starting with desired outcomes in terms of embedding over the longer term minimum acceptable living standards for broad, readily identifiable sections of the population facing lifecycle vulnerabilities, and seeking to realize those outcomes at minimum cost. Reducing poverty in the short term may take you to poverty targeting in the first instance, but when you consider wider agendas, especially political support, and add in the difficulties and inaccuracies involved, the case for poverty targeting using proxy means testing becomes weaker and weaker, even in terms of short-term cost effectiveness.

I think back to that 2004 course and how I enjoyed visiting Washington DC and sitting in the World Bank's shining headquarters listening to Margaret Grosh, Martin Ravallion and Lant Pritchett. And I think about how I do not envy World Bank staff their mission of ending extreme poverty. It creates a pressure and incentive structure which the institution as a whole should be blamed for, or even the wider world, but not individuals among World Bank staff. That pressure and incentive structure means that, looking back to 2004, the World Bank was in the early stages of starting a proxy means testing bandwagon that has now reached more than sixty low- and middle-income countries, and is likely to be accelerated by the promotion of social registries.[71] In countries where social protection spending has stayed low and the infrastructure to deliver social protection schemes is getting skewed away from simple national systems towards the paraphernalia of difficult-to-do poverty targeting, the development of effective and sustainable social protection systems may have been impeded for years, if not decades.

Chile: a brief revisit

In Chile, the birthplace of the proxy means test, there were mass protests in 2019. According to the website *Open Democracy*, 'the largest, most intense, and most extensive mobilizations exploded.'[72] Branko Milanovic, the world-famous Serbian-American economist and expert on inequality, observed that the government shot and killed '16 people in two days of socially motivated riots'.[73] Inequality of incomes and wealth was a key motivation for the protests.[74] As Milanovic describes it, 'The bottom 5% of the Chilean population have an income level that is about the same as that of the bottom 5% in Mongolia. The top 2% enjoy the income level equivalent to that of the top 2% in Germany.'[75]

Why was inequality in Chile so high? When General Augusto Pinochet was in power, from the US-supported military coup in 1973 until 1990, his government turned Chile into the poster child of neoliberalism, of economic liberalization and privatization. Chile eventually became a high-income country, though much growth came after the dictatorship ended when a coalition of centre-left parties ruled for two decades and partially reversed some of the neoliberal reforms.[76] But while poverty fell during this growth, inequality remained high and even increased.[77] The social protection system, along with other government support, was not sufficient to prevent this. In the development of the social protection system, as well as introducing proxy means testing around 1980, Chile, encouraged by the World Bank, pioneered pension reform in Latin America, in 1981.[78] It introduced contribution-financed private accounts where private companies manage pension funds and benefit levels are based on investment performance.[79] Milanovic says it was a switch to 'roulette capitalism'.[80]

On 19 December 2021, Gabriel Boric, a thirty-five-year-old former leader of demonstrations in 2011 against private education, won the presidential election by 12 percentage points, replacing billionaire Miguel Juan Sebastián Piñera Echenique.[81] In January 2022, Chile established a new near-universal pension for those aged sixty-five or older, which excluded only those in the richest 10 per cent of the population. The pension replaced two schemes, one targeting older persons in low-income households and one aimed at those in the poorest 60 per cent of the population.[82] Boric has declared, 'If Chile was the birthplace of neoliberalism, it will also be its grave.'[83] Perhaps to the list of countries that have demonstrated the positive link between universal social protection schemes and political support can be added the birthplace of the proxy means test itself.

Chapter 5

INDONESIA

HOW TO HELP A QUARTER OF A BILLION PEOPLE

The arrival of proxy means testing

In 2010, the Australian Government asked Stephen to go to Indonesia. There he would see the government collaborate with the World Bank, and others, to develop a social protection system intended to serve 250 million people, and proxy means testing would be at the centre. Stephen's job, which he did through regular visits, as in Fiji, involved working in a team funded by an Australian government programme. Called the *Poverty Reduction Support Facility*, it had a budget of more than AUS$100 million.[1] It was being run by a consultancy company called Palladium, and its purpose was to support the National Team for the Acceleration of Poverty Reduction – based in the vice president's Office under an influential vice president, Mr Boediono – to improve existing tax-financed social protection.[2] At that moment, tax-financed social protection comprised relatively small programmes spread across various ministries. The World Bank already had staff looking at social protection in their office in Jakarta. They were also part-funded by the Australian Government, and when Stephen arrived, he got on with them.

> I went out drinking with this World Bank bloke from New Zealand. He was doing interesting work on people with middle incomes that were left out of government support. He called them the 'Scooter Class'. They couldn't afford a car and were stuck between the small formal sector, where people paid into social insurance, and poverty-targeted programmes aimed at the poorest.

Proxy means testing arrived in Indonesia in 2005, promoted by the World Bank. It was used to poverty target a short-term cash transfer for nineteen million households, introduced to compensate for a cut in fuel subsidies.[3] Reducing fuel subsidies is generally a progressive measure where higher-income groups are the greater users of fuel. However, in response to the programme compensating for the subsidy cuts, there were protests in more than a third of affected villages about the amount of benefit received, and about how recipients were selected.[4] There was also an increase in the crime rate of 5.8 per cent in response to the poor targeting.[5]

While the programme had success, achieving its goal of avoiding an increase in poverty, the challenges of poverty targeting had been laid bare.

Short-term, poverty-targeted cash transfers were provided again in 2008 and 2013, following more reforms in the fuel sector. The proxy means test was also used to target a relatively small World Bank-supported conditional cash transfer programme, Program Keluarga Harapan (PKH), in which households below the poverty line defined as 'very poor' and containing children or pregnant mothers were targeted, and received their benefit in return for using specific health and education services.[6] PKH was small, but it was going to get much bigger.

Thinking big: the Unified Database

Proxy means testing had ownership within the Indonesian government which, supported by the World Bank and the Australian government, had big plans for expansion. In 2011, the government developed the Unified Database, which would come to contain socio-economic and demographic information for 40 per cent of the population, or approaching 100 million individuals.[7] After its launch in 2011, the Unified Database was managed, from 2012 to 2015, by the National Team for the Acceleration of Poverty Reduction, home to the programme Stephen was a part of, before moving to the Ministry of Social Affairs. Up to 2015, registration data was collected by the government statistics agency using a survey every three or four years of households identified as 'poor', based on existing data sources such as current recipients of programmes as well as community knowledge. Since then, on-demand registration has been piloted and is being rolled out nationally via local government.

The Unified Database has grown in importance. 'It became a central part of government', Stephen says. Data collected, in surveys and through on-demand registration, is used in a proxy means test for determining eligibility for a range of programmes at national and decentralized level, including tax-financed social protection schemes. 'Around 2015 the government used it to award people social protection cards which gave access to various government-funded programmes. And, if you were on the Unified Database the government would pay your contribution to health insurance, which was probably the biggest programme of all. It was kept on servers, with analysts continually trying to enhance and improve it.'

Unified Database or not, poverty targeting through proxy means testing remained a huge challenge to do accurately. Using survey data that may be out of date was one source of error, as was the process of developing a model in the first place to estimate who is for eligible benefits. World Bank research on the cash transfer introduced to compensate for lower fuel subsidies shows that while most of the benefits went to the poorest 40 per cent of households, more than a third did not.[8] Program Keluarga Harapan (PKH) *appeared* to be doing slightly better when the World Bank found 'over 70 per cent' of recipients were in the poorest 40 per cent of the population.[9] But it is misleading to look simply at the proportion of recipients that are poor, not least because, as mentioned in the previous chapter, it allows you to score small schemes targeted by proxy means testing higher than relatively simple universal programmes with national coverage.[10] It is more meaningful to look at the proportion of intended recipients mistakenly excluded from (or included in) the programme, and from that, at the proportion of recipients correctly targeted.[11] Following this approach, Stephen and Diloá Athias found that *less than 20 per cent* of those in PKH were correctly targeted.[12] The difference in the estimates is explained by the fact the programme covered just 7 per cent of the target group of 'very poor' households containing children or pregnant mothers – so it was easy to be outside this group but still within the poorest 40 per cent of households in Indonesia.[13] The finding of high targeting errors was no fluke: a previous estimate of PKH's targeting errors, from the World Bank, was even worse.[14]

And there were targeting issues elsewhere. 'The largest tax-financed social protection programme in Indonesia was a rice voucher programme called Raskin', Stephen says. 'It was targeted to the poorest households using the Unified Database. But there was opposition in many of the rural areas, and villagers reacted to the targeting by taking the vouchers from the government officials and distributing them on a more even basis.' As the government has reported, 'many communities disagreed with the practice of poverty targeting and distributed the rice to everyone in the community.'[15] The government adds, 'Although 15.6 million families were officially registered as beneficiaries of the food assistance programs in 2017, in practice, around 28.6 million households were benefitting.' Communities had taken matters into their own hands to ensure greater equity, and presumably greater social peace. But even with the communities' actions, the government's own analysis still found that '45 per cent of the poorest 15.5 million households were excluded from the scheme in 2017'.[16]

The need for social protection in Indonesia

The enthusiasm of the Indonesian government for poverty targeting through proxy means testing reflects, in part, being close to the World Bank. This goes back several decades. Further back than that, in the sixteenth century, Europeans were attracted to Indonesia by the potential for spice production. Indonesia became a Dutch colony but eventually gained independence at the end of the Japanese occupation in the Second World War. Its new leader, President Sukarno, was replaced by General Suharto in the late 1960s following mass killings that mostly targeted members of the Indonesian communist party. Between half a million and a million people died.[17] Fearing a communist Indonesia, powers in the Global North, including the UK and USA, had been involved.[18] The World Bank, with Robert McNamara, US Defence Secretary at the start of the Vietnam War, as its president, re-established lending to Indonesia with the arrival of now President Suharto, and Indonesia became one of the World Bank's most important country programmes.[19] Australian government engagement in Indonesia was also to become significant and long-term. Stephen says, 'When I was there, they were putting in AUS$1 billion a year into Indonesia.'

Since the 1960s, Indonesia has enjoyed an extended period of growth that was only interrupted by the Asian economic crisis of the late 1990s, when President Suharto finally left power. There were corresponding falls in poverty, though one-fifth of the population remains under the international poverty line of US$3.65 per day, or US$1.20 in real terms. On the global scale of richest to poorest countries measured by income per capita, Indonesia is below Fiji, at two-thirds of the way down.[20] It also has higher inequality than Fiji, though it is below the extremes of Chile.[21]

Apart from poverty, the Indonesian population has a number of challenges, over and above those normally associated with the human lifecycle. More than one-third of children under five years of age experience stunting, which can affect cognitive development, schooling and productivity in later life.[22] And female participation in the labour force is lower than for women in other East Asian countries.[23] Indeed, women's economic potential remains a large untapped resource for sustainable growth across the world, not just in Indonesia. According to the OECD, 'If women participated in the [global] economy identically to men, it would add up to USD 28 trillion, or 26%, to annual GDP in 2025.'[24] Moreover, when resources are in the hands of women, this can have a big impact on children's nutrition, health and school attendance – all good for sustainable growth – because women tend to invest more in families and communities.[25]

Another challenge in Indonesia is its vulnerability to the climate crisis, which is high and rising. The country is made up of more than 17,500 islands and is the world's largest archipelago. According to the World Bank, the fact that much of the population lives in 'lower elevation coastal zones' puts Indonesia in the top third of countries in terms of climate risk, with its high exposure to flooding and extreme heat.[26] Indonesia is also within 'the highly seismic Pacific Ring of Fire which experiences 90 per cent of the world's earthquakes'.[27]

A new government strategy

Despite this context, help that included support to the poorest and most vulnerable in Indonesia only started relatively recently. Poverty-targeted support began in response to the 1997–8 financial crisis. Before then, government help to those in need centred on things like stabilizing food prices, developing rural infrastructure and implementing credit programmes.[28] But the government's view of social protection was broadening with the development of the Unified Database, despite targeting challenges.

In 2014, a new president of Indonesia was elected, Joko Widodo, nickname 'Jokowi', who was seen as progressive and accessible. The Vice President Mr Boediono left office and was replaced by Jusuf Kalla. Over the next four years, the Vice President's Office supported the development of a new vision for social protection. Within the office, the programme of support funded by the Australian government was ending. Stephen was included in the team designing a new phase for the programme called *Mahkota*, Indonesian for crown, which started in 2016 though with a reduced budget. Cardno, another private company, won the bid to implement the programme with Stephen's company Development Pathways as junior partners. Stephen hoped to contribute to reform, and in his role as programme technical director supported those in government arguing for a more universal approach to tax-financed social protection schemes. This was at a time when every programme of significance was poverty-targeted, so the task for advocates of universality was large and would take time.[29]

And World Bank support to social protection in Indonesia was expanding. A team led from World Bank headquarters in Washington DC became more prominent within the country than the World Bank team in Jakarta that Stephen had got on with. A US$200 million loan to the Ministry of Social Affairs was agreed, in 2017. Its purpose was to expand Program Keluarga Harapan (PKH), the World Bank-supported and poverty-targeted conditional cash transfer, despite its high targeting errors. The press release announced, 'Due to PKH's high impact, the government decided to scale up its coverage from 3.5 million families in 2015 to 10 million, or 15 percent of the population, by the end of 2020.'[30] This massive expansion would be targeted using the Unified Database and proxy means testing. The press release argued, 'Among Indonesia's social assistance programs, the PKH, implemented by the Ministry of Social Affairs, has the highest impact per dollar spent in terms of poverty and inequality reduction but has the lowest budget allocation.' It was saying that PKH offered the best value for money among existing programme and needed more resources. But is this true? There is good evaluation evidence that PKH has had some positive impacts, as you would expect, but the question of whether benefits set against costs – in other words, value for money – outperforms, for example, universal programmes, given targeting errors and all the other costs that we have seen, appears to be unresolved.[31] Notwithstanding this, the Indonesian government put significant funds of its own into the expansion of PKH to make a total budget allocation of US$5.5 billion over five years.[32] By 2018, PKH had expanded to reach ten million households.[33]

There was also progress on wider social protection reform. A full strategy for social protection in Indonesia was under development among officials in the Vice President's Office, with Stephen and others in support. *Mahkota* recruited Karishma Huda, a collaborator of Stephen who had worked for organizations including the BRAC Development Institute and Development Pathways. 'It took Karishma and I a bit of time, but we started making some really interesting contacts', Stephen says. 'There were people in government with enthusiasm for universal lifecycle social protection. We had one meeting at the Ministry of Social Affairs where I showed staff how challenging poverty targeting was in terms of errors, and they were interested.' Within the Vice President's Office, Bambang Widianto, Executive Secretary of the National Team for the Acceleration of Poverty Reduction in the

Vice President's Office, was happy to consider the evidence that Stephen presented to him on errors in targeting.

In 2018, a new vision for social protection was published, drafted by a team in the Vice President's Office called the Social Assistance Working Group, led by Sri Kusumastuti Rahayu.[34] It describes a comprehensive, multi-tiered system of tax-financed and contributory schemes, with a combination of universal and poverty-targeted schemes for the former. Bambang Widianto says in the foreword that there are major gaps in social protection coverage, 'especially for the emerging middle-income groups who typically work in the informal sectors.' This is the Scooter Class that the local World Bank team had identified. In an endorsement of lifecycle social protection, he says that the future social protection system in Indonesia will 'protect children through inclusive child grants . . . (and) ensure social protection for the elderly and guarantee the availability of protection for people with disabilities across all age groups.'[35] The strategy also reminds everyone that the Indonesian constitution stipulates the right to social security for *all* Indonesian citizens.

Implementing the strategy

The government's 2018 social protection strategy was developed and published but has it had any impact? I ask Sri Kusumastuti Rahayu, known as Kus, when we speak over a link to Jakarta. 'The impact of the strategy is actually massive', she says. 'Before it, the government rarely discussed the concept of social protection as a system.' Indonesia has a 2004 law defining social insurance, for employment and for health, but does not have a law for social protection as a whole. The strategy begins to fill the gap. 'Now we need government and Parliament to introduce a new social protection law and to get the institutions in place.' Kus knows it will be a long road, but the strategy means there is a clear plan. 'We are proposing a universal pension, to help with our aging population, and a universal severe disability grant. Support to school age children will be poverty-targeted as now, and we want to expand social insurance for employment through to the informal sector, especially women, to make it universal.'[36] So the plan contains poverty targeting, but within a framework of universality. This reflects wider social policy in Indonesia where there is near-universal access to education, at the primary level, and near-universal access to health.[37]

The strategy also has wider backing. 'The biggest supporters of our strategy have been the Ministry of Finance and inputs were also received from Bappenas', Kus says. Bappenas is the Ministry of National Development Planning in Indonesia. 'The now Deputy Minister of Finance and chair of the Fiscal Policy Agency, Professor Suahasil Nazara, even suggested the title of the strategy, 'Social Protection for All.' But there are also challenges. 'I've been really optimistic about social protection reform until recently', Kus says. 'But then the pandemic hit and now times are tight. And in its response to the pandemic the government has had to use existing social protection programmes of course, which has made reform more difficult.'

Aside from the pandemic, a challenge is that only 10 per cent of GDP in Indonesia is collected in tax.[38] This is low by international comparisons, and low tax revenues and low spending on social protection can be mutually reinforcing. The social contract is an agreement between citizens and government: Stephen and his colleagues say, 'when it functions well, citizens pay taxes to the government and, in return, the government should use these revenues to provide their citizens with good quality public services, infrastructure and protection.'[39] In Indonesia, universal social protection schemes may have an important role to play in strengthening that social contract. For now, government spending on social protection remains, as the World Bank and government concede, 'low as a share of GDP and by international comparison.'[40] Before the pandemic, spending on tax-financed social protection in Indonesia was just 0.35 per cent of GDP with the largest programmes Program Sembako, a poverty-targeted food voucher programme that replaced Raskin, and PKH.[41] This figure includes World Bank loans, to be repaid in the future. The government's response to the pandemic, including new programmes, raised this to 1.6 per cent of GDP, but much of this is temporary. In terms of the wider social protection system, spending on contribution-funded social insurance is 0.2 per cent of GDP.[42] Contributory social insurance is, at the moment, mainly for civil servants and military and police personnel. There is scope for expansion, but this is made more difficult by the fact that most of the labour force in Indonesia work in the informal sector where there is less regulation and contributions are harder to collect and harder for people to afford.

With the strategy, there are signs that a collective will to broaden tax-financed social protection is opening up. The World Bank itself has hinted wider reform may be needed. It has recently argued for 'guaranteed minimum protection across a person's lifecycle', suggesting improving 'the protection for the elderly and disabled by providing cash transfers', though it is unclear whether it is still thinking in terms of poverty-targeted benefits.[43] The Ministry of Finance review of the government's response to COVID-19 still promotes poverty targeting, but it also says that 'the Indonesian government needs to . . . think of ways to expand [social protection] coverage beyond the poorest 40 per cent of families in the country', in line with the government's social protection strategy.[44] It argues, 'Other countries have a much lower GDP than Indonesia but invest approximately 2 per cent of GDP on tax-financed social protection.'

Indonesia is a slow burn in terms of reform. We can argue about whether the World Bank has been a force for or against progress towards a comprehensive, multi-tiered social protection system for a population of a quarter of a billion people. We don't know what the government would have done in the World Bank's absence. Though we can undoubtedly make a strong case that a good part of World Bank and government resources for tax-financed social protection would have been better spent on universal schemes. But the government itself has been committed to the development of the Unified Database, and it has invested major resources in the expansion of the conditional cash transfer PKH.[45] Yet it has been encouraged along this route by the World Bank, which has a clear bias towards poverty targeting. Now the government, along with the World Bank itself, has raised the issue of significant gaps in support. There is a clear appetite for a more comprehensive system, and to fill the 'missing middle' between the formal sector and poverty-targeted benefits. But steps to fill those gaps could have started much earlier. Looking ahead, 'The journey is not going to be easy', Kus says. 'The government needs to be ready for the next fifty years. We are worried about that. But Stephen helped us with that strategy. It's a start. We have the ingredients.'[46]

Chapter 6

ISTANBUL

THE WORLD BANK'S LOVE FOR CONDITIONAL CASH TRANSFERS

Origins

The World Bank has promoted common design features for tax-financed social protection schemes in low- and middle-income countries, as we have seen. These include poverty targeting using proxy means testing and applying conditions to benefits - such as requiring families to attend health clinics or send their children to school - both of which are part of the PKH programme in Indonesia, as well as poverty-targeted public works programmes which we will come back to. We have seen significant concerns about costs and the overall rationale for proxy means testing. What about for conditional cash transfers?

I discuss the origins of the World Bank's obvious enthusiasm for conditional cash transfers with Stephen. He starts with the evolution of social protection more generally in the World Bank, beginning with contributory schemes, which are, as mentioned, the complement to tax-financed benefits in social protection systems. 'They worked on pension reform in the 1980s and 1990s. They did serious damage to social insurance by encouraging private pensions, individual accounts rather than pooled schemes.' As we have seen, Chile was a pioneer. 'It was an experiment that failed.' The late Michael Cichon, former director of the ILO's Social Protection Department, concurred when I spoke to him, arguing that those reforms, including what he calls the 1981 'Pinochet-World Bank' reforms in Chile, 'pushed tens of millions of people into poverty'.[1] The World Bank itself now concedes that the reforms 'did not lead to the expansion in coverage that early reformers envisioned, and the systems are also increasingly failing to deliver adequate pensions'.[2]

'Then they tried Social Risk Management in the 2000s', Stephen says. The head of social protection in the World Bank at the time, Robert Holzmann, and another World Bank member of staff, Steen Jorgensen, wrote a paper on Social Risk Management in which the focus was on the risks households and communities face, from local household risks such as disability to wider risks such as floods.[3] 'It was an important and interesting contribution which still has relevance today. But it was more of an analytical technique than a blueprint for future social protection systems. So, there was still a gap.' Stephen goes on,

> In the 2000s, Steen Jorgensen on the social development side of the World Bank and Robert Holzmann on the social protection side tussled for ascendancy. The social development side in the Bank was much more creative, and not dominated by economists, and pushed back against conditional cash transfers when enthusiasm for them started. But then social development was put under 'infrastructure' during a Bank reorganisation and all the innovative people left. There was no internal challenge left when Robert Holzmann took over social protection in its entirety. And there wasn't much to promote following the failures on pensions. So, they latched onto conditional cash transfers.

The two original poverty-targeted conditional cash transfer programmes were the mentioned PROGRESA programme in Mexico, renamed Oportunidades and then PROSPERA, which started in 1997 – the one that was the World Bank's 'Model from Mexico for the World' and was summarily ended by President Andrés Manuel López Obrador in 2019 – and Brazil's Bolsa Familia, which started in 2003.[4] According to Professors Sam Hickey and Jeremy Seekings, of Manchester University and Cape Town University respectively, 'In 2002, the World Bank hosted a conference on [conditional cash transfers] in Mexico, and took participants on a "pilgrimage" to [PROSPERA] facilities. This was the first "rallying point for the true believers, founding fathers of what would become the [conditional cash transfer] movement."'[5] The attraction of conditional cash transfers lay in their apparent encouragement of greater human development and economic growth, to generate additional impact or an extra bang for every buck spent on benefits. Though evidence on whether this has happened would be disputed. The examples of PROSPERA and Bolsa Familia led to the World Bank latching onto and advocating for conditional cash transfers until they became 'an unquestioned part of World Bank policy'.[6] It is a relationship that appears to be half reasoned and half a love affair.

Istanbul

In 2006, Stephen, as head of the Social Protection Team in DFID, along with his colleagues and international collaborators, pushed back against the growing movement for conditional cash transfers. They said that they were still an unproven model and questioned the 'effectiveness and moral appropriateness of placing conditions on entitlements'.[7] Battle was joined in Istanbul when the World Bank asked Stephen and his team for funding for an international conference on conditional cash transfers.[8] Stephen agreed to provide £50,000 on condition – the irony was conscious – that there be sessions in the conference that provided arguments both for and against conditional cash transfers. He also wanted DFID to decide who would argue in opposition. The World Bank was uneasy. 'It didn't exactly project confidence in their case', Stephen says. But it complied, and Stephen brought in social protection expert Michael Samson to make the case against. 'He's a great speaker.'

The Istanbul conference opened in June 2006 in front of the Prime Minister of Turkey. When it was Michael Samson's turn to speak, he argued there was lots of evidence of positive impacts of conditional cash transfer programmes, but there was no evidence that the impact is a result of the conditions themselves. It was more likely the cash transfer on its own or the fact that programmes were simply raising awareness of issues such as health, nutrition and education. Raising awareness is something that can be done more cheaply with an information campaign, rather than applying conditions which need monitoring and enforcement, so this was an important point. In addition, it can be argued that raising awareness rather than applying conditions is more consistent with respecting human rights. To Stephen's surprise, the World Bank speaker putting the case *for* conditional cash transfers largely agreed with Michael Samson's argument. 'The rest of the World Bank team there weren't happy with him', Stephen says. 'They became visibly upset during the meeting and stood up to insist that they would robustly look at the evidence and show that the conditions themselves made an impact.'

Three years later, in 2009, the World Bank published the product of its staff's efforts, a 361-page book on conditional cash transfers.[9] The book concluded that, in terms of impact, 'there is limited evidence on exactly which feature of (conditional cash transfer) programs matters most – the cash, the conditions, the social marketing of the program, the fact that transfers are made to women'. Given that monitoring conditions and sanctioning non-compliers takes significant administrative capacity, this was a problem. The authors added, 'There . . . may be good arguments against conditioning if the same result can be achieved at a lower cost.' The book argues for more research but, essentially, it was saying that Stephen and his collaborators including Michael Samson were right.

Back to the lab

Despite producing the 2009 book, the World Bank was not ready to give up. It funded experiments in Burkina Faso, Kenya, Malawi and Morocco to measure the additional impact of conditional cash transfers, over and above unconditional transfers, to see if the extra cost of administering conditions was justified. The initial results of the Malawi experiment were published in 2010.[10] The experiment looked at school enrolment, attendance and drop-out rates among adolescent girls in the city of Zomba in southern Malawi, using 'randomized conditional and unconditional treatment arms'. The authors announced unambiguously they 'do not detect a higher impact in the conditional treatment group'. In other words, for all their additional cost, conditions made no difference. However, the same authors published a paper in the *Quarterly Journal of Economics* the following year, from the same experiment, and changed their findings. This time they said that conditions *did* have a bigger impact.[11] In 2012, Stephen and his collaborator Rebecca Calder, a former adviser in DFID, investigated. They found that the research method had been changed and raised concerns about the new approach 'focusing on ... teacher reporting and school ledgers ... (and) dismissing self-reporting by girls as unreliable', despite issues of reliability with the former.[12] They were also concerned about small sample sizes and differences between the conditional and unconditional groups and the fact that 'it is unclear whether this was reliably controlled for'. They said of the revised approach, 'it is not possible to conclude that the revised methodology is superior to the original one'. Stephen is dismissive of the second paper. 'It was just intellectual dishonesty'.

Notwithstanding issues with the Malawi research, Berk Özler of the World Bank, a co-author of the two Malawi papers, announced in a co-authored blog in 2011, 'Conditions work! But are they a good thing?'[13] In other words - presumably - conditions result in a greater impact, but does the extra benefit outweigh the extra cost? Referring to quasi-experimental evidence from Ecuador and Mexico, the experimental evidence from Malawi and additional experimental evidence from Burkina Faso, the blog says, 'you get a big bang for your buck in terms of enrolment and attendance ... if you condition the transfers on school attendance'.[14] It implies, though does not say explicitly, that you gain extra impact with conditions *and* the extra impact is worth the extra cost. Nicholas Freeland, a long-time collaborator of Stephen, thought the picture was less clear. Looking at the experimental results for Burkina Faso and Malawi, as well as for Kenya, he said results were 'contested, controversial, but ultimately rather disappointing'.[15] He was arguing the case for conditions had not yet been made.

Berk Özler and his blog co-author Francisco Ferreira raised questions about conditional cash transfers in a second blog in 2011, which returned to Michael Samson's argument: 'would a (unconditional cash transfer) plus a social marketing campaign aided by communication scientists, psychologists, and behavioural economists perform better than a (conditional cash transfer)?'[16] They concluded, 'alternative designs should be squarely on the table when the next generation of cash transfer programs is being designed'. This is a shift. It is also in line with the World Bank's 2009 book. But there is a problem here. While these blogs were being carefully drafted, conditional cash transfers were being promoted, including on a large scale in Indonesia. It is all too easy to talk about the 'next generation of cash transfer programmes', but when you start down a road the short-term so often becomes the long-term. The Indonesian government's massive investment in PKH is evidence of that. Governments, especially low- and middle-income country governments, investing precious resources in programme design and delivery, cannot quickly change direction. Stephen says, 'It was all about privileging small experimental pilots, not developing national systems.'

It is also about privileging conditional cash transfers above other schemes. The Bolsa Familia programme in Brazil is probably, with PROSPERA in Mexico, the most celebrated conditional cash transfer in the world. Stephen refers back to his meeting with the late Martin Ravallion in Canberra in 2012, when the latter was still head of research at the World Bank and acting chief economist. 'I asked which social protection programme in Brazil has had the biggest impact on inequality.' The question was prompted by Martin Ravallion giving a talk extolling the virtues of Bolsa Familia. When Ravallion said he did not know, Stephen said,

'It's the Previdencia Social.' This is the long-established near-universal pension, part contributory and part tax-financed. Stephen explains. 'Donors including the World Bank don't have anything to do with Brazil's pension, so Martin Ravallion had no idea. Their only interest was in the conditional cash transfer, they had no interest in what was at the core of the social protection system.' In 2013, Stephen and Karishma Huda published a paper pointing out Bolsa Familia has less than half the number of recipients of the Previdencia Social and a fraction of the spending: 0.4 per cent of GDP compared with 7.5 per cent of GDP.[17] Citing an International Social Security Association study, it says the pension system has 'brought about a 12 percent reduction in inequality, Bolsa Familia's contribution was 0.6 percent'.[18]

Back on the trail of evidence, in 2012 the question of whether an unconditional transfer, with an information campaign, would be better than a conditional cash transfer was answered by experimental results from Morocco, which Nicholas Freeland once again scrutinized.[19] An initial report in 2012, Freeland says, showed unconditional transfers had a *larger* impact on student participation than conditional cash transfers, not the other way around. Not only did they cost less, unconditional transfers had a bigger impact. But this result was muddied when, as in Malawi, a further paper was released, in 2013, which renamed the unconditional transfers as 'labelled cash transfers' because they were accompanied by a positive message on education encouraging school enrolment.[20] The goal posts had been moved. The report was then able to conclude that the research 'tells us little about . . . how an unconditional and unlabelled cash transfer would compare to a [conditional cash transfer]'. Nicholas Freeland was scorning. 'If a programme does not have [a condition], then it is unconditional, pure and simple.' He adds, 'there exists an earlier version of the report . . . And in this version . . . there is no mention whatsoever of a [labelled cash transfer].'[21] Stephen says, 'More intellectual dishonesty.'

In 2014 Berk Özler and others published a systematic review of the evidence for conditional cash transfer and education which says, 'The effect sizes for [school] enrolment and attendance are always larger for [conditional cash transfers] compared to [unconditional cash transfers] but the difference is not statistically significant.'[22] This appears to be at odds with the Morocco result, which showed a bigger impact for unconditional transfers. In addition the review compares programmes that are chalk and cheese in the real world. These include, on the unconditional side, national old age pensions in Brazil and South Africa and, on the conditional side, a cash transfer pilot in China aimed specifically at children and reaching just 150 students. And the review *still* does not answer the question of whether the supposed extra impact of conditional cash transfers justifies the extra cost, so it leaves us no nearer a conclusion of whether they offer better value for money. Adopting a more realistic tone, a 2021 summary of evidence on cash transfers, also co-authored by Berk Özler, gives qualified support to conditional cash transfers but emphasizes that unconditional support is becoming more popular.[23]

In 2016, a rigorous literature review carried out by the UK Overseas Development Institute went some way to answering the question on impact and cost. It says, 'while there may be a role for including an element of conditionality in certain contexts, it is increasingly apparent that encouraging beneficiaries of cash transfers to take certain actions, which may involve considerably lower financial and other costs than strict monitoring and enforcement of sanctions, can contribute to progress towards intended outcomes.'[24] This is careful language, but the ODI was saying unconditional cash transfers, with a positive message, may be the better way to go. A 2023 review of global evidence on the impact on adult and child mortality, published in *Nature* concurs, describing 'similar effects for conditional and unconditional programmes'.[25] Another 2023 review, on the impact of mental health, found larger effects for unconditional schemes compared to conditional schemes.[26]

Negative side effects, human rights and scalability

But the story does not quite end there: there are three additional concerns relating to conditional cash transfers that should be mentioned briefly.

Negative side effects. Conditional cash transfers can have inadvertent effects. A Yale University study points out, 'An unintended consequence of conditionality may be the distortion of recipients' behaviour in ways that lower social welfare.'[27] The second of Berk Özler's blogs acknowledges this, pointing to the fact that, in Malawi, 'girls given [unconditional cash transfers] were significantly less likely to suffer from psychological distress in comparison to girls who were offered [conditional cash transfers].'[28] The 2023 review of evidence on mental health talks of the 'potential adverse effects of conditionality on mental health.'[29] And a recent review of evidence in the *Journal of Adolescent Health* says, 'imposing conditions may be actively harmful for the mental health of adolescent girls.'[30] There is also an issue of potentially imposing gender norms. Development Pathways argues, 'conditional programmes... risk perpetuating gender inequalities by placing further care responsibilities on women. This is because benefits are tied to conditions such as providing nutrition and education for their children.'[31] A Tanzania study found an increase in 'depressive symptoms' for women and points to 'conditions which rely on stereotypically female roles'.[32] And the Yale study describes an example from Brazil where women moved away from formal employment in Brazil to meet time-consuming health check-up conditions.[33] Stephen adds another inadvertent cost. 'In the Philippines, the low value of the Pantawid [conditional cash transfer] programme's transfers has generated increased child labour, as families need higher incomes to cover school costs and avoid being sanctioned.'[34] Özler's blog concedes, 'Such trade-offs may well start stacking the deck in favour of . . . unconditional support.'[35] It adds, 'many families do not take up a [conditional cash transfer] offer' because of the side effects.

Human rights. The non-take-up of conditional cash transfers brings up the question of whether they are humane and defensible from a human rights standpoint. Can it be justified, threatening to withdraw benefits if certain behaviours are not carried out? Stephen points out that, 'Sanctions . . . tend to exclude the most vulnerable children – including those with disabilities – since they find it most difficult to comply with the conditions.'[36] Social protection expert Ian Orton articulates the argument that 'human rights are unconditional, universal and indissoluble in character, their fulfilment cannot be based on supposed "deservingness". In this sense, [conditional cash transfers] . . . are clearly detrimental to securing human rights.'[37] Conditional cash transfers can also be seen as ideological to the extent that they advance the view that poverty is the fault of 'the poor'. But in reality, sanctions may not be strictly enforced. I observed myself uneasiness with enforcing conditions in Brazil. In the state of Bahia in the north, I met a local council worker administering Bolsa Familia who refused to stop people's benefit if they did not meet the conditions. 'I know these people and there is often a good reason for their children not going to school. How could I deprive them of money they need?' However in other contexts, such as Indonesia, the World Bank has pressed for a strengthening of sanctions.[38]

Scalability. Brazil, Indonesia and Mexico have administered conditional cash transfers at a national level, enforcing conditions with, no doubt, varying degree of strictness. But monitoring and enforcing conditions may be impracticable in other contexts. Berk Özler concedes 'scalability remains an open question' and that evidence he has cited is from 'small experiments'.[39] Stephen and Rebecca Calder point out,

> Some of the most telling evidence on conditions comes from programmes such as the [Cash Transfers for Orphans and Vulnerable Children] . . . programme in Kenya and the [Livelihood Empowerment Against Poverty] . . . programme in Ghana. Both have attempted to implement conditions yet, even at a small scale, the resulting programmes have been far too complex to manage due to the relative weakness of both countries' administrative systems.[40]

And both Kenya and Ghana are classed as middle-income, not low-income where capacity is likely to be lower. There is little point in developing conditional cash transfers if they cannot be part of a national system.

Not letting go

At the same time that fundamental questions have been raised on conditional cash transfers, inside the World Bank and out, the World Bank's love affair has continued. In 2016, the same year as the Overseas Development Institute report containing a strong critique of conditional cash transfers was published, World Bank president Jim Yong Kim, known as Jim Kim, was quoted in the UK newspaper *The Guardian* describing the success of a conditional cash transfer programme to tackle stunting in children in Peru. He drew a broad conclusion. 'We're going to say to every country in the world that has a problem with stunting, we're ready to bring you the Peru formula. We're willing to provide financing for these conditional cash transfers. Conditional cash transfers are great anyway. They help poor people. They stimulate the economy, they are a great thing to do.'[41] The

Peru model may have been successful on its own terms, though even there, would an information campaign have been better? In any case, given the evidence, Jim Kim's enthusiasm for applying conditional cash transfers to 'every country in the world' that has a problem with stunting – which is a widespread issue, as we see with the countries in this story – is a significant cause for concern.

It may be appropriate to support conditional cash transfers in some places, where the political economy points in this direction, even if the World Bank has been less than rigorous in its use of evidence supporting their use. The World Bank's 2009 book points out, 'Political economy considerations . . . may favour conditional over unconditional transfers: taxpayers may be more likely to support transfers to the poor if they are linked to efforts to overcome poverty in the long term, particularly when the efforts involve actions to improve the welfare of children.'[42] We have seen how, in 2017, in Indonesia, the World Bank doubled down on its love for conditional cash transfers with its US$200 million loan to expand the conditional cash transfer Program Keluarga Harapan (PKH), and how there has been significant investment from government. Bolsa Familia in Brazil may be another example. Though even here, Stephen is dismissive. 'In both countries, donors were all over those programmes.'

The big picture is that, just as with proxy means testing, there has been a massive expansion in the use of conditional cash transfers, notwithstanding fundamental issues with their use. The Yale University study describes how between 1997, when the first conditional cash transfer programme in Mexico started, and 2014, the number of (non-OECD) countries with conditional cash transfers went from three to sixty-four.[43] In terms of expenditure, in Latin America and the Caribbean, the region where the movement started, spending on conditional cash transfers is more than a fifth of the total for tax-financed social protection.[44] It has been harder to secure reliable estimates for other regions.[45] But the evidence suggests that, in many countries, the World Bank and other advocates – including DFID where I worked for a number of years – have wasted much precious time and resources encouraging this expansion. Social protection institutions and systems take time to build and simplicity and doability are important principles to follow. That is true for high-income countries, and it is especially true for lower-income countries.

Yet as we have seen, some of the World Bank's own blogs and publications have pointed out that *un*conditional cash transfers are quite likely to give better value for money. Where is the connection between those blogs and publications and the design of programmes in countries? Where is the internal learning within the World Bank? Martin Ravallion published a paper in the 2016 Journal of Economic Perspectives ruing the lack of that internal learning. He described World Bank research showing low levels of public services, including health and education, in countries which 'advocates (of conditional cash transfers) did not always pay proper attention to'.[46] He was referring to the futility of having complicated schemes obliging people to attend a health service or go to school when a sufficient level of health and education services does not exist. We will return to the issue of lesson learning.

It was a landmark moment when the Mexican government ended PROSPERA, the original World Bank-supported flagship conditional cash transfers, in 2019. It was a sign that the ship may be turning. Margaret Grosh from the World Bank has also said recently, 'I observe that conditionalities are becoming both less common and lighter, and more social messaging in many cases now.'[47] Is this evidence that the World Bank's love of strictly sanctioned conditional cash transfers is fading? Perhaps, but love embers surely still glow.

Chapter 7

UGANDA

IN THE HEART OF AFRICA

In Uganda, something unusual happened. A donor, DFID, helped a national government fund the introduction of a universal social protection programme. I saw the beginning of the process when one Friday afternoon in 2009 I sat in the study of my family's bungalow, just after starting as the new economic adviser in the DFID office in Kampala. I was reading bids for a multi-year DFID contract to work with the government on social protection in Uganda.

DFID's global interest in supporting the development of government-funded social protection schemes was high at that point. The Social Protection Team's paper on social transfers had been published four years earlier, and Jo Bosworth, DFID Uganda's social development adviser, was one of many advisers in country offices that wanted to support governments in getting something done. One of the consultancy firm bids was from Maxwell Stamp and HelpAge International. It was written, unbeknown to me, by Stephen and Steve Barrett, who Stephen had worked with at HelpAge International.[1] I sent my bid scores to the DFID office, to be added to others, and Stephen and Steve Barrett's bid duly won. So began a decade-long engagement for Stephen on social protection in Uganda and a battle between different parts of the Ugandan government around the establishment of a national tax-financed universal social protection scheme.

From Colville to Kony

The World Bank is involved in this story, but it was not initially. At that time, they had a different focus: supporting the north of Uganda which had recently been damaged by conflict.

I knew of course Uganda had conflict in its recent past when I arrived for my new job. I knew about Idi Amin, whose grass airstrip for his helicopter was around the corner from where we lived. And I knew Amin trained at the Royal Military Academy Sandhurst, in England. But going further back, I did not know that, in 1894, according to a report in the *Irish Times*, 'British soldiers, under the command of Henry Colville, consul of Uganda, waged a bloody campaign of oppression as

Bunyoro (a Bantu kingdom in western Uganda) was annexed under the British Protectorate of Uganda.'[2] Nor that Bunyoro 'subsequently suffered from starvation, malnutrition and diseases that reduced its population from 2.5 million to a mere 100,000 by 1900'.

Nor did I know that the south of Uganda, where the British settled, benefitted the most from colonialism and that other areas, including the north, lagged behind and that this would be important background to conflicts to come.[3] Nor that Buganda, a Bantu kingdom in the favoured south, once visited by the explorer Henry Morton Stanley, was awarded a chunk of Bunyoro land by way of a thanks for siding with the British. I wished I had been more diligent in my reading though – or that I was better briefed – when, in 2009, a senior Ministry of Finance official pulled me to one side to say that the land dispute was still current and that the British government needed to take responsibility and compensate descendants of the aggrieved parties. Needless to say, the British government of which I was a part was not interested.[4]

The story of British colonial rule in Uganda – Uganda was a protectorate of the British Empire from 1894 to 1962 – is a typical one of divide and rule. Division was added to when people from South Asia were invited to Uganda to be a cushion between the British and Africans, by occupying the middle rungs of commerce and government.[5] Before this, 32,000 indentured labourers had been brought from India to work on the Uganda Railway. I have heard it said that people from South Asia were housed in Kampala in such a way as to create a physical buffer between the British and the local black population. Whether this is true or not, sufficient resentment appears to have been created for Idi Amin to exploit when he expelled the ethnic South Asian population in 1972.

The UK has damage to make up for, and some recompense is being delivered through its aid programme, but nowhere near enough. And that aid is not without conditions. In the year I worked there, much time was taken up by DFID, me included, and the British High Commission, complaining to President Museveni's government about human rights. There was a point here, in that there were plenty of suspected abuses and corruption, and a lack of democracy. Uganda is 99 out of 167 in the Economist Intelligence Unit's world democracy rankings, with President Museveni described as an autocrat who likes to 'crack down on the opposition and hold on to power'.[6] But the historic irony of the British government, also responsible for the 1950s suppression of the Mau Mau Uprising in neighbouring Kenya, complaining about human rights abuses was lost.

President Yoweri Museveni started as a figure of admiration for the West. In 1981, he headed the Popular Resistance Army (PRA), a group of twenty-seven men, among them the future president of Rwanda, Paul Kagame.[7] Having learned about guerrilla warfare in Mozambique, Museveni led the PRA in an attack on the Kabamba Military Barracks in southern Uganda, to capture guns and vehicles. This was an echo of Castro's high-risk attack with a small group on the Moncada Barracks in 1953 which helped start the Cuban Revolution. An insurgency started in Uganda during which the PRA merged with other resistance groups to form the National Resistance Army (NRA), which became and remains the national army of Uganda. The NRA fought Milton Obote's oppressive government that had superseded Idi Amin's violent reign, with support from the left-behind north of Uganda, and took Kampala in 1986.[8]

A terrible legacy of national division came in 1987, the year after Museveni became president, when the rebel Lord's Resistance Army (LRA) was born among those in northern Uganda who had been left behind and subsequently abused by Idi Amin and Milton Obote.[9] The LRA abducted, mutilated and killed thousands of civilians, with children suffering particularly badly. Support fell as a result, and when I worked in Uganda two decades later, the LRA was on the run and northern Uganda was opening up. The World Bank, DFID and other donors sought to help the recovery. But the gloss on Museveni, who was a darling of the international development community in the 1990s as his government sought to build the nation, was fading with his suppression of political opponents. The risks he had taken in liberating and unifying a country the UK had helped to divide were apparently forgotten.

Seeking government approval

Amid Museveni's fading lustre, Stephen, with others, sought to assist the government in starting to build a social protection system. In 2010, he arrived as head of the design team for DFID's social protection programme in Uganda.[10] The programme would support the government in developing tax-financed social protection. The design team in Kampala had consultants that included Charles Langwa-Ntale, Jane Namandu, Emily Wylde, economist and a collaborator of Stephen's, Steve Barrett and Richard Chirchir.

Richard Chirchir, from Kenya, was on his way to becoming a global expert in social protection management information systems and digital technology. In that role he has worked in Angola, Cambodia, Fiji, Indonesia, Kenya, Nepal, Rwanda, Slovakia, Somalia, Uganda, Uzbekistan, Zambia and many other countries. Along with Stephen and others he is a co-founder of Development Pathways, which was to become an important voice challenging the World Bank on social protection.[11] Stephen reflects, 'That first breakfast in the hotel on the first morning was when I met Richard Chirchir and when Development Pathways was born.' Richard concurs when I speak to him on a link to Kampala. 'Yes, that's where it started, it was the restaurant in Mosa Court Suites. I had been doing contracts for the World Bank in Kenya and Pakistan and then worked on a programme in Kenya with Steve Barrett: that was the connection.'[12] I ask Richard for his first impressions of Stephen.

> Driven, passionate, organised, strategic, a leader – but also relaxed, he had a sense of humour, he wouldn't put a suit on unless he had to. He was knowledgeable as well; he was capable of analysing policy issues and then presenting things convincingly. He thought logically, was strong in debate and was strong in recalling facts and information. He could relate to people, to people from

any particular background. He had a strong inclusion agenda. And he was a risk taker. He could have stayed in HelpAge International and continued as a director, but he didn't.

Stephen is honest when he thinks back to the start of his time in Uganda. 'I thought, let's help the government get a universal tax-financed social protection programme up and then maybe other governments across Africa will want to do the same.' The plan was to help the government pilot a programme, with DFID funding at the outset and with the government taking over as the scheme expanded.[13] Existing tax-financed social protection in Uganda was piecemeal to say the least. The government was wary, having rejected a social protection pilot proposed by the UK Overseas Development Institute the previous year.[14] So, there was a task ahead.

The design team that Stephen led had meetings with government, local government, donors and NGOs. It met the permanent secretary at the Ministry of Finance, which had a reputation in Uganda and beyond as a tough institution.[15] Ministry of Finance officials are close to the president, and many are wary of the expense of tax-financed social protection. When Stephen made the case for expanding it, the permanent secretary said, 'Can I stop you, young man? Surely you haven't come here to tell me giving cash to people is a good thing! It's obvious giving cash to people that need cash is a good thing. The question is, can Uganda afford it?' Ministry of Finance officials apparently thought it could not. But luck intervened. The recently appointed minister of finance, Syda Bbumba, had been in the ministry for social protection in Kampala and was sympathetic to the cause.[16] HelpAge International's Africa Regional Office had been engaging with her for some time on the issue of a tax-financed pension, work which Stephen was part of. The minister overrode any staff opposition to piloting tax-financed social protection, and the DFID programme of support was given an initial green light.

Poverty and vulnerability in Uganda

Syda Bbumba had good reason to be sympathetic. There was a clear need for social protection, leaving aside for a moment the issue of affordability. On the global scale of richest to poorest countries, Uganda is near the bottom.[17] Inequality is as high as in Chile and 72 per cent of the forty-six million population are under the international poverty line of US$3.65 per day, or US$1.22 in real terms.[18] People face low wages, job insecurity and a dependence on subsistence agriculture, among many other challenges.[19] As ever, women and girls face additional obstacles. Uganda has the eighth highest fertility rate in the world, with an average of 5.6 children per woman, and is in the top ten countries for maternal, newborn and child mortality.[20] One in three girls in Uganda experience sexual violence during their childhoods, and one in ten are married before the age of fifteen.[21] For women between twenty and fifty-nine years, physical violence has been experienced by the majority.[22] Social protection can help in these areas, as mentioned, by increasing household wellbeing and reducing the stress that can lead to male violence, and by giving women and girls more choice in what they do with their lives.[23]

Another challenge, as in Indonesia, is that approaching a third of young children are stunted.[24] Food insecurity is particularly bad in the east and in the long-suffering north. And Uganda has been affected by conflict in the region and hosts 1.5 million refugees, more than any other African country.[25] Also, around *half* the population in Uganda are school age or pre-school age. This creates a 'demographic dividend', an opportunity to grow more strongly when these people reach working age. But there is a corresponding risk of social conflict if young people cannot find work. And like everywhere else, Uganda is increasingly vulnerable to the climate crisis. It needs greater resilience to drought – a bad one hit in 2016 – as well as to floods and landslides. There is also an ongoing vulnerability to disease: Uganda has faced thirty epidemics over the past two decades, including cholera and Ebola.[26] Social protection can help in all these areas too, as well as with normal Lifecycle vulnerabilities, working as part of wider government support. Yet tax-financed spending on social protection, including donor support, is currently just 0.14 per cent of GDP, less than half of the level in Indonesia, itself a low performer.[27] Hence the interest in its expansion. And this figure includes World Bank loans. Spending on contributory programmes such as contributory retirement schemes is 0.76 per cent of GDP, but as in other countries, this is mostly for formal sector workers including civil servants.

The programme gets underway

The details of the DFID programme were now addressed. Stephen and the design team knew that DFID and the government were interested in poverty targeting and suggested testing two design options: a universal pension for sixty-five-year-olds and over and a benefit for the most vulnerable 15 per cent in each community.[28] Another donor, Irish Aid, came on board to fund the programme in Karamoja, a particularly conflict-affected region in north-eastern Uganda, where the pension age would be sixty, reflecting higher poverty.[29]

As the programme took shape, two officials in the ministry for social protection became important. One was Beatrice Okillan, who was involved with the programme from the start, the other was Stephen Kasaija, who joined after a year or two. Both were involved in designing, getting high-level approval for and implementing the programme, and both are still doing so. Stephen Kasaija had been on Michael Samson's 'there is an alternative to the World Bank' training in Cape Town, where he had met Stephen and discussed the merits of universality.

The final programme details were completed, and the government formally agreed to the US$80 million in DFID funding.[30] There was not enough money to go fully national straight away, but districts were selected from each region of the country to avoid accusations of regional bias. The plan was that Members of Parliament for districts without the programme would see it operating in the district next door and advocate for domestic funding for its expansion. 'Every decision we made was politically-informed', Steve Barrett says when I talk to him over a link to Malaysia, where he was working for UNICEF.

Implementation of the programme, which would be led by the government that would also co-fund it with DFID and Irish AID, got underway in 2011. Steve Barrett led operations for piloting the two design options, in a unit within the ministry for social protection containing DFID-funded staff and government officials, all under the head of the programme, a role eventually taken by Stephen Kasaija.[31] As in Indonesia, Stephen provided technical support.

The programme had a cleverness of design that colleagues and I would come to admire later on, when I worked in DFID headquarters in London. It had the two components common to such programmes, a part paying for benefits going to households, and a part for policy development, supporting government planning for the future. But there was an unusual third part which was helping MPs and civil society lobby for change. The three parts were mutually supporting: the transfers would show that social protection worked; the policy side would support the ministry in getting social protection into future government plans; and the lobbying part would defend and expand the government budget to pay for the benefits.

But did it work? A few years later, in 2017, I was back in Uganda, working as a consultant with Development Pathways. I was asked by DFID Uganda adviser Ben Cattermoul to give a presentation to his head of office to defend DFID's support to social protection in the country. The UK Brexit referendum had happened the year before and new DFID ministers seemed less interested in aid being used for social protection. By this point, the programme had become purely a universal pension. The poverty-targeted part had been dropped by the government in 2015, in part because of its targeting errors and lack of popularity within communities.[32] Stephen Kidd says,

> Even in the relatively undemocratic context of Uganda, where there is less accountability, the government, in the end, wanted a universal not a poverty-targeted programme when they saw how poverty targeting worked in reality. We did our best to improve the design but any poverty-targeted programme would have failed because of all the inaccuracies and unfairness. The difference in Uganda compared to other countries is that the government, having been given two options, had somewhere else to go, they could turn to the universal pension.

I made the presentation one Monday morning in 2017, in a large meeting room in DFID's modern, high-security compound in Kampala. The head of office and other DFID advisers sat before me. But arguing for the continuation of DFID support to social protection in Uganda was relatively easy. The universal pension, worth US$7 per month, had grown to nearly 160,000 recipients, and it was having an impact.³³ Perhaps most importantly of all, government financing had increased from nothing at the start of the pension to over 40 per cent by 2017 and would exceed donor contributions the following year.³⁴ This is textbook development for donors: funding a programme at first and then withdrawing as the government takes over. It is the holy grail in terms of making a sustainable impact, and often not reached. But in Uganda it was.

Defending the universal pension

Despite its success, the universal pension needed defending within the government. There was something of a war of attrition between the Ministry of Finance and the ministry for social protection.³⁵ Even small amounts of government money for the universal pension had to be fought for, month after month, year after year. The part of the DFID programme helping MPs and civil society lobby for resources was important in this battle. It was led by a Ugandan working in the government and funded by DFID, David Tumwesigye.

David was born in Fort Portal in the foothills of the Rwenzori Mountains in western Uganda and raised on the family farm in Kitagata, in southwestern Uganda. He moved to Kampala in 1994 to study at Makerere University. David was working for the Uganda National Social Security Fund (NSSF) when he was persuaded to join the programme in 2010 by George Beekunda, Director of Social Protection in the ministry for social protection. He stayed in it for the next decade. David was sceptical about the move at first but attended a workshop where Michael Samson, whom he knew from earlier work in Ghana, and Stephen spoke persuasively about the programme. Stephen told David they needed someone like him in the programme.³⁶ 'And the rest is history', David says when we talk on a link to Kampala. 'The strategy for the programme for addressing the institutional and advocacy challenge was so precise. I was impressed.'

In his decade working for the programme, I saw David use charm and patience to encourage and cajole high-level government officials, ministers, MPs and prominent members of civil society to promote and defend the universal pension. Much of this work was in collaboration with Bernie Wyler who took a managing role from Steve Barrett for the second phase of the DFID programme, directly under Stephen Kasaija. David and others arranged strategic messaging to be delivered through public events, newspapers and radio and TV shows to raise the profile of the universal pension. Politicians were challenged for not supporting the scheme and then taken to villages to see it in action, to bring them around. Soon after one such visit, a cabinet minister defended the universal pension in a critical cabinet meeting in 2014, when support for it was teetering.

A Uganda Parliamentary Forum for Social Protection was set up by David and others, led by the Honourable Flavia Kabahenda Rwabuhoro. The Forum organized MPs across parliament to threaten to veto the entire government budget for 2015–16 if proper resources were not committed to the universal pension, and the MPs won. The Forum did the same thing in 2017–18 and again were successful. The president's wife came on board saying the government wanted *everyone* in the country to have an income, so the pension was needed. In 2016, Stephen helped HelpAge International arrange a trip, part-funded by Development Pathways, for some of those MPs to go to London, to meet senior DFID officials and UK MPs and to lobby for DFID's support to the universal pension to continue.[37] 'To come up with that idea and arrange that trip – that level of commitment is amazing', David says.

But not everyone was swayed, and DFID's funding was not without controversy. From the start, the universal pension was intended as a government scheme, not a donor scheme. Steve Barrett says, 'We nailed the flag of the universal pension to the government mast from the start. We built ownership. There wasn't a DFID logo anywhere to be seen.' But some other donors and some officials in the Ministry of Finance argued that it was a programme driven by DFID and Irish Aid, not government. It is an ongoing debate. DFID had been central to the whole process. But who represents the people of Uganda? Is it those officials in the Ministry of Finance and others in government that have been sceptical of the universal pension? Or is it the ministry for social protection, MPs, civil society organisations, the minister of finance Syda Bbumba and the president and his wife, that have supported it?

I saw one official in the Ministry of Finance berate David Tumwesigye for being good at activism rather than good at winning the technical argument for the universal pension. Many, though by no means all, Ministry of Finance officials argued that Uganda was at too early a stage of development for significant investment in government-funded social protection, as the permanent secretary had apparently said to Stephen. This was the same argument I had heard among many DFID economists. But in 2017, the IMF's Resident Representative in Uganda, Clara Mira, said the country was behind its neighbours, Kenya, Rwanda and Tanzania, on human development, which is a key issue for the development of the country's labour supply.[38] Uganda was also falling behind on economic growth. Health, education and social protection needed to be invested in, along with other areas such as power and infrastructure. The IMF pointed out that current government spending on social protection in Uganda, with donor support, was less than half the spending of its near neighbours, as a proportion of GDP. In terms of affordability, all four countries are at a similar level of development: Kenya is ranked 172 in the world in terms of income per capita, Tanzania 185, Uganda 187 and Rwanda 191.[39] So the dismissal of social protection as unaffordable because Uganda is at too early a stage of development cannot be appealed to on evidence from countries in the region. The IMF were saying that David Tumwesigye and other supporters of greater government spending on social protection had the macroeconomic argument on their side.

Supporters had another thing on their side in that, as mentioned, the universal pension was having an impact. As well as increasing household incomes directly, it was increasing the ownership of productive assets. It was also enabling working-age adults living with pensioners to work more, as well as pensioners themselves.⁴⁰ The myth among some economists in DFID and elsewhere, that 'free money' might make people lazy, was being rebuffed in Uganda. And this was in line with international evidence which shows that tax-financed social protection programmes across low- and middle-income countries, where they have an impact, result in people working *more*, not less, as it encourages people to diversify and helps with things like the cost of finding work.⁴¹ There are instances where programme design can have a negative effect on particular groups of people, as we saw with women in Brazil that received conditional cash transfers and moved away from formal employment to meet health check-up conditions, but the overall picture is positive.

The universal pension in Uganda was also improving education among the young and reducing child labour. Perhaps above all, it was putting in place a hard-fought-for foundation stone of a comprehensive social protection system.

Keeping the World Bank at bay

Around the same time that Stephen and his team began designing the DFID programme of support, in 2009, the World Bank designed the second phase of its programme providing support to the north of Uganda. It was changing it from a system of giving grants to communities to a workfare programme, workfare being poverty-targeted public works, in other words cash or food transfers for doing manual labour.⁴² The switch was a route into the social protection sector for the World Bank.⁴³ 'They called it social protection from there', Stephen says. 'It became known as a productive safety net programme. They're clever with their use of words.' The model, which contains workfare plus unconditional cash transfers for those that cannot work, drew on Ethiopia's Productive Safety Net Programme, which had started in 2005.

Later, around 2014, the World Bank designed the *third* phase of its programme supporting northern Uganda. The ambition was to use it as a launch pad for a national-scale poverty-targeted 'productive safety net', working through government and financing the programme, at least in part, through World Bank loans. The World Bank looked for a rationale for going down the poverty targeting rather than the universal route. Steve Barrett describes how he was up for the ensuing battle. 'I had pretty heated debates with the World Bank team in Uganda, the head of which had worked on the Productive Safety Net Programme in Ethiopia. Meeting after meeting. It went on and on.' The World Bank brought in a consultant to provide analysis that the poorest 10% in Uganda were a coherent group on which support could be focused. Steve Barrett remembers,

> It was pretty obvious and pre-meditated. They were trying to show there was this group that was sufficiently static and distinct from the rest that it should and could be reached by poverty-targeted social assistance. We told them, you need to think about how people's incomes move up and down, about vulnerability,

and get away from the idea that it is possible to poverty target with any degree of accuracy. We also said that approach would not build nationwide political support for social protection system building. They were just regurgitating a pre-determined policy position that came direct from Washington that was grounded, I think, in their intended proposal for a new loan. They tried to use a review of the social protection sector the government was doing to reverse the policy debate on poverty targeting. But they failed. They weren't in tune politically. The DFID programme was.

David Tumwesigye remembers the World Bank being closed in their dealings with the ministry for social protection in which he worked.

You would have thought it would want to engage with what we were doing, putting in the first building blocks of an inclusive and sustainable social protection system. But they were very closed about what they were planning and what analysis they were doing. I think it's the culture in that organisation, keeping your cards close to your chest. I told them we'd tried poverty targeting and it hadn't worked. And no one wants to do it, it's not politically popular.[44]

The World Bank allegedly went on to brief vociferously against the universal pension to MPs, at a regional training event, though evidence for this is not available and it remains an allegation.

The World Bank had another go at influencing national planning of tax-financed social protection in another review of the social protection sector, in 2019. It apparently tried to take control of the review from the ministry for social protection, and it failed. Working in Uganda as part of the team that eventually carried out the review, I witnessed the World Bank's subsequent lack of interest in the work, despite it being an official, government-led process. In fact it even went so far as to draft a separate review of the issues.[45] That World Bank draft asserted that tax-financed social protection that was poverty-targeted offered the 'highest cost-benefit ratio'. But this assertion seemed to take no account of the extra costs of targeting errors, administration and potential loss of political support.[46] The World Bank review did acknowledge that the 'political and implementation feasibility of such a benefit is an open question', which is progress of a sort.

In any case, the universal pension stayed intact. 'It was ironic', David Tumwesigye says. 'World Bank-supported public works programmes in Uganda spent all that money and were never evaluated properly and yet the World Bank was happy to attack the well-evidenced and popular universal pension.'

The World Bank successfully lobbied for Stephen *not* to be the leader of the 2019 review of the social protection sector, although Development Pathways, without Stephen, led on the review.[47] Then DFID asked for bids to implement the next stage of their social protection programme of support, starting in 2020. Stephen, David Tumwesigye and Bernie Wyler were together in a bid, but were unsuccessful.[48] That marked the end of a decade of engagement. 'And just as things were really getting going', Stephen reflects. Stephen, David Tumwesigye and Bernie

Wyler had been working with Stephen Kasaija, Beatrice Okillan and the young and dynamic senior official James Ebitu, who headed social protection policy across the ministry, to develop a vision for a comprehensive, multi-tiered social protection system, a process I was involved in. But the lost bid marked a change of direction and two years later, in 2022, DFID's programme of support for social protection in Uganda came to an end, leaving it to other donors to fill the gap in support.

A partial success

The universal pension, predominantly funded by government, was rolled out nationally across 146 districts from March 2020, helping 350,000 people, including other people living in recipient households.[49] It can be seen as a partial success. The pension is not yet available to everyone sixty-five years and over outside the fifteen original pilot districts – elsewhere the age of eligibility is eighty. But MPs are pushing for this to be lowered to seventy. David Tumwesigye says, 'COVID and other global economic crises mean government revenues are low, and debt is rising, so it's difficult just at the moment, though putting money through the universal pension would help revive the economy.'

Stephen reflects, 'It could all have been bigger, faster, if there was a proper democracy there. Progress was made with MPs, but not enough with Museveni.' I say that he did support the universal pension. 'Yes, but only weakly and he just doesn't fear losing elections. If he needed to win an election, to properly compete, he'd have put much more money into the universal pension much sooner. It would have been his vote winner from the start.'

There are lessons to learn. David Tumwesigye reflects that donor support could have been used to build capacity better. 'I have been supporting the World Bank lately on their work helping the government to develop a new social protection strategy. The World Bank have actually been better than they were – they said let's go and find out what the government want to do and that will be the framework we can all support.' Now with Save the Children International, David was brought in by long-time consultant on social protection Steve Ashley, working with World Bank staff member Fatima Naqvi, an ex-DFID adviser.[50] The World Bank's more progressive approach shows moving forward can depend on individuals, not just an organization's official line. 'But the ministry hasn't engaged very well', David says.

> It hasn't responded. We showed leadership before when we got the universal pension going but we should have built more capacity, maybe had a separate social security agency, but that idea was blocked. We should have lobbied higher up for that. Officials in the ministry switched off when daily allowances stopped from the funding DFID provided. There was no more pecuniary advantage and that can be a big distraction.

These issues are a constant challenge for reformers in government and the donors supporting them. People look for opportunities to earn, understandably, given extended family members often depend on their relatively low government pay. They can lose interest when per diems disappear. 'In the end you need reform of the civil service', David says. 'But that's a much bigger exercise.'

The World Bank will stay in Uganda of course. It has in-built advantages over bilateral donors like DFID: greater resources and not being vulnerable to the winds of political change in home countries. And notwithstanding encouraging signs, the World Bank is promoting workfare and proxy means testing, and the development of a social registry, a record of household characteristics which allows poverty targeting across a range of programmes.[51] But the universal pension is likely to stay, not least because it is government run and government funded, and it is popular. It looks likely its future will continue to be wrangled over. But Steve Barrett is upbeat. 'In little over a decade, things have moved from the government refusing to approve even small, NGO-implemented, donor-funded pilots to a universal government funded national programme. That must be some sort of record.'

Chapter 8

SUPPORT THE POOR BUT MAKE THEM WORK FOR IT

The World Bank promotes workfare, or poverty-targeted public works programmes, in the development of social protection systems, as we have seen in Uganda. This represents the third component in its preferred menu of approaches to tax-financed social protection, along with proxy means testing and conditional cash transfers. Surely workfare breaks a pattern and can be clearly justified by the evidence.

The British legacy

Public works, where employment is created and assets or services for the public good produced, are not new. As Arup Banerji, then Director of Social Protection and Labour at the World Bank, announced in the foreword to a 2013 World Bank 403-page textbook on public works, 'From the Victorian Poor Laws in nineteenth century Britain . . . public works programs have historically played an important role as . . . interventions to address seasonal and short-term unemployment.'[1] However, the history of poverty-targeted public works is not something to draw encouragement from.

In early nineteenth-century Britain, support to the poor was provided by local church districts. But the middle class in the British population complained about the rising expense of the Poor Law.[2] In 1832, a body called the Royal Commission into the Operation of the Poor Laws recommended a change of approach. This was to expand public works in the form of workhouses, which gave accommodation and food in exchange for work. Workhouses were intended to *deter* the poor from seeking support and cut costs. The Commission suggested that able-bodied inmates be 'subjected to such courses of labour and discipline as will repel the indolent'.[3] Its intention was to make life unpleasant.[4] An ILO history of public works refers to 'deliberately low paid and unattractive work intended to deter all but the most needy from claiming support'.[5]

In 1834, the Poor Law Amendment Act made entering a workhouse compulsory for all those wanting help including children, except under special circumstances.[6] In Britain, the number of workhouses expanded massively, and by the end of the nineteenth century, *a third* of the population of pension age would reside in one for at least a part of the year.[7] Stephen sees the 1834 Poor Law as a turning point.

'The idea of the undeserving poor came in. The implication was that they are lazy and potentially dependent.' This lack of trust, the view that poverty is the fault of 'the poor', is arguably mirrored in the development of conditional cash transfers, of which workfare is perhaps a particular type. The workhouse approach was exported during the Irish Potato Famine in the mid-nineteenth century, during which, under the oversight of the UK's ministry of finance, public works 'compelled a semi-starved population to toil for ten hours per day for a meagre relief wage'.[8]

Public works in developing countries

Since these origins, public works have been used in different forms, including in countries that are now high-income. According to the ILO history, *these* public works were generally *not* punitive and off-putting, and were aimed at producing infrastructure of real value.[9] Public works became a large part of the 'New Deal' in the United States during the Great Depression, helping to employ the excess supply of labour, and they were also implemented in the same period in Belgium, Czechoslovakia, Finland, France, Germany, Hungary, Italy, Japan, Lithuania, the Netherlands, Poland, Portugal, Spain, Sweden, Switzerland and the UK. The ILO says there were also 'similar large-scale, but less well known, programmes implemented widely across north Africa, Asia . . . and Latin America'.

Today, public works in low- and middle-income countries appear to fit the two fundamental models of the American New Deal and the nineteenth-century British workhouses. The first model is known today as labour-intensive infrastructure programmes, in which building infrastructure is the priority at the same time as generating employment. These schemes sit in non-social protection sectors such as transport and agriculture. The second model is public works programmes with specific social protection objectives, which sit in the social protection sector. Where they are poverty-targeted, they are known as workfare, and these programmes are our focus.[10]

Workfare schemes, where those in the programme build for example rural roads, irrigation systems or terraces to grow crops, can be short term in response to temporary shocks, and give as little as twenty days employment per year. Or they can be longer-term, giving for example 80 to 100 days employment a year.[11] Commonly supported by donors, workfare schemes are widespread, especially in certain regions of the world. They make up 13 per cent of total spending on tax-financed social protection in sub-Saharan Africa and 17 per cent in the Middle East and North Africa.[12]

That is serious investment. But what is their impact? A 2019 summary of research on workfare schemes says, 'The evidence shows limited impacts even in the short term, with very little evidence to show post-programme benefits in the medium- to longer term.'[13] It goes further. 'There is no robust empirical evidence of [workfare schemes] generating medium to long-term sustainable extra employment, improved nutrition or education outcomes, or asset accumulation.'

In 2013, the World Bank's 403-page textbook *Public Works as a Safety Net* conceded that 'the overall record of achievement is uneven'.[14] Yet, in that year, it was estimated the World Bank had supported more than eighty social protection public works schemes, predominantly workfare, in forty-five countries in the previous decade.[15] The book explains why: workfare schemes are 'Popular for maintaining worker dignity and improving the status of vulnerable groups'. And, 'the public and politicians tend to like [their] potential to contribute to a productive economy and create public goods'.

Stephen is scathing of the point about worker dignity. 'No employer pays contributions to social insurance for these individuals', he says. 'They just make people work in humiliating circumstances. All the rules of decent employment are undermined.' A 2021 paper in *World Development* concurs, saying that people are 'neither officially employed nor adequately compensated for their labour'.[16] Chiming with the 2019 review of evidence, Stephen also takes issue with the quality of assets created by workfare schemes.

> The infrastructure – the public goods bit – is mostly rubbish. There is often no proper budget for maintenance, the focus is all on the transfers. No one ever goes back to look at what's happening to what's been built. I went on a field trip to look at public works in Laos with the World Food Programme. Their vehicle got stuck on a collapsing bridge which had been built by the workfare scheme. Then we saw some dam irrigation system that was of such poor quality, it was leaking water through the concrete.

A 2018 review of evidence for workfare schemes in Africa and the Middle East talks along the same lines. '[A] striking feature of the literature reviewed is that it contains almost no evidence on impacts stemming from the assets created through the public works.'[17]

There is some evidence of public works having a positive effect, albeit an indirect one. The MGNREGS is famous in the social protection world. Started in the state of Maharashtra as an anti-drought measure, it gives rural employment of 100 days per household per year for all of those that want it.[18] There is evidence of MGNREGS indirectly increasing wider agricultural wages and productivity.[19] That said, we must be careful on definitions: it is a national employment guarantee at a set wage level which is open to everyone, not a poverty-targeted workfare scheme.

International expert on public works and workfare Anna McCord has pointed out that part of the explanation for the general lack of impact of workfare is that short-term public works, designed to address short-term shocks such as a temporary weather event, are being supported by donors in areas where there is long-term unemployment and poverty, that is more deep-seated and chronic challenges.[20] Workfare in Uganda is an example, as is workfare in neighbouring Rwanda. But surely research in these countries is finding impacts to justify all the resources being ploughed in by donors as well as governments? You would think so. But in line with David Tumwesigye's experience, I have found no reliable estimates of impact at all for the workfare scheme in Uganda, in which the World Bank has been investing for more than a decade.

The programme in Rwanda, as elsewhere, has unconditional transfers for households without labour and workfare for others, the 'productive safety net'.[21] Steve Barrett, who after leaving Uganda headed the team of social protection experts in government in Kigali, funded by DFID, says of Rwanda, 'The direct support component, cash transfers for those unable to work, seemed to have consistently reduced poverty among its recipients while the public works component consistently appeared to be having only a very small positive impact or no discernible impact at all.'[22] An evaluation published after Steve Barrett left Rwanda, which we will come back to, paints an even less flattering picture.

It gets worse because public works cost more than simple cash transfers. They have capital costs, the expense of buying equipment and materials, as well as the cost of planning and overseeing the building of roads, irrigation systems and so on and the cost of maintenance, if maintenance happens at all. Those extra costs are fine if it is clear the infrastructure lasts and the programme has an impact justifying the cost. But it is not clear. As Anna McCord and Rachel Slater point out, 'from a fiscal perspective, such a [cost] premium is acceptable only if the value of assets created and any other benefits specific to [public works] provision . . . are commensurate with this premium, a question which remains largely unexplored in the literature and evaluations to date.'[23]

Is the World Bank saying all of this? Is it objectively setting out the options for donors and governments? In the 2013 World Bank book, the benefits and costs of workfare are not laid out, as far as I can see, and the term 'value for money' does not appear once in its 403 pages.[24] There is simply a presumption that this is an appropriate way to spend valuable resources.[25] The 2018 review of evidence in Africa and the Middle East says, 'the case for (public works) vis-à-vis alternative social protection instruments such as cash transfers mainly rests on assumed benefits and theoretical deliberations'.[26]

The most famous public works programme in Africa

And it gets even worse than that. Because there is evidence that public works can make people poorer. Stephen points to the predominantly donor-funded Productive Safety Net Programme (PSNP) in Ethiopia. PSNP is probably the most famous workfare programme in Africa, and surely the largest donor-funded workfare scheme in the world. It is worth a closer look because it shows that, while the evidence points away from investing in workfare, history and politics can get in the way. PSNP was set up by the Ethiopian government in 2005 with help from donors, including the World Bank, to support millions of people that would otherwise be dependent on humanitarian aid each year. The programme operates in the most food-insecure districts and uses community-based targeting. It is another scheme which Stephen and Diloá Athias have found, in terms of targeting, provides 'little better than random selection'.[27] The programme provides cash and food to eight million people in exchange for seventy-five to eighty days of work a year, with, as per the productive safety net model, unconditional transfers for those who cannot work.[28]

In terms of impact, a 2011 independent evaluation found *reductions* in consumption for beneficiary households, of US$1.86 per month.[29] Why? The evaluation says, 'PSNP is making some people dependent on aid . . . people who were not included in the PSNP worked hard to increase the amount of payment they obtained from off-farm employment . . . while many PSNP beneficiaries waited for low-paying public work, which they saw as less risky.' This appears to be another instance of programme design negatively affecting work incentives, going against the predominant trend, for cash transfers, of being good for work incentives where they have an effect. Stephen adds, 'Another thing is poor households are forced to participate in the programme when they should be working on their own land. There is a massive opportunity cost to these households.'

There appears to be evidence of negative impacts in other countries. For example, in Rwanda, a 2019 evaluation shows poverty in households receiving unconditional cash transfers fell between 2014 and 2017, but *increased* from 69.2 per cent to 80.9 per cent for those engaged in workfare.[30] And in Malawi, while the proportion of those receiving the government's unconditional cash transfer that were able to eat three meals rose 13 percentage points between 2018 and 2020, the proportion of those engaged in workfare able to do so *fell* 9 percentage points.[31]

Children and women can pay a particularly high price for participation. The same 2011 evaluation for PSNP found, 'The [workfare] . . . requirements of the programme meant that they (children) engage in work at the expense of their schooling and leisure.' There is also evidence of them spending more time on household chores, apparently substituting for parents engaged in workfare. Anasuya Sengupta, a former senior adviser at Development Pathways, writes about the 'silent scandal' of women's labour in workfare generally, pointing out how 'many women are obliged to work . . . without receiving a wage'.[32] This is a result of targeting by household rather than individuals. Any adult can participate, and it is often women who are sent to work. But, payment often goes to the household head, who is frequently male. As with benefits paid to households generally, it is all based on the 'simplistic assumption that these payments will be fairly allocated within the household'. Sengupta adds that, ironically, these usually donor-supported programmes often make claims to boosting 'women's economic empowerment'. There are a 'range of initiatives to increase their participation . . . special quotas . . . flexi-working hours . . . creches to balance childcare responsibilities'. This may increase women's participation, but often at a big price.

Since the 2011 study, evidence of a positive impact for PSNP remains patchy. And this is before we consider whether the impact justifies the considerable cost, which was US$2 billion for the fourth phase of the programme, running from 2015 to 2021.[33] The 2018 review of evidence for Africa and the Middle East says results for PSNP are 'positive' relative to other public works, with evidence, notwithstanding the 2011 evaluation, of increased food consumption and food security and asset accumulation, but 'it has not been investigated whether the benefits gained by participating households extend beyond the latter's time on the programme.'[34] A 2020 paper in the Development Policy Review is more critical: 'The programme has been successful on some fronts – such as saving lives, reducing distress sales and providing community-level services – while on others, such as household asset building and livestock accumulation, it has failed to deliver.'[35]

Saving lives is, of course, a hugely significant achievement. Famines in Ethiopia in 1974 and 1984 led to hundreds of thousands of deaths. I visited PSNP myself in 2011, travelling three hours southeast of Addis Ababa, to Boset district in the Great Rift Valley. I was with various people including Kalanidhi Subbarao, main author of that World Bank textbook on public works. The area was arid and one of the poorest parts of Ethiopia, and I remember the infrastructure built by the scheme to manage the local water supply was large and impressive. I wrote in my diary that day, 'This is a nationwide programme providing food and cash for the poor, in exchange for work for those who are able. An incredible achievement. No more *Live Aids* required.' I might have added the caveat that such trips always show you the programme highlights not the failing bits. But this is a key defence of PSNP: it has replaced humanitarian aid for people in the programme, and there has been no return to past disasters. A respected DFID adviser based in Ethiopia told me that the drought that East Africa suffered from 2011 and 2012 would have been calamitous but for PSNP. 'It stopped another famine.'

However, the weak wider impact of PSNP, at least in regular times, is unarguable. Wouldn't it have been better value for money, including for preventing disasters, to start building a tax-financed social protection system based, at least in part, on simple and universal lifecycle benefits? This is in a country where two-thirds of the population live under the international poverty line of US$3.65 per day, or US$1.40 in real terms, and presumably a much higher proportion in the programme target areas.[36] Apart from PSNP, there is very little tax-financed social protection in Ethiopia.[37]

Stephen says, 'PSNP has all been done through the Ministry of Agriculture. Talk to the ministry in charge of social welfare and you'll get a different view. PSNP wasn't set up as social protection.' But what would the government have supported in the absence of PSNP? Is workfare in Ethiopia defensible because it is better than nothing? Democracy is still under development in Ethiopia. It sits 116 out of 167 in the Economist Intelligence Unit's world democracy rankings.[38] It may be that as a result, anything close to a comprehensive multi-tiered social protection system is a distant dream.

But the troubling fact remains that there is a lack of government funding for PSNP. This is an obvious impediment to the programme lasting into the long term. In 2018, thirteen years after the start of the programme, the Ethiopian government was still only funding 15 per cent of the scheme.[39] In Uganda, the government was funding *the majority* of the universal pension within seven years. There is an apparent misalignment between the vision of donors and the vision of government. Stephen says, 'Donors say there's lots of government buy-in for PSNP. I say there isn't.'

8. Support the poor but make them work for it   89

It is not just the World Bank

Much of the proliferation of workfare schemes is politics, as the World Bank pointed out in its public works textbook. Governments often see it as the acceptable option for social protection in support of those of working age, even if they do not always put much of their own money into it. And you cannot blame governments for liking the idea of creating assets at the same time as providing support. But you *can* blame donors for not setting out the international evidence on workfare clearly, for governments to use as they see fit. And you can blame donors for using the leverage of their resources to encourage governments in an ill-advised direction. I am culpable, having worked in DFID which has supported workfare. Though I also remember when I worked there my frustration in trying to get information out of major global donors including the World Bank on the cost of schemes, in terms of capital spending and building and maintaining assets and so forth, so that value for money comparisons with simple cash transfers could be made. I and others were always met with a shut door.

'Donors have a responsibility to offer something beyond public works, and beyond poverty-targeted benefits and conditional cash transfers', Stephen says. 'And they have a responsibility to be honest about the evidence. But the World Bank keep pushing the same 19th century workfare model.' Fault does not lie only at the door of the World Bank and DFID. The World Food Programme describes how its Food Assistance for Assets schemes – food in exchange for work to build assets such as wells and roads – have, since 2013, 'in more than 50 countries . . . helped between 10 and 15 million people each year.'[40] And the list of organizations supporting workfare includes the African Development Bank, the Asian Development Bank, the Canadian International Development Agency CIDA, the European Union, the German Development Agency GIZ, the IDB, the Japan International Cooperation Agency JICA, the Swedish International Development Cooperation Agency SIDA, the United Nations Development Programme UNDP and the United States Agency for International Development USAID.[41]

I ask Stephen, if donors' support for public works is so at odds with the evidence, where are the feedback loops to tell them what they are doing wrong? Where is the accountability?

> If you criticise programmes, say they're not working, like the short-term public works programme in Rwanda, the response is, we'll redesign it to make it work. That's what the World Bank said in Rwanda. The presumption is that the approach should not change, it must just be improved. It's the same with proxy means testing. When you point out the poor results it's always, oh we'll redesign it.

A recent World Bank blog on the impact of public works in fragile and failing states supports Stephen's view. It says, 'we find little evidence (so far) of an impact of [workfare] programs on economic welfare outcomes in the long-run'[42] But it adds, 'Nevertheless, there is still potential to redesign these . . . programs through better targeting of beneficiaries, and add-on interventions such as capital infusion, training and mentoring, and behavioural therapy.'

As with proxy means testing, the bandwagon rolls on. The World Bank's most recent social protection strategy contains an objective to consolidate and expand the coverage of workfare schemes.[43] But Stephen is adamant that all donor-supported workfare programmes need to go.

> Countries need to invest in high quality infrastructure and provide proper jobs and training when building the infrastructure, with the aim of improving economic growth and mitigating the impacts of the climate crisis. But we need to forget these hopeless workfare schemes, some of which are now called productive safety nets, completely. We need to ditch the idea of them providing social protection. But *nobody* within the donor community funding these schemes is making these arguments.

Chapter 9

A MEETING IN GENEVA

THE ADVANCE OF UNIVERSALITY

In looking at events in countries in the fight for universal social protection, we must also look where Stephen was only peripherally involved. It goes without saying that a vast cast of people and organizations have come together in the fight and this story describes only a small part of it. On the global stage, this includes many staff in the ILO, whose opposition to the World Bank's social protection agenda started in the 1990s in response to the World Bank's support for pension privatization. It has also included staff in UNICEF, in governments in the Global North, in international NGOs, in academia and of course in low- and middle-income country governments themselves. Telling everyone's story is impossible, but a couple of people in the ILO that played a key role, with others, in creating a global vision for social protection are worth mentioning. They are referred to, as is everyone in this book, including Stephen, as representatives of a much wider effort.

The Social Protection Floor

The ILO has its headquarters in Geneva, Switzerland and was set up in 1919 to promote social justice, as part of the Treaty of Versailles. Following the First World War and the Russian Revolution, social justice was considered central to universal and lasting peace. For the ILO, the main way to achieve social justice has been to promote full employment, with decent salaries and working conditions, along with universal social security and other equitable social policies. To help this process, governments, employers and trade unions from all countries, which make up the governance structure of the ILO, agree international standards in what are known as Conventions and Recommendations, which we will come back to.

One of the ILO's strategic objectives is to 'Enhance the coverage and effectiveness of social protection for all'.[1] Its support for universal social protection goes back to the 1944 Declaration of Philadelphia, adopted at the 26th Session of the ILO, which aims at 'the extension of social security to provide a basic income to all in need of such protection'.[2] As mentioned, social security is equivalent to social protection in this book. Stephen and others argue that social security is better and the label social protection is 'poorly understood by policy makers', and organizations define it in different ways.[3] Social security, a term embedded in human rights discourse and more conventionally used in high-income countries, is a clearer phrase. Nevertheless, social protection remains the term in common use.

In 1946, soon after the United Nations was created, the ILO became a UN agency and was in tune with its new institutional home. Because in 1948, the UN Universal Declaration of Human Rights was adopted. It stated, 'Everyone, as a member of society, has the right to social security.'[4] In 1952, ILO Social Security Convention 102 was passed, setting international standards for different types of benefit.[5] Later, the 'right of everyone to social security' was written into the UN's 1967 International Covenant on Economic, Social and Cultural Rights.[6] So, the institutional foundation was strong.

The late Michael Cichon was director of the Social Security Department at the ILO - soon to be the Social Protection Department - from 2005 to 2012.[7] Early on, he and his team collaborated with Stephen and the Social Protection Team in DFID including in estimating the cost of high coverage programmes in countries across the world.[8] But there was a gap. International efforts to oppose the World Bank's agenda on tax-financed social protection, the promotion of poverty targeting, conditional cash transfers and workfare, were somewhat fractured. There was no overall framework. Michael wanted to facilitate the development of a global vision for social protection, to meet the ambitious aims of the ILO and the wider UN.

I discussed the development of the vision with Michael in May 2022, over a link to his home in Germany. Having worked on social protection his whole working life and having been in the ILO since the mid-1980s, Michael was semi-retired, though still working as a professor at Maastricht University. He had a glint in his eye that I remembered from working with him in the early 2000s. He still radiated good-natureness, reminding me of the toymaker in the Disney production of *Pinocchio*.

In 2006, Michael collaborated with Stephen to call together, with funding from Stephen's team in DFID, a group of international experts in Geneva. The idea was to form a collective view on the global vision for social security. The group brought together included, apart from Michael and Stephen, Michael Samson from the Economic Policy Research Institute in Cape Town, with whom Stephen collaborated on social protection training, Peter Townsend, Professor of International Social Policy at the London School of Economics, Peter Lindert, Professor of Economics at the University of California (Davis), Chris de Neuborg, Professor of Economics at the Maastricht Graduate School of Governance, Rüdiger Krech from the German development organization GIZ, Timo Voipio from the Government of Finland who was a close ally of Stephen, Francie Lund from the University of Cape Town, who had played an important role in expanding social protection in post-apartheid South Africa and who was then working at the UN Research Institute for Social Development (UNRISD) and Thandika Mkandawire, also at UNRISD, who was such an important influence on Stephen through his seminal paper on universality.[9] The group, comprising mainly experts from the Global North, with exceptions, met at the Inter-Parliamentary Union building in Geneva for what became a landmark meeting. The building was a short walk from the ILO's headquarters for Michael Cichon and his team, which included long-standing advocates of universal social protection Christina Behrendt and Krzysztof Hagemejer, among others. Some of the events in the meeting have become hazy with the passing of time, but as Michael recalled, when the group were asked for ideas on the vision, Stephen said it should contain universal benefits across the lifecycle aimed at older people, children and persons with disabilities. Peter Lindert then added that support was required for the unemployed, and others spoke and made contributions including Thandika Mkandawire. The vision was discussed and began to take an initial shape and was given a name, the Social Security Floor.

Going through the UN system

From there, Michael Cichon needed to take the first draft of the vision through the labyrinthine UN system. Part of the job was obtaining the support of the ILO Director General Juan Somavia. But the Director General had other pressing matters at hand and the going was tough. 'Then the 2008-09 global financial crisis happened', Michael said.

> The Director General wanted solutions. In 2009, he chaired a meeting of the director generals of all the UN organisations, which came up with nine responses to the global crisis. One of these was what became known as the Social Protection Floor Initiative, the next iteration of the Social Security Floor. The Initiative would be a global coalition of UN agencies and development partners.[10]

Its aim would be to support the creation of universal social security systems around the world. Contributing to the cause, lawyer Magdalena Sepulveda Carmona, United Nations Special Rapporteur on Extreme Poverty and Human Rights from 2008 to 2014, published a paper in 2009 about human rights and social protection. It argues that cash transfers must be 'grounded by solid legal and institutional frameworks framed by human rights standards and principles'.[11]

Michael and colleagues held a large series of meetings with other UN agencies including the World Health Organization (WHO), UNICEF and the World Food Programme (WFP).[12] These were three to four-day meetings, held two or three times a year up to 2011, and took place mostly at the ILO's large and leafy training campus in the middle of Turin, which had been donated to the ILO by the city in 1965. 'We were defining concepts and looking at affordability', Michael said.

> It was a seminar atmosphere, it was great. It was a massive exercise in collaboration, looking at how things would work within countries with the UN providing support to interested national governments. I hadn't seen anything like it. You have to remember, we were bringing together people working on social protection who had been quite lonely in their separate organisations, they'd never been connected like this before.

Ambition was high. A 2009 meeting in Turin said of the Social Protection Floor, 'The approach is not just a short term, ad hoc response to the consequences of the [2008] crisis but also the basis for a long-term strategy to promote development, reduce vulnerability and prepare ... countries for future shocks.'[13] The World Bank and IMF joined the meetings. 'But they sat on the fence', Michael said.

> They attended online rather than in person. They were remote in every sense. The World Bank just wanted to keep an eye on things, to see if there was anything they needed to react to. They weren't going to help to make it happen. I have never seen so many quiet observers. The IMF representative would literally only speak up when someone insulted the IMF.

Beyond the meetings in Turin, the ILO governance structure, divided, as mentioned, between employers, employees and governments, also needed persuading. Michael and his colleagues attended meetings in Asia, Africa and Latin America telling governments, employers and workers, as well as NGOs, about the Social Protection Floor. 'It was an enormous process', Michael said.

Next, an instrument for the Social Protection Floor had to be chosen. The ILO's role is to set global standards in the workplace and on social protection. It does this in part by approving instruments. These are those Recommendations, which are guidelines for countries to follow, and Conventions, which are legally binding international treaties. 'The original game plan was a Convention', Michael said. 'Either a UN or an ILO Convention, we didn't care. Then we thought the UN road was too heavy, it would have taken a decade, so we thought, take the ILO route.' An ILO Convention was planned and in 2011, Michael and colleagues got the Social Protection Floor on the agenda of the International Labour Conference, in front of its 3,000 delegates from governments, employers and workers. The conference took place, as it did every year, at the vast Palais de Nations in Ariana Park in Geneva. The gathering in 2011 delivered a strong message which resonates today, that 'national solidarity-based social security systems' must be strengthened to 'foster economic development, strengthen economic resilience and neutralize ... systemic global risks'.[14]

The Social Protection Floor came back to the International Labour Conference in 2012, having been sped through the normally 3-year ILO approval process in 12 months because of its urgency. But the decision was taken to put a Recommendation forward for approval rather than a legally binding Convention. 'We knew we couldn't get a Convention through', Michael said. 'It was a step too far. We wouldn't have got support from the formal sector workers' side and governments.' Ironically there was a wariness among unions, especially in Latin America, which were fearful that the focus on a Social Protection Floor, including those in the informal economy, would divert attention from the need to formalize workers and strengthen social insurance systems. Latin America had been particularly affected by reforms promoting labour flexibility, as well as the privatization of social insurance pensions.

The Recommendation's primary purpose, according to Michael, would be 'to provide an international legal instrument that civil society organisations (CSOs) could use to hold their governments to account when delivering on their right to social security'.[15] To construct the wording of the Recommendation, a questionnaire was sent to workers, employers and governments in all countries. Respondents were reminded that there is an estimated '80 per cent of the world population without adequate income security and/or access to medical care'.[16] Somewhat confusingly, health financing is within the ILO's definition of social security, though it is outside the definition of social security in this book.[17] All a further taste of the language minefield in this area.[18] In the 2012 conference, amendments were made to the draft wording of the Recommendation. Then, on 14 June 2012, governments, employers and workers from 184 countries adopted Social Protection Floors Recommendation No. 202 (SPF 202). In doing so, they enshrined an international commitment to universal social protection. Stephen says, 'Before the Social Protection Floor our thinking was all a bit unarticulated.' The dial on how social protection would be talked about in subsequent global dialogue had been moved and the Recommendation set a new international standard.

The World Bank and the IMF had attended the 2012 International Labour Conference as observers with speaking rights. 'They were mildly supportive', Michael Cichon said. 'They weren't enthusiastic, but they didn't really take it seriously, which actually helped getting it through. Thank God they didn't realise what was coming.'[19]

The Recommendation

The wording of the Recommendation draws on the Universal Declaration of Human Rights and is aimed at building comprehensive systems, containing tax-financed and contributory schemes and protecting people throughout their whole lifecycle. It says social protection systems in each country should comprise 'basic income security' for children, people of working age – including those unemployed, sick or living with a disability – and older people, and it says, in line with how the ILO defines social security, countries should also provide essential healthcare.[20] Other principles in the Recommendation include 'a rights-based approach based on entitlements', 'universality of protection based on social solidarity' and the 'protection of rights and dignity of beneficiaries'. As Stephen's colleague Daisy Sibun wrote later, the Recommendation goes wide, it is about 'the building of nations'.[21]

The power of the Social Protection Floor is that it is not a blueprint. Flexibility is built in, and it is up to populations and their representative governments, as it should be, to determine the specifics of social protection systems for their countries and the speed at which programmes are introduced. The Recommendation allows for the 'progressive realisation' of universal social protection, striking a balance between state accountability – to both non-state actors and to other states – and state sovereignty. Its role is to set the framework and direction of travel. It allows for means tested schemes, if that is what populations and their representative governments want. This highlights the important point that the Social Protection Floor is about moving towards universal social protection *systems*. Within universal systems, there may be individual *programmes* that are aimed at poorer members of society who need support, in addition to lifecycle schemes. Daisy Sibun points out that many countries, including high-income countries with 'strong entitlements-based universal benefits for their citizens as they progress across the life course . . . have . . . means-tested programmes to provide supplementary support for those on low incomes.'[22] So the Recommendation reflects the global reality that systems are typically a mix of universal and means-tested schemes.[23] It also reflects the views of Mkandawire, Stephen and others, as we have seen, that means-tested schemes are not wrong per se, as residual programmes within a universal framework for those needing additional support - on condition of course that they are invested in to an appropriate level and function effectively.[24]

Getting World Bank commitment

The next stage was to try and gain wider public commitment to universal social protection, especially from the World Bank. Isabel Ortiz took over from Michael Cichon as Director of Social Protection at the ILO in 2013. Like Michael, she was also a long-time critic of the World Bank's approach. When we talk on a link to Nairobi, she says,

> I was in UNICEF before the ILO as Associate Director of Policy. I was on the train from New York to Washington D.C., in May 2012, for one of our annual consultations with the World Bank. I and others were with Geeta Rao Gupta, Deputy Executive Director at UNICEF, who wanted to raise the issue of conditional cash transfers. In line with human rights and UN values, I wanted to raise universality. At the end of the meeting, which was attended on the World Bank side by Arup Banerji, Director of Social Protection, and Tamar Manuelyan Atinc, Vice President for Human Development, amongst others, I raised my hand. When the meeting heard what I had to say on universality there was a silence, the whole room looked at me and started laughing. The laughter wasn't nasty in any way, there was no malice. They said don't take it badly. But it was as if a fool had spoken.

In 2014, two years after Recommendation 202 was adopted, Isabel Ortiz, by then Director of Social Protection at the ILO, attended a meeting, with others, between Guy Ryder, Director of the ILO, and Jim Yong Kim, president of the World Bank. It was part of the World Bank and ILO's regular dialogue. Travelling to the meeting at the World Bank headquarters, Isabel asked Guy Ryder about raising the issue of the World Bank publicly committing to universal social protection. In 2013, Jim Kim had committed the World Bank, with the World Health Organization, where he had previously worked, to universal health coverage. 'I got goosebumps when I saw that announcement on health', Isabel says. 'I thought, it was such an important move politically.' Guy Ryder looked at Isabel and said, 'Why not.' 'In the meeting arguments were put forward', Isabel says. 'But Jim Kim didn't need to be convinced. He knew there would be difficulties with his staff, but he committed, though both he and Guy Ryder knew achieving universal social protection would take time.'

Much discussion followed the meeting. As expected, World Bank staff came back arguing that universal social protection was difficult for low- and middle-income countries, and that it was only an ideal. Isabel Ortiz retorted with examples of where countries had implemented universal social protection schemes. In the end, after much debate, the World Bank and ILO co-authored studies on a range of countries to show how they had achieved universal, or at least wide-coverage programmes. The studies looked at pensions for older persons in Argentina, Azerbaijan, Bolivia, Botswana, Brazil, Cabo Verde, China, Georgia, Kosovo, Maldives, Mongolia, Namibia, Nepal, South Africa, Thailand, Trinidad and Tobago and Zanzibar; at benefits for persons with disabilities in Nepal, Timor-Leste and Ukraine; at maternity benefits in Argentina; and at child benefits in Argentina, Mongolia and South Africa. They provided evidence that universal or wide-coverage social protection schemes are feasible and achievable, even in a low-income context like Nepal, which we will return to in the next chapter.

In 2015, Jim Kim and Guy Ryder took the next step and launched the Universal Social Protection Initiative saying, 'We are proud to endorse the consensus that has emerged in the early 21st century... The African Union, ASEAN (Association of South East Asian Nations), the European Commission, G20, OECD and the United Nations have all endorsed universal social protection. Now, it is time to join forces to make it happen.'[25] 'Imagine my pleasure when I heard that', Isabel says. 'After that first meeting in Washington D.C. where there was all that laughter.'

After that, in 2016, the World Bank and ILO launched the Global Partnership for Universal Social Protection to Achieve the Sustainable Development Goals.[26] The partnership, co-chaired by the World Bank and ILO, 'brings together governments, international and regional organisations, social partners and civil society organisations'.

The Sustainable Development Goals, which the Global Partnership would help to achieve, are internationally agreed development targets, to be met by 2030. There were many international consultations to forge a global consensus on those goals. Isabel Ortiz and her team at the ILO hosted meetings in different global regions to advocate for universal coverage and ensure that Social Protection Floors would be part of the picture. Target 1.3, which addressed social protection, was eventually developed. The target says, 'Implement nationally appropriate social protection systems and measures for all, including floors, and by 2030 achieve substantial coverage of the poor and the vulnerable.' When I was in DFID, I remember the language in target 1.3 being tortuously negotiated, before the announcement of the Goals in late 2015. It appeared to end up as a mixture of ILO staff and World Bank staff visions. Isabel confirms it was a difficult process. 'That was a big battle between the World Bank, the IMF and the ILO.'

Isabel adds,

> Another issue was who would monitor Sustainable Development Goals (SDG) target 1.3. The World Bank could only offer data on their targeted programmes, covering selected countries, but not all countries in the world. We had to make the case endlessly, but finally we managed to get agreement that SDG 1.3 will monitor *overall* social protection coverage using administrative data from all governments that the ILO had been collecting since the 1940s and which is presented in the ILO flagship The World Social Protection Report. The monitoring would look at the degree to which social protection schemes are covering *all* children, *all* mothers with new-borns, *all* poor and unemployed, *all* older persons and *all* persons with severe disabilities. This was a fundamental step because it committed all governments in the world to monitor progress towards universality. And it meant the world could observe that progress.[27]

And the process of negotiating target 1.3 sparked other important work, as Isabel Ortiz describes.

> Ultimately World Bank and IMF staff act as if there are minimal resources for social protection. These organizations prioritise resources for economic growth, for debt servicing or to reduce fiscal deficits. This is why they advise small poverty-targeted safety nets instead of universal and comprehensive social protection systems. We had to show that there are many financing options available to all governments, even in the poorest countries. We set into motion many national dialogues to agree publicly how to expand social protection, together with feasible financing options. This work on fiscal space for universal social protection was started by ILO, UNICEF and UN Women and is fundamental to advancing social development, particularly now at these times of austerity cuts.[28]

World Bank backtracking

Jim Kim may well have believed in universality. But in 2016, at the same time as the World Bank was publicly committing to universal social protection, he advocated, as we have seen, for poverty-targeted conditional cash transfers for 'every country in the world' that has a problem with stunting.[29] Was this advocacy a sign of World Bank staff fighting back? Stephen wrote in a blog in response, 'If Kim really is committed to universal social protection, he needs to adopt a more critical ear when receiving advice from his staff, who are evidently still finding it difficult to embrace a more inclusive vision.'[30]

The push against universality from within the World Bank, despite its high-level endorsement of universality, continued. In 2018, it began to refer to 'progressive universalism', which it argued meant promoting poverty targeting in the short term as a first step to achieving wider coverage.[31] It is similar wording to the 'progressive realisation' described in Recommendation 202, but with the intent of continuing to prioritize poverty targeting. As Daisy Sibun describes it, what clearly emerged was a 'disconnect between the discursive endorsement of universal social protection at the leadership level of the Bank and the types of social protection programming that the Bank finances and promotes on the ground'.[32] Again, the World Bank was not alone. The UK government says in its 2023 White Paper on International Development that it supports universal social protection, but gives the Public Safety Net Programme (PSNP) in Ethiopia, built on poverty targeting and workfare, as a prime example.[33]

Daisy Sibun challenges the concept of progressive universalism. 'Means-tested benefits are simply not able to realise all people's right to social security when used in isolation.' She adds, 'A human rights-based approach to social protection entails framing social protection policy decisions and programme design around legal entitlements instead of charity or handouts.' Speaking to a long-standing ILO official and champion of universal social protection, they think the World Bank's approach is unconvincing. 'There has to be scope for progressive realisation, but there are certain principles which should be followed. In the World Bank's conceptualisation, you don't see progressivity. It's still a poverty-targeted safety net approach.'

In 2019 a new Call to Action was released by the Global Partnership for Universal Social Protection.[34] It said, 'We urge countries and international partners to support the global commitment to implement nationally appropriate social protection systems and measures for all.' This time, the ILO official thinks the World Bank deserves some praise for its involvement. 'To their credit, the World Bank were trying to accommodate universal social protection. If you look at that wording of the Call to Action it reflects the Recommendation. It is actually a major step forward.'

But in 2022, in its 539-page book on targeting, the World Bank appeared to regress again by questioning whether there was any need for universal programmes at all. It argues that everyone would have access to poverty-targeted schemes if their income drops below a certain level, based on the assumption that poverty targeting is working effectively. In its thinking, a poverty-targeted scheme giving a guaranteed minimum income provides insurance for the whole population. It is 'universal in insurance terms'.[35] 'They are framing tax-financed benefits as an insurance product', Stephen says.

> The idea being that the benefit is there when you need it. If you can access it when you need it, then the Bank argues that that is universality. There's a degree of logic to this, leaving aside political economy and dignity arguments. But the logic breaks down in practice. If you don't have the means of identifying

when someone falls below the income threshold, then you can't make it work. If your best attempt to do that is a proxy means test, which is a static measure, the whole insurance argument fails. Your income falls but you still can't access the programme because you've got tiles on your roof, or you've got a brick wall or a university degree, whatever proxies are being used to measure the welfare of the household. In addition to this the proxy means test has very large inherent errors. Furthermore, you cannot run continuous surveys. Even in a country like the UK it is very hard to measure incomes continuously. That's why we have seen all the scandals with people getting tax credits and being asked to pay back large amounts of money, and why you see the huge numbers of people eligible for means tested benefits not receiving them. In lower- and middle-income countries it's just not going to happen.[36]

The insurance argument looks like a turnaround worthy of a circus unicyclist. In World Bank thinking, poverty-targeted programmes have now become universal entitlements. To add to this, Stephen points out that an equivalence is drawn in the World Bank's 2022 book between poverty-targeted and universal schemes. Universal programmes, where entitlement is often determined simply by age, are labelled 'categorically targeted'.[37] Stephen says, 'Categorical targeting is a nonsensical concept. Who would choose an old age pension if the priority is to reach the poorest with just one scheme? Advocates of this do not understand the difference between what they call categorical targeting and a lifecycle scheme as part of a broader lifecycle system.' The upshot of it all, for the World Bank, is that poverty-targeted programmes have become universal and universal programmes targeted. It is social protection through the looking glass.

The World Bank raised hopes again by publishing the aforementioned *Charting a Course Towards Universal Social Protection*, also in 2022.[38] The report says, 'comprehensive and effective coverage can only be provided by a suite of programs that span the domains of social insurance, labour and economic inclusion, and social assistance and care, ensuring that all people are effectively protected at different points in the lifecycle.' This is progress, as is, 'How social protection systems evolve in each country depends on a number of factors . . . perhaps most importantly, the political and institutional context as well as the social contract.' But then we return to earth with a bump, as we saw in Chapter 4: 'the progressive realization of [universal social protection] implies the need to start by prioritizing the poorest and most vulnerable for support.' We appear to be back to excluding universal programmes at the outset. This, apparently, is the way to 'maximize both the equity and efficiency of public spending'. Despite recognizing the World Bank's engagement in the Global Partnership's Call to Action, the ILO official cannot help but be critical of this wordsmithery. 'It's old wine in new bottles.' Since 2022 the World Bank has, as mentioned, published similar messages including in the *State of Social Protection Report 2025* which states that 'social assistance should be focussed on those in the poorer quintiles'.[39]

A decade since the Recommendation

While the World Bank's positioning of itself has rumbled on, a decade after the Social Protection Floors Recommendation was passed, hopes of a Convention have not gone. 'We tried pushing for it at the last ILO conference, in 2021', Michael Cichon said when I interviewed him in 2022. 'The General Secretary of the International Trade Union Confederation, Sharan Burrow, the first woman to hold the post, banged her fist on the table and said, "It's our responsibility as trade unions to ensure that all workers, whether in the formal sector or not, enjoy social protection for themselves and their families."' But a Convention has not happened yet, and Michael wished it had all gone further.[40] 'A Convention would force the government to engage, since it either has to ratify and take action or explain to the ILO at regular intervals why it cannot ratify. A Convention would have been better.'

But the Recommendation is there and is now being pushed by an alliance called the Global Coalition for Social Protection Floors. The Coalition, made up of more than a hundred NGOs and trade unions, was set up at the prompting of Michael Cichon and colleagues so it could support the Social Protection Floor during open hearings at the 2012 conference, and it has since become permanent.[41] 'The Coalition is pushing the Recommendation at the G7 and the G20, focussing on how to get Social Protection Floors funded', Michael said. 'They're quite good at getting the word out.' More recently, following a meeting between Stephen and Human Rights Watch in 2023, a group of over ninety economic justice, human rights, and faith-based organizations from all over the world have joined forces to advocate for the right to social security. In a 2024 letter to World Bank and IMF executive directors, the group called for 'a more inclusive and rights-aligned universal approach' which 'sets the tone and leads the way toward more just societies and economies'.[42] With leadership from local organizations, many based in the Global South, the group has also started documenting the impacts of World Bank and IMF social protection policies at the country level.[43]

And social protection continues to go up the agenda of the United Nations. In late 2021, the UN publicized an enhanced effort to widen coverage. An announcement said:

***UN Secretary-General calls for accelerated action on jobs and social protection*[44]**

Deeply diverging recoveries [from the COVID-19 pandemic] threaten to undermine trust and solidarity and make the world more vulnerable to future crises, including climate change. In response the UN and ILO have established a 'Global Accelerator' to help ensure global financing to create 400 million jobs and extend social protection to 4 billion people currently without coverage.

The Global Accelerator is a call to action rather than a commitment of new resources. But it is a direct appeal to governments and international institutions to step up their efforts. It is scathing of how 'the wealth of billionaires increased by over US$3.9 trillion between March and December 2020' while the number of extremely poor increased by between 100 and 200 million, the first increase in poverty in over 2 decades. And it calls for 'US$1.2 trillion annually for social protection floors in low- and middle-income countries.'

In May 2022, a meeting of labour and employment ministers from the G7 group of wealthy countries took place in Germany, addressing the climate crisis again and the issue of a just transition to a green economy. It released a communique which said, under the headline 'Strengthening Universal Social Protection', 'we welcome the UN Secretary-General's initiative for a "Global Accelerator on Jobs and Social Protection for [a] Just Transition" to . . . extend social protection including floors to the people currently not covered by any social protection system or measure by 2030.'[45]

In June 2022, the UN said, 'billions of people face the greatest cost-of-living crisis in a generation.'[46] It said, 'The current climate crisis and impact of the conflict in Ukraine have compounded the pandemic's already devastating effects on food, energy, and finance globally.' On 23 September 2022, UN secretary-general António Guterres hosted a meeting of world leaders and senior staff from the World Bank, African Development Bank, UN agencies and others to help strengthen 'the collective response needed to urgently address the global job crisis and support the billions of people that continue to be excluded from social protection'.[47] The March 2023 United Nations Conference on the Least Developed Countries, with fifty heads of state, set out a strategy for the next ten years with 'universal social protection' at the top of the list of specific goals.[48] And Global Accelerator Dialogue has continued since then, including in 2025 when the ILO and World Bank hosted a meeting of twenty-one donors to commit to accelerated progress on universal social protection.[49]

It is indisputable that social protection in international dialogue has come a long way from the days when Michael Cichon and colleagues, with Stephen and other allies, first worked on a coherent vision. And it has come a long way from when Isabel Ortiz and her team helped to get all governments and agencies, including the World Bank, to commit to universal social protection. The ILO official says, 'Social protection has entered the main stage. We used to talk about just the economy and employment, now social protection has been put right up there on a par.' Michael Cichon agreed. 'We've made it to the front burner of the policy debate.' Though Stephen points out, 'We're really only back in 1948, with the Universal Declaration of Human Rights. That's when high-income countries took up universality. It is only now that it is being recognised that it is also relevant, and essential, for low- and middle-income countries today.'

A long way to go but we're on our way

The much-respected Michael Cichon died in December 2022. I did not know he was ill when we talked seven months earlier. I can only admire his generosity and commitment to the fight for universal social protection in agreeing to be interviewed. I enjoyed hearing him reflect on the collaboration with others outside the ILO, beyond Stephen. 'There was Peter Townsend from the London School of Economics in the early years. And he was very sick at the time.' The book that came from the original meeting in Geneva in 2006, edited by Peter Townsend, was published in 2009, the same year the internationally respected academic died.[50] 'Then later there was Isabel Ortiz, UNICEF and the UN generally. There's a whole circle of people, they all signed up. We felt we had nothing to lose.'

But no one is celebrating yet. Michael Cichon said,

> The Recommendation has influenced the global debate, and no doubt helped to align the leading global NGOs behind the concept of the Social Protection Floor. The trade union support outside Latin America is also quite substantial now. So, there are reasons to hope. It all still has to trickle down into national policy debates, but we are on our way.[51]

Stephen says, 'The real work is at country level and that is where the World Bank has a very large advantage.' Everyone knows there are battles ahead. And the ILO official I talk to also remains measured.

> The Social Protection Floor Initiative has been successful, yet there is a need to see the wider picture in the ongoing low coverage of social protection in lower- and middle-income countries. And, in addition to establishing Social Protection Floors, attention also needs to be given to the adequacy of social protection provision in protecting the sick and healthy, people with and without disabilities, men and women and those with and without children.

But international standards help to set the framework and direction of travel. Isabel Ortiz, now working outside the ILO to stop austerity cuts and to promote investments in people, echoes Juan Somavia, former ILO Director General, in saying that the world does not lack the resources to promote universal social protection, it lacks the right priorities.[52] She also cautions against being discouraged by World Bank staff backtracking on its commitment to universality and encourages a sense of perspective.

> Guy Ryder and Jim Kim knew at that meeting in 2014 that universal social protection would take time. They were aware that World Bank staff didn't want to do it; like most bureaucrats, staff were reluctant to embrace change. No matter, today we have the World Bank officially committed to universal social protection, we have Recommendation 202 on Social Protection Floors and an internationally agreed Sustainable Development Goal target 1.3. Governments are monitoring progress towards universal social protection and citizens are demanding it. Institutions remain very active in the Global Partnership for Universal Social Protection, and Civil Society Organisations are pushing hard.

So, there is great progress – and change will continue gradually. Look at the bigger picture. The 1948 Universal Declaration of Human Rights was signed by a number of countries committing huge human rights crimes, but the Declaration was signed, and it has become the standard moving forward. No matter small temporary reversals, universal social protection and the right to social security are not going away.

That is a fitting legacy for Michael Cichon.

Chapter 10

NEPAL

MAOISM AND THE MYTH OF UNAFFORDABILITY

Universal benefits during and after a civil war

Another important arena where Stephen has been involved in a peripheral way is Nepal. Between 1996 and 2006, the country suffered from a civil war which led to the deaths of more than 16,000 people.[1] Nine days before the Nepali government and Maoists signed a peace agreement, on 21 November 2006, I was on my first trip outside Kathmandu as the new economic adviser in DFID Nepal. I and two officials from the Norwegian Embassy were being driven by Save the Children through a forest in the west of the country. On the journey we passed through a government checkpoint and after that an opposing checkpoint, belonging to the Maoists. There were sand-bagged positions, but no guns and no danger. The fighting had ended seven months earlier and we were looking at the aftermath. Our trip meant driving up a rough track on the side of a long valley, with nothing between our Toyota pick-up and a 1,000-metre drop. At the top, we stopped at a local government office. The compound had been fortified during the fighting, against the Maoists who had taken pot shots from the surrounding hillsides. We were told how local government officials had handed out payments for Nepal's universal pension to the local population right through the civil war. Other offices across the country did the same.

The trip was an insight into how, despite adverse circumstances, Nepal has shown a strong commitment to universal social protection schemes. A number of universal benefits were introduced by the minority government led by the Communist Party of Nepal (Unified Marxist-Leninist) in 1995 and 1996, despite tight resources: Nepal was then a low-income country. These include a pension for all those seventy-five and over, which grew from 170,000 recipients around the beginning of the conflict to nearly a quarter of a million by its end; a benefit for widows aged sixty and over with a similar level of recipients; and smaller scale benefits for persons with disabilities.[2] All were, and remain, funded by the government. Dr Dilli Raj Khanal, a member of the National Planning Commission in those early years, says when we communicate by email,

> Given the high level of vulnerability of the population and the perpetuating social injustice driven by longstanding inequalities, I together with senior leaders in the government and party pushed for universal social protection schemes. A

strong political commitment to protect the elderly and others made it possible for such a historic decision which is continuously admired by the Nepali people.

It was indeed a significant moment. Nepal has, in many ways, come to represent the spirit of what the ILO is trying to achieve in its campaign for global universal social protection.

When fighting in the civil war stopped, in 2006, universal benefits continued to be popular across political parties. This is evidence for the argument that universality can attract strong political support. In 2008, a Maoist-led coalition government was formed when the Maoists became the largest party in the election for a Constituent Assembly Election, formed to write a new national constitution. Baburam Bhattarai, a prominent Maoist leader during the civil war, became finance minister. He more than doubled the value of the universal pension and lowered the age limit, from seventy-five to seventy.[3] The benefit level was also increased by subsequent governments, and the age limit lowered to sixty-eight.[4] Recipients of the universal pension, currently worth 4,000 Nepali rupees – or US$31 – per month, now stand at 1.2 million.[5] In the region, this compares with the poverty-targeted pension of 200 Indian rupees per month, or US$2, in India.[6] Over the period, the widows benefit has also been expanded, to all single women over sixty as well as widows of any age, and is worth 2,600 rupees (US$20) per month. The disability benefit is now worth between 1,600 (US$12) and 3,000 (US$23), depending on the severity of disability.[7] And other benefits have been introduced including, in 2009, a universal child grant for Dalit children under five and other children under five in the poorest districts, worth 400 rupees (US$3) per month.[8] The child grant was expanded to a third of all districts, with a benefit level of 532 rupees (US$4) per month, and the government has plans to expand it to all districts.[9]

Today, more than a third of households in Nepal receive tax-financed social protection, on which 2.2 per cent of GDP is spent.[10] On top of this, 2.5 per cent of GDP is spent on contributory schemes, though these are dominated by the pension for ex-public sector employees, available to relatively few.[11] By way of comparison, for the two countries in this story that are much wealthier than Nepal, Fiji and Indonesia, spending on tax-financed social protection is 1.1 per cent and 0.35 per cent of GDP respectively.[12] For the country with GDP per capita closer to Nepal, Uganda, it is 0.14 per cent.[13] How has Nepal done this? The answer is politics. Nepali governments of different parties have prioritized tax-financed social protection.

Progress and challenges in Nepal

My family and I lived in Nepal between 2006 and 2009. We took in the temples, prayer flags in the mountains and the ringing of small bells in the morning amid the busy-ness of Kathmandu. But we also learned that underneath what you can see and hear, there is a complicated history of diverse ethnicities and feudalism.

Part of that history is a punitive caste system, systematic discrimination against women and a population that is often remote and hard to reach. Power has been concentrated in few hands.[14] Nepal was closed to foreigners until, in 1951, a revolution ended the totalitarian regime known as the Rana dynasty. Since then, it has moved by fits and starts towards a modern state.

The civil war, between 1996 and 2006, was at least in part an attempt, albeit a violent one, to address embedded issues of inequality and exclusion. In 1996 Baburam Bhattarai, later to become finance minister, handed the prime minister of Nepal a letter setting out forty Maoist demands.[15] It was a calm and analytical communication that said 'people living below the absolute poverty line has gone up to 71 per cent' and 'the gap between the rich and the poor . . . is growing wider'. Some of the demands could have been drafted by the United Nations:

- 'exploitation and discrimination against women should be stopped'
- 'the system of untouchability should be eliminated'
- 'land under the control of the feudal system should be confiscated and distributed to the landless and the homeless'
- 'an unemployment allowance should be provided'
- 'orphans, the disabled, the elderly and children should be . . . protected'
- 'free . . . health services and education should be available to all'

The letter goes on, 'We would like to request the present coalition government to immediately initiate steps to fulfil these demands.' The letter was a prelude to a decade of fighting, but the polite tone of the letter is maintained. 'If there are no positive indications towards (fulfilling the demands) from the government by 17 February, 1996, we would like to inform you that we will be forced to adopt the path of armed struggle against the existing state power.'

The civil war was violent, and progress since the end of the war has been rocky. But Nepal has taken steps forward in areas beyond social protection. At the first meeting of the new Constituent Assembly in 2008, the decision was taken to abolish the monarchy, which had been in place since the founding of the Kingdom of Nepal in 1768.[16] The ex-king moved into an ordinary-looking house in the city and his palace was turned into a museum. Lots will have disapproved, but I remember reading the newspaper and wondering how there had not been more protests. More recently, according to the World Bank, 'The 2017 elections represented a significant turning point. Local elections were held after 20 years filling a void in popular representation.'[17] It says that with moves towards a more federal state, 'greater political stability is expected that provides a basis for a positive shift in Nepal's development path.' Of course only time will tell.

Another step forward has been the reduction in poverty: the proportion of the population below the international poverty line of US$3.65 per day, or US$1.21 in real terms, fell from 84 per cent in 1995, just before the civil war, to 40 per cent in 2010, the latest year available.[18] A big factor has been workers travelling abroad, typically to the Middle East, and sending remittances home.[19] Inequality has also gone down to close to the level in Fiji and well below Indonesia and Uganda.[20]

But many large challenges remain. Nepal is disproportionately affected by the climate crisis, which affects mountainous regions like the Himalayas more than elsewhere.[21] To quote a World Bank-supported study, 'One of the more spectacular effects [of the climate crisis] ... has been the creation of meltwater lakes on the lower sections of many glaciers ... [which] has produced catastrophic flood surges ... that have destroyed infrastructure and taken human lives in the valleys below'.[22] Floods in Nepal in 2017, this time caused by heavy rainfall, were the worst in decades.[23] And Nepal is vulnerable to earthquakes: 9,000 people died in the last major one, in 2015.[24] Nepal's dependence on remittances from abroad is also a source of vulnerability, as is being sandwiched between the two giants of India and China. And the country needs much more infrastructure and power generation and transmission to reach remote parts of its 30 million population.[25]

There is also the historical legacy of needing to maintain social cohesion across disparate castes and ethnic and social groups.[26] Women and girls in Nepal face traditional practices like the dowry system, early marriage, the stigmatization of widows, the seclusion of women (purdah), polygamy and the segregation of women and girls during menstruation (chhaupadi).[27] A quarter of the female population aged fifteen and older suffers domestic violence. This is violence which gets worse during crises such as the 2015 earthquake and COVID-19 when women are stuck at home with their abusers.[28] Nepal also suffers from stunting among young children, which has come down significantly in the last two decades but still affects nearly a third of those under 5.[29]

Donors get involved

With all of these ongoing challenges, what have donors done to support the government on tax-financed social protection? As in so many places, donors have been divided along familiar battle lines. Kristie Drucza from Deaking University in Australia describes how donors in Nepal have been 'ideologically at odds with one another on social protection's key points such as targeting [and] conditionality'.[30] Stephen, who was briefly engaged in social protection in Nepal, observed donor divisions. He worked with Rebecca Calder, who arrived in Nepal as DFID's social development adviser in 2009, shortly before I left, and who like so many DFID advisers came across as determined and committed.[31] Stephen describes how Rebecca challenged the World Bank on social protection, wanting it to focus on improving the systems for *existing* government-funded programmes.[32] True to form, the World Bank was encouraging the government towards poverty targeting. Kristie Drucza describes how, 'DFID funded the World Bank to complete a [social protection] report in 2009 but felt the methodology was weak and the findings were biased towards poverty targeting. DFID withheld the report's publication for two years.'[33]

In 2010, the World Bank published its *Nepal Public Expenditure Review*. As elsewhere, it describes transfers from the universal pension going to the non-poor as 'leakage'.³⁴ No value was attributed to benefits going to the non-poor. This is in a country where most older people live on very low incomes.³⁵ The World Bank concedes in the review that universal pensions are 'politically and administratively easier to implement than targeted programs'. This was, in fact, demonstrated in an earlier trial of poverty targeting in Nepal. According to Larry Willmore in the journal *World Development*, when the universal pension was introduced in 1995, there was so much demand for it that 'Nepal decided to abandon universality, instructing village development committees to limit payments to persons below the poverty line. The committees complained that means testing was difficult to carry out fairly and effectively, so universality was quickly restored.'³⁶

None of this stopped the World Bank recommending in its 2010 publication 'Targeting benefits specifically to the poor'. This is in spite of a civil war having ended just four years earlier, a war motivated according to the Maoists' original demands by pervasive exclusion, and in spite of cross-party support for universal benefits. And it is in spite of additional evidence that universal benefits were playing an important role in strengthening the social contract, stabilizing the peace and laying the foundations for future development.

The social contract

In 2018, Minouche Shafik, former president of Columbia University in New York and at different times director of the London School of Economics, IMF deputy managing director, permanent secretary in DFID and vice president of the World Bank, said, 'universal benefits have a social logic which we economists have lost.'³⁷ This logic relates to how nations function, to the social contract between citizens and government. A strong social contract, as mentioned, helps governments increase tax revenue to pay for government services. But strengthening it is easier said than done, as we saw in Indonesia where tax revenue as a proportion of GDP is relatively low. Stephen and colleagues cite Western Europe after the Second World War as a successful example of strengthening the link between people and government after conflict. 'Progressive politicians were elected who, as a priority, established universal public services, including schemes such as universal old age pensions and child benefits. In a relatively short period of time they built trust among their citizens, enabling governments to vastly increase levels of taxation.'

In 2010, when the World Bank talked of targeting benefits to the poor, universal benefits were providing an important link between the citizens of Nepal and the government. Kristie Drucza argues that, 'Giving excluded citizens access to government benefits enables them to feel part of the system of the state and to have a relationship with the government. It gives them a sense of citizenship, rights consciousness, and of feeling included, respected, and cared for.'³⁸ According to research carried out in Nepal less than three years after the 2006 peace agreement by the UK Overseas Development Institute (ODI), 'Cash is seen as a visible and direct transfer from government to people.'³⁹

ODI research in 2012 found 93 per cent of beneficiaries feel social protection 'is an indication that the government cares about their socioeconomic situation' and, 'for 85 per cent it has improved their opinion of the government of Nepal'.[40] Further evidence of a strengthening social contract in Nepal is that tax revenue as a proportion of GDP grew from 9 per cent at the start of the civil war to 20 per cent in 2019, before COVID-19 hit and brought it down to 16 per cent.[41] Stephen writes, with Gunnel Axelsson Nycander from Act Church of Sweden and colleagues at Development Pathways, 'The case of the Indian sub-continent is particularly interesting. Nepal is the only country in the region to offer universal social security schemes: Bangladesh, India, Pakistan and Sri Lanka have focused on providing poor quality, poor relief. Over the past 20 years, government revenues in Nepal have more than doubled while elsewhere in the region there has been little change No doubt other factors such as improved tax policy and administration have contributed to rising tax revenues in Nepal, but these will have happened elsewhere as well and it is likely universal social protection schemes have played an important role.'[42]

A change of direction

Some donors and international organizations in Nepal got behind universality. I remember, during my time there, UNICEF collaborating with the ILO to advocate for 2 per cent of GDP being spent on tax-financed universal lifecycle social protection programmes. This was a position I was sceptical about at the time, in perhaps typical economist fashion, but it has now come to pass.

And DFID went into print with Development Pathways in 2011 when Stephen, Emily Wylde and Rebecca Calder published a paper critiquing the idea of poverty targeting in Nepal. They described the risk of increasing social conflict, rather than establishing citizen's entitlements and building social cohesion.[43] Stephen and Rebecca Calder also published a critical paper on implementing conditional cash transfers, which was also being advocated by the World Bank for Nepal.[44] The papers were published jointly by DFID and Development Pathways. Stephen says, 'We had to water down the language to get the papers through DFID processes.' But who could blame them if their tone betrayed some impatience, even anger?

Through all of the donor debate, the government stayed in control. It found a way of handling the World Bank. Stephen says,

> In 2018, I was presenting a paper in Bangkok. I met a Nepali government official and asked him what's been happening on social protection in Nepal. He said, 'The World Bank have spent the last ten years trying to convince us to do conditional cash transfers and poverty targeting. We placated them, we needed funds, we allowed them to test it. They tested it, we tolerated them, but it never

worked. We let them get on with it, we knew they were going to fail. And we kept on with our universal programmes.'

In 2016, the World Bank changed direction, at least to some extent. It agreed a loan to the Nepali government for US$150 million to 'help the Government of Nepal expand coverage of civil registration and modernize the delivery of social security allowances.'[45] The World Bank would support the delivery of the government's universal benefits. According to Stephen's colleague Daisy Sibun, 'This is a positive example of the Bank using their financing capabilities to strengthen the delivery of existing government-led initiatives and build systems to credibly help realise universal social protection coverage.'[46] The World Bank spoils it somewhat by continuing to advocate for poverty targeting through the development of a social registry, a record of household characteristics allowing poverty targeting across a range of programmes, discussed further in Chapter 12. And it still cannot stop itself from being critical of the government, saying in 2021 that Nepal's set of universal schemes 'does not effectively target' the poor and vulnerable.[47] But the shift in approach is significant.

Posh Raj Pandey and the net impact of benefits and taxes

Posh Raj Pandey is a Nepali academic and an expert on macroeconomics. He helped negotiate Nepal's entry into the World Trade Organization from 2006 to 2008 and, like Dr Dilli Raj Khanal was at one point one of the eleven member National Planning Commission in Nepal, a committee headed by the prime minister which establishes priorities for national development. He is currently chair of the NGO South Asia Watch on Trade, Economics and Environment. I speak to him on a link to Kathmandu in 2023 to gain a local view on social protection in Nepal and its fit with wider development. I expect to hear some celebration of what Nepal has achieved in social protection, but I get something slightly different.

Posh Raj Pandey, he is happy to be called Posh, emphasizes he is not a social protection expert but warms to the subject. He points out that the new 2015 Constitution of Nepal contains the right to social security and mentions the laws and programmes that have been put in place to flesh that out. But he points to the level of government spending on social protection, at 1.9 per cent of GDP in 2010 and 4.8 per cent in 2019.[48] 'And for the budget for the current year the spending allocation is 5.2 per cent of GDP.' As mentioned, more than half of this is contributory schemes that relatively few have access to. In any case, Posh says total spending is quite high, above other South Asia countries and is equal to two-thirds of the budget for capital spending, that's money for investments for long-term benefits, like schools, hospitals and roads. Posh argues that, 'For nation building, health, education and infrastructure need more resources.' The overall quality of government services is low. These are services that are also part of the social contract, along with social protection, though arguably they are more complex to deliver and so slower getting to the people. Posh points to roads and rail links, electricity generation and transmission, digital connectivity and making young people literate in digital technology as critical priorities. He believes that with continued low investment it will be difficult to develop the country.

This is a useful sense check. Nepal is held up as proof that a country low on the global scale of rich to poor countries can afford tax-financed universal lifecycle social protection. Is this evidence that it cannot? Here, your answer depends on the extent to which you believe universal social protection schemes have been important in helping to stabilize Nepal, strengthen the social contract and allow economic growth, which in turn is the key to sustained poverty reduction over the long term.[49]

Posh is also concerned about the universal pension being received by wealthier people while the poor are included in the tax system and have money taken away from them. 'Half of government revenues in Nepal come from indirect taxes on goods and services, which the poor pay. So, you've got the poor paying taxes to spend on support for the non-poor.'[50] This is another useful check, because it is the combined impact of taxes and benefits that matters.[51] I heard a similar argument from the World Bank in Washington DC in 2024, during a seminar in which I was presenting messages from this book. Low-income countries – as Nepal was until recently – in contrast to middle-income countries, do not have progressive tax systems and so the benefit system must be poverty-targeted. However, Stephen and his colleagues at Development Pathways have shown that the combined impact of taxes and tax-financed social protection schemes in Nepal is, in fact, progressive and reduces inequality.[52] According to their analysis, the net impact of taxes and benefits on households is positive for those that are poorer in Nepal, and negative for those that are richer, because they pay more in taxes than they gain in benefits.[53] [54]

Stephen and his colleagues' analysis extends to other countries in Asia. They find, where there are 'elements of a universal lifecycle system' as opposed to the domination of poverty targeting, the net impact of taxes and benefits is *more* progressive and the impact on reducing inequality is much greater. This is explained, in part, by the fact that emerging universal lifecycle systems are associated with a much higher level of investment in tax-financed social protection, further supporting the 'paradox of redistribution' mentioned in Chapter 1. This states that the more benefits are targeted at the poor, the less likely taxes and benefits are to reduce poverty and inequality.

But Posh's implied point, that there is somewhere an upper limit to spending, is clearly true. That said, it is up to the sovereign decision-making of populations and representative governments, not the World Bank, to decide when this point is reached. Democracy is under development in Nepal, which sits at 98 out of 167 countries in the Economist Intelligence Unit world democracy rankings.[55] But this surely means it is up to donors including the World Bank to help strengthen government accountability to the population and the social contract, not cut across it by attempting to import approaches to social protection developed elsewhere. And these are approaches with significant problems, as we have seen.

Reaching middle-income

At the end of that trip in 2006, we returned down the valley to a Maoist stronghold town to meet the Maoist leader of the district. He was a bearded, middle-aged man sitting with a male and female colleague. All three shook hands warmly and gave a single fist salute. But they looked edgy. Three big red flags were on the wall behind where they sat and two men sat on the veranda outside the open shutters. It had a vaguely Wild West atmosphere. The leader talked a lot, through an interpreter. Some of what he said did not sound right to me, but there was a lot that sounded reasonable and in line with the policy of our DFID office as well as that original letter of Maoists demands. Back in Kathmandu, on the television, I saw Prachanda, the Maoist leader who in 2024 finished his third spell as prime minister of Nepal, also look edgy after his many years of living underground. But the Maoists, despite all their nervousness, had uncovered a truth, with other political parties, that had apparently eluded the World Bank. This is that universal social protection schemes can be introduced and expanded, and contribute to national development, even in a country with limited resources and struggling with conflict and its aftermath, if they are a political priority.

Recovery from the civil war in Nepal has been messy, there have been ups and downs, and there are still many deep-seated and legitimate grievances to satisfy. But the country is holding together, and progress is being made. Economic growth averaged 4.9 per cent a year from the end of the civil war until COVID-19 in 2020, despite the setback of the 2015 earthquake, and national debt is 39 per cent of GDP, lower than India and significantly below the level of countries like the UK, France and the United States.[56] Progress has been such that Nepali newspaper *The Himalayan Times* was able to report in 2020 that Nepal had become a middle-income country.[57] The precise contribution of different factors to progress will always be a debate because this is nation-building, huge and complex. And there will be future challenges in allocating resources across health, education, infrastructure, social protection and other areas, as there always is. But, the evidence suggests significant investment in tax-financed social protection in Nepal has helped, and even been crucial to the country moving forward.

The myth of unaffordability

It is worth stopping again briefly on the issue of affordability, given universal social protection schemes have been considered by many as unaffordable in a country like Nepal. Unaffordability is something of a myth, or at best it is highly misleading. This is because populations and representative governments decide spending priorities, given the resources available. Of course decisions are affected by resources available. And responsible fiscal policies and debt management along with macroeconomic stability are vital. Instability and high debt servicing affects poor people at least as much as the wealthier. But within that constraint, only local populations can appraise the relative benefits of spending options, only they can judge how best to balance resources across government sectors. Their choice may include universal schemes that start small and grow to remain within the bounds of responsible fiscal management. And universal schemes can go on to help strengthen the government-citizen relationship and widen the resource envelope itself through collecting a greater proportion of GDP in tax, as Nepal appears to have shown. Above all, it is not down to outsiders to take a preconceived view on what is and is not affordable.[58] Daisy Sibun says of the World Bank, 'a policy consensus on poverty targeting has largely defined the policy problem of "no fiscal space" as inalienable, which risks shutting down the debate before it has even begun.'[59]

Part of the jump to 'no fiscal space' appears to draw on another myth, that high-income countries only invested significantly in social protection when they were at a later stage of development than current developing countries. Today, high-income country governments' spending on social protection averages 16.2 per cent of GDP, including both tax-financed and contributory schemes.[60] We might argue that some countries need to manage their social protection systems better, and there are no doubt lessons to learn. But that does not detract from the core need to balance spending across government sectors appropriately and build towards comprehensive social protection systems: there is little point in spending on health and education if people cannot afford to eat. At what stage did high-income countries begin to seriously invest in them?

For this it helps to look first at long-term trends in spending, which are shown in a study by Peter Lindert, Professor of Economics at the University of California (Davis). Lindert sets out the history of 'social transfers' in twenty-one high-income OECD countries, as a share of the national economy.[61] 'Social transfers' are defined as tax-financed social protection plus health spending and housing subsidies. The study shows that starting from a 'negligible base' in the late eighteenth century, spending 'rose haltingly over the next one hundred years, then accelerated between 1880 and World War II'. A report from The Economic and Social Commission for Asia and the Pacific (ESCAP) and Development Pathways fleshes out the picture: 'Progress toward universality dates to the late 19th century when a shift from old "poor relief" programmes that directed social protection benefits to the poor, toward new programmes, including redistributive, tax-financed programmes for old age, disability, and unemployment, occurred.'[62] Lindert says spending then 'boomed between World War II and about 1980', after which it was relatively flat.

Building on this analysis, the ILO has looked at GDP per capita in high-income countries at the point when their social protection systems were being established and spending started to accelerate, generally well before the Second World War, and compared it to low- and middle-income countries now. It concludes that 'today's developing countries have a similar level of GDP per capita to high-income countries when they established their social security systems'.[63] To give specific examples, Indonesia is similar, in terms of GDP per capita, to the UK when its main social security system was being established in 1911; India is richer than Denmark in 1892 and France in 1905 when their main systems were being established; Cambodia, Congo and Mozambique are richer than Italy in 1919; Benin, Cameroon, Liberia and Sierra Leone are richer than the Russian Federation in 1922; Nigeria and Pakistan are wealthier than Portugal in 1935; and Jordan is wealthier than the United States in 1935. The ILO analysis shows that, overall, low- and middle-income countries are in a position, now, to begin to lay the foundations of comprehensive lifecycle systems, with national programmes based on individual entitlements, instead of donor-influenced poverty-targeted schemes. This is not to say that low-and middle-income countries are ready for a post-Second World War boom, nor that progress will be easy. Individual countries will have their own challenges, and will have to build at an appropriate speed. But based on historic evidence, the assumption that low- and middle-income countries today are at too early a stage of development for system building to get underway in earnest is misleading.

Incidentally there is another myth which is used to undermine the case for social protection. This is that Europe, from which sixteen out of the twenty-one countries in Peter Lindert's study are drawn, spends a lot on welfare but that countries such as those in East Asia rely more on the free market. Countering this, Lindert says, 'East Asia is not different from the earlier industrialising countries of Europe and North America. For all the talk of a separate Asian cultural approach to welfare . . . East Asia has been following the same path.'[64]

In short, wealthier countries across the world have known, through a century and a half of history, that addressing vulnerability, inequality and the development of human capital, through social protection and other means, is essential to supports social cohesion and national development.

Chapter 11

MAURITIUS, ZANZIBAR AND KENYA

EAST AFRICA TAKES CONTROL

The conversion

In southern Africa, universal pensions have existed in countries like Namibia and Botswana for a number of years, but not further north.[1] However, on 1 June 2016, a British Broadcasting Corporation (BBC) report announced that Zanzibar, an island with a 1.5 million population twenty miles off mainland Africa and a part of Tanzania, is 'the first [place] in East and Central Africa to roll out a 100 per cent government funded universal pension'.[2] This groundbreaking moment was a result of the considerable efforts of the autonomous Zanzibar government, with the support of others, including a man called Smart Daniel.

Smart Daniel is from Bukoba, in north-west Tanzania. A few years before the Zanzibar pension was introduced, he was a sceptic, not just of universal programmes but of social protection in general. 'I didn't believe in social protection to be frank, giving cash to people', he says when we talk over a link to Dar es Salaam. Then, in 2008, he met Stephen, when he was working for HelpAge International as Director of Policy and Communications. Stephen had arrived in Tanzania to train HelpAge's staff. Smart Daniel was one of them and Stephen sat down with him to talk. 'I had an hour with him', Smart Daniel says. 'He had all these ideas. He converted me. He explained the case for social protection. It was a very interesting discussion which really opened my eyes.' The meeting was energizing. 'I had the energy of the converted. Something had to be done in Tanzania. I had a cause.'

Smart Daniel was further fired up by attending one of Michael Samson's 'There is an alternative to the World Bank' training courses. He went on to lead a team that, in 2010, published a study on introducing a universal pension to mainland Tanzania and Zanzibar.[3] It was prepared with government officials and it made an impact. 'We campaigned across the country, both mainland Tanzania and Zanzibar', Smart Daniel says. 'It started discussion, it really changed the mood.'

For Tanzania, including both the mainland and Zanzibar, the case for social protection, as elsewhere, is compelling. With a population of around sixty million, it is ranked 185 in the world in terms of income per capita, besides Nepal and Uganda.[4] Tanzania has many sources of vulnerability, including the climate crisis and a colonial history affected by arguing between European nations. Just under three-quarters of the population are below the international poverty line of US$3.65 a day, or US$1.23 in real terms, with a similar proportion in Zanzibar compared to the mainland. Inequality is between the levels in Indonesia and Chile.[5] Smart Daniel's feasibility study says, 'In the past, security in old age was provided through a range of social protection mechanisms based on the extended family and community structures.'[6] As in so many countries, fast social and economic change has undermined that. The study says, 'only 6.5 per cent of the workforce is currently covered by formal social security.' It adds that a universal social pension to those sixty and over, were it to be introduced, 'would reach almost one in four households', with expected impacts – in conjunction with other government sectors – on poverty, health, education, livelihoods and social cohesion.

'We used the evidence to continue to push a universal pension', Smart Daniel says. This included a series of educational activities between 2012 and 2014 for government officials, politicians and civil society.[7] One game-changing part of this was a 2013 study tour to Mauritius, funded by Irish Aid, the Swedish International Development Cooperation Agency (SIDA) and the Zanzibar government, and organized by Smart Daniel.

The Mauritian Miracle

Mauritius is in the Indian Ocean, more than a thousand miles off the south-east coast of Africa. Smart Daniel's study tour was organized for officials from the Tanzanian and Zanzibari governments. The Tanzanian government sent senior people but Zanzibar raised the stakes by sending their top government official, the Chief Secretary Dr Abdulhamid Yahya Mzee, who was close to the president. They also sent the permanent secretary in the Office of the Second Vice President in Zanzibar, Dr Khalid Salum Mohamed, a man who had also attended one of Michael Samson's social protection courses and would become the Minister of Finance in Zanzibar when the universal pension was introduced.[8]

Mauritius is a small island country with a population, at 1.3 million, similar to Zanzibar. Unlike Zanzibar it became a high-income country, in 2020, though COVID-19 has since caused it to dip back to middle-income status.[9] It is a success story, and IMF staff have sought to explain 'The Mauritian Miracle'.[10] Progress has been despite a typical colonial legacy of ethnic division. Slaves were imported under the French, and indentured labour, from the East Indies and India, when Mauritius became a British colony.[11] Winner of the Nobel Prize in Economic Sciences James Meade has described the 'envy felt by the Indian and Creole underdog for the Franco-Mauritian top dog', caused by minority French domination of the sugar sector.[12] IMF staff have identified a number of factors behind the remarkable record of economic growth in Mauritius after independence in 1968.[13] One is how 'diversity and ethnic fragmentation' were addressed. Profits from the sugar sector were shared, by having a large and relatively well-paid civil service, dominated by the Indian community, and by 'a generous system of social protection'. The latter was predominantly the civil service pension and a universal pension going to everyone 60 years of age or over. The pension had been introduced as a means-tested benefit in 1950, but after public resentment of the means test, it was made universal in 1958.[14] According to IMF staff, the universal pension, because it was given to everyone on an equal basis, had helped reduce racial tensions in Mauritius. This had strengthened the national social contract, which was critical for the structural reforms that were required to move Mauritius away from its dependence on sugar cane to a more prosperous and diverse economy.

Notwithstanding the universal pension's record of supporting growth, in 2004 the World Bank lobbied for it to be means-tested once more. It pointed to its rising cost because of the ageing population, and it didn't hold back. 'The un-funded nature of the universal scheme, together with the . . . civil service (pension), are endangering the country's economic stability.'[15] At the time the universal pension cost 1.7 per cent of GDP, though, by accident or design, the World Bank were using an artificially inflated figure of 3 per cent to advocate for reform.[16] The civil service pension cost 1.3 per cent. Mauritius means-tested the universal pension in August 2004.[17] However, according to Sheilabai Bappoo, one-time government minister for tax-financed social protection, this second go at means testing 'caused a lot of trauma to our people'.[18] Soon after, in July 2005, there was a general election and the sitting government lost. The opposition had campaigned to once more universalize the pension, and the new president of Mauritius announced that the 'Government will end the humiliation previously imposed on pensioners by abolishing the targeted approach and reinstating universal pension to all pensioners'.[19]

However the World Bank, with the support of the IMF, has continued to lobby for reform, including poverty targeting, because of rising costs. The pension currently has a transfer value of US$300 per month and costs 5.6 per cent of GDP.[20] This cost places it somewhere between middle-income countries such as Namibia (1.0 per cent of GDP), Lesotho (1.7 per cent) and Georgia (4.6 per cent) and high-income countries such as United States (6.4), Germany (8.0) and France (11.9).[21] This could be regarded as reasonable enough for a country on the cusp of high-income status. But the World Bank and IMF clearly do not think so, though it is surely a matter for the government and population of Mauritius to decide what is an appropriate level of spending for a scheme that has been so important to its recent history.

In what is perhaps a sign of progress, both the World Bank and IMF have recently suggested raising the age of eligibility and gradually scaling back the value of the universal pension as alternatives to means testing.[22] Whether they have any right to influence policy at this level of detail at all is another matter. In the meantime, the government has reinforced its support for universality by introducing a universal child benefit for those under three years of age, worth US$44 per month, in June 2023. This was extended to a second year and raised to US$56 per month.[23]

Back in Zanzibar

In Tanzania, after Smart Daniel had taken officials to Mauritius, things looked up during the general elections held in 2015 in both Zanzibar and on the Tanzanian mainland: plans for a universal pension were mentioned in party manifestos. However, after the elections the two governments went different ways.

In Zanzibar, 'The Chief Secretary arranged more meetings on the universal pension', Smart Daniel says. There were reservations about the universal pension in the Zanzibar cabinet and a seven-person task team of senior officials was set up to look at it in more detail, with Smart Daniel being brought in to advise as required. The World Bank argued Zanzibar did not have the capacity to introduce a universal pension. 'We briefed officials on how to respond', Smart Daniel says.

> And I went back to Mauritius and got the person who had been in the engine room of the social protection system there, the ex-permanent secretary in the ministry for social assistance, Anbanaden Veerasamy, to come back to Zanzibar and have one-to-one meetings with the permanent secretaries in different ministries. That was the key, getting all the ministries on board, because they all have an equal say in the cabinet. Anbanaden Veerasamy explained how obstacles were overcome in Mauritius. It worked very well.

Professor Jeremy Seekings of the University of Cape Town has studied the evolution of the Zanzibar universal pension and says, 'Veerasamy told Zanzibari officials that "it was feasible" . . . He said, don't lose hope . . . just be positive.'[24]

Things progressed well from there to the point when the president of Zanzibar instructed the Minister of Finance to find the required budget. The new pension started in 2016 and would be paid to all people aged seventy years of age and over and be worth US$9 per month.[25] Smart Daniel was driving his car when an official at the ministry for tax-financed social protection phoned on the day of the decision and said, 'yes, yes, yes, yes, we made it.'[26] The new Zanzibar minister of finance, Dr Khalid Salum Mohamed, part of Smart Daniel's visit to Mauritius, handed over the first universal pension payment to a Zanzibar pensioner at the Kiembe Samaki paypoint, close to the island's airport. Professor Seekings describes the introduction of the universal pension in Zanzibar as 'the boldest pension reform in Africa north of the Zambezi.'[27]

In developing the universal pension the Zanzibar government had learned directly from a fellow government, rather than listening to international donors which too often set the terms of the discussion and recommend policy. The government had seen how the universal pension in Mauritius had been around for decades and the sky hadn't fallen in. Indeed, Mauritius has become the second richest country in Africa, in terms of income per capita, after the Seychelles.[28] Smart Daniel's support had been important. Professor Seekings reports an official in the ministry for social protection saying, 'we only started to talk about universal pensions after Smart's intervention.' He points out the significance of

Smart Daniel being Tanzanian and not an outsider, and how he 'crucially, spoke Swahili'. Importantly, 'most of the government officials in the [ministry for social protection] in Zanzibar saw the initiative as theirs . . . they "owned" it'. This contrasted with 'other cases in the poorer countries of East and Southern Africa, where reforms were seen by government officials . . . [as being] pushed by outside players.'[29]

Professor Seekings adds, 'Perhaps the most important aspect of . . . [HelpAge International's] influence was in emphasising that pensions should be universal, rather than means-tested (as was conventional wisdom in circles linked to the World Bank at the time).'[30] Stephen, in HelpAge International, had played his role in influencing Smart Daniel and Stephen was an 'outside player'. But his indirect influence appears to have worked with the grain of government and local political processes, not against it.

On the mainland

On mainland Tanzania, the social protection sector moved in another direction. A poverty-targeted productive safety net, such as those seen in Ethiopia, Uganda and Rwanda, was started in 2012, supported by the World Bank and other donors such as Sweden. This is notwithstanding Sweden being, at home, a champion of universality.[31] The scheme covered both the mainland and Zanzibar, and comprised 'a package of integrated conditional cash transfers': workfare, a conditional cash transfer for children, dependent on health and education behaviours, and additional, small unconditional transfers.[32] The conditional cash transfers were later under the spotlight, as mentioned in Chapter 6, being suspected of reducing women's mental health through gender stereotyping.[33] Targeting of the productive safety net was undertaken by a combination of geographic and community-based targeting and a proxy means test. It was all that the World Bank holds dear and, as for other similiar programmes, little better than a lottery in selecting those eligible.[34] Nevertheless, by 2016 the programme had expanded to cover 10 per cent of the entire population.[35] Total programme spending was more than US$400 million.[36] The cost grew to 0.3 per cent of GDP, and it was largely met by World Bank loans and other donor support.[37]

I visited Tanzania myself in late 2010 as a DFID staff member, with another colleague from London. Asked to give DFID Tanzania advice, we recommended that it invest in the productive safety net rather than a universal pension. Why did we do that? Because DFID Tanzania wanted to mobilise resources in the next financial year, it had an aid budget to spend. We wanted to suggest a universal pension, which was being discussed by Smart Daniel and others, and indeed, the DFID office was gearing up to make a significant investment in this direction. But the mainland government gave insufficient signals of positive intent. They may well have been discouraged by the World Bank. I don't have concrete evidence for this, though so much happens on the quiet. In any case, we recommended the productive safety net. And that is part of the reason the World Bank model of social protection prospers. For donors that want to spend money now and not take a risk with something with a potentially high return that may or may not happen in the future, it is so often the only game in town.

But being the only game in town does not make the World Bank's programme a good one. Evaluation evidence has shown some positive impacts of the scheme since it began, as we would expect from the simple fact of delivering cash transfers.[38] But could things have been done better? What more could have been done, for example, if workfare, on which evidence of value for money is so thin, had been ditched? Even at the outset in Tanzania, the World Bank admitted to there being 'little empirical evidence to demonstrate the long-term impact of public works programs (as stand-alone programs) on poverty reduction and human capital accumulation'.[39] And what if the roulette wheel targeting, which the World Bank itself found was unpopular with the majority of affected communities in Tanzania, was removed?[40] Were universal, unconditional transfers even considered by the World Bank, at any point? A study of the development of social protection in Tanzania says of a high-level conference in the early stages of programme implementation, in 2014, 'it is . . . noteworthy that potentially controversial issues were ignored, such as the questionable impact of conditionalities and the challenges of targeting in countries where the majority is poor and administrative capacity is limited.'[41]

Perhaps most concerning of all is that, although the World Bank gained the agreement of governments on the mainland and in Zanzibar for the productive safety net, only a relatively small amount of government money was put into the first stage of the programme, beyond World Bank loans.[42] It seems things have been pushed off in the wrong direction, against what the government is prepared to spend its own money on, as in Ethiopia. And now the programme is continuing with a second stage, with more than double the budget at US $883 million.[43] Again, most of the money is coming from the World Bank and other donors. The scheme looks like a donor programme that will come and eventually go, leaving a country with higher debt and too little to show for it. It makes me reflect on how donor influence can misdirect things, but also on the incentives that donor staff including myself have faced in administering the spending of overseas aid.

A stop in Malawi

In the country that neighbours Tanzania to the south-west, Malawi, Smart Daniel met Andrew Kavala, CEO of the Malawi Network of Older Persons' Organizations (MANEPO). 'I travelled there. The idea of a universal social pension was new to them. After that I helped them prepare their own feasibility study, as we'd done in Tanzania, which Andrew Kavala coordinated.'[44] The work on the universal pension is unfinished. 'They've pushed the agenda', Smart Daniel says. 'But it hasn't happened yet.'

I visited Malawi in 2018, with a colleague from Development Pathways. Our job was to support the modernization of the payment system for the main tax-financed social protection scheme. The capital Lilongwe is a pretty quiet place and Malawi is a very poor country, 99 per cent down the scale of richest to poorest countries in the world, in terms of income per capita.[45] Inequality is similar to Indonesia and poverty is high: 89 per cent of the population are estimated to be under the international poverty line of US$3.65, or US$1.40 in real terms.[46]

What did we find donors supporting in such a poor and low-capacity environment? Poverty targeting of course, though this time it had been driven, in the first instance, by UNICEF. The main social protection programme, predominantly funded by the World Bank and other donors, aims to reach the poorest 10 per cent in districts in which it operates.[47] This is nonsensical in an environment where pretty much everyone is poor, and there have been tensions. In a pilot district for the programme, Mchinji, more than a fifth of recipients reported an increase in conflict in their community.[48]

Not put off by all of this, the World Bank approved a US $142 million programme in 2019, a grant rather than a loan this time, in part to support and expand the programme.[49] Other funding is provided by Germany and the European Union. Once again, the low spending from the government's own resources – just 6 per cent of total programme costs – rings alarm bells about where the programme is going and whether it is hurting rather than helping long-run system development.[50] Perhaps there is a clue to whether this is happening in the motion passed by the Malawian parliament in 2018, a year before the World Bank grant was approved, calling for a universal pension.[51]

From Zanzibar to Kenya

Soon after the universal pension in Zanzibar started, in 2017, a delegation from the Kenyan government visited to see it in operation. They stayed for three days, meeting government officials and seeing what was possible with their own eyes. The year after that, in 2018, the Kenyan government introduced its own universal pension. As I witnessed myself, the World Bank fought them every step of the way. And it even attacked the pension after it had started, in 2019, as we saw in Chapter 1 when Stephen read that email from the Kenyan government in the training room in Entebbe.

Two years before the pension was introduced, in 2016, Stephen and Development Pathways were contracted to work in Kenya on a review of the social protection sector. UNICEF and the World Food Programme (WFP) were funding the work. 'They wanted to push a different agenda on social protection to the World Bank's approach', Stephen says. I was included in the team that Stephen led, having recently left DFID, and in Nairobi we built good relations with Cecilia Mbaka and John Gachigi, head and deputy head of the Social Protection Secretariat in the ministry for social protection.[52] 'That work gave us a seat at the table', Stephen says. But inevitably, the World Bank, which knew Stephen well enough by now, was unhappy. I recorded in my diary for 26 October 2016 the inevitable: 'World Bank has complained about Stephen leading the Social Protection Review.'

In its work, our team highlighted progress that had been made in establishing tax-financed social protection in Kenya, with the support of donors like UNICEF, DFID and the World Bank, over more than a decade. Programmes were reaching a million households and were also increasingly government funded.[53] The World Bank had provided considerable loans to central government, partly in return for extra government spending on tax-financed social protection. And donors had helped strengthen and streamline programme administration systems. Some of this work was done by Stephen's colleague and a co-founder of Development Pathways Richard Chirchir, who worked on programme management information systems and the single registry, which is a publicly accessible store of detailed information on different programmes.[54]

But the team also pointed to coverage of tax-financed social protection in a population of 55 million falling a long way short of anything approaching universal access. Also, on the contributory side, only 10 per cent of workers in Kenya are covered by the state contributory pension scheme.[55] The context for this is a country whose vulnerability to the climate crisis was demonstrated in the 2022 Horn of Africa drought which affected four million Kenyans.[56] Kenya is also 83 per cent of the way down the scale of richest to poorest countries in terms of income per capita, and more than two-thirds of the population are below the international poverty line of US$3.65 per day, or US$1.55 in real terms.[57] More than a quarter of children under five are stunted.[58] And women and girls across the welfare distribution face their own particular challenges, as they do elsewhere.

In terms of history, Kenya is another ex-British colony. In the 1950s, the Mau Mau Uprising took place in response to white farmers forcing down the wages of farm workers.[59] According to research by American Pulitzer Prize winner Caroline Elkins, during the Uprising 'the British detained nearly the entire Kikuyu population – some one and a half million people – for more than eight years. Inside detention camps and barbed-wire villages, the Kikuyu lived in a world of fear, hunger, and death.'[60] UK writer and journalist Richard Dowden adds that during the rebellion, there was violence on both sides. However, 'Only thirty-two white settlers were killed but 3,000 African police and soldiers, 12,000 alleged Mau Mau supporters and 1,800 African civilians died.' Dowden says, 'It took twelve battalions of the British army and a squadron of . . . bombers to defeat it.'[61] To make things worse, just before Kenya gained independence in 1963, the British authorities did their best to destroy evidence of its behaviour.[62] But this didn't stop the UK government being defeated at the High Court in London in 2012 when three elderly Mau Mau veterans claimed damages for what Al Jazeera called 'a systematic campaign of torture'.[63]

Getting away from donors

This was the environment in which donors in Kenya worked. Anyway, the review team that Stephen led raised concerns about the core cash transfer programmes being poverty-targeted using a combination of community-based targeting and proxy means testing.[64] For two of the programmes, for orphans and vulnerable children and for older people, only around half of the beneficiaries were found to be in the poorest fifth of the population. And for a third programme, for vulnerable households in more arid parts of the country, targeting was, as elsewhere, a roulette wheel with 'only a little better than random selection'.[65] Inevitably, the World Bank didn't agree with the team's assessment and in a later document described the same programmes as 'well-targeted', though it is not clear what evidence this is based on.[66]

In tense meetings the team continued to critique existing programmes and describe the potential of more universal, lifecycle schemes, as part of a comprehensive, multi-tiered social protection system.[67] The World Bank, working closely with DFID, criticized the team's work and argued universal schemes were unaffordable.[68] Both the World Bank and DFID had made significant investments in poverty-targeted schemes in Kenya, so this is perhaps understandable. But I was taken aback by how donors dominated discussions when government officials were present. There was an obvious uneasiness in government about the extent to which policy was being driven by donors, though this could not be said publicly. International expert Marion Ouma, from the Nordic Africa Institute in Sweden, has authored a paper with Professor Jimi Adesina from the University of South Africa, analysing the development of social protection policy in Kenya, a sector Ouma has worked in herself. The paper argues, 'social relations between international and national actors were non-egalitarian and asymmetrical.'[69] Our team's review of social protection adds, 'senior members of government have expressed the view that . . . development partners [donors] have had greater influence over social protection policy than the national government and that this should change.'[70]

To get away from donors, Stephen's team did a four-day training course for government officials at a hotel on Lake Naivasha in the Great Rift Valley, funded by WFP. Cecilia Mbaka, head of the Social Protection Secretariat, and her deputy John Gachigi were there. Away from Nairobi, people could avoid distraction by visitors, meetings and donors. Stephen says, 'Having government officials together for that long meant we could really get into things. It got a lot of messages across about how the World Bank approach was not the only way.'

Soon after that, in late 2016, Stephen and I went to Mombasa to make presentations to senior Kenyan politicians and parliamentarians, again without donors. The event was organized by David Kamau from WFP. Susan Mochache attended, a junior government minister in charge of tax-financed social protection who Stephen says 'clearly wanted to drive things forward'. So did her boss, the Cabinet Secretary at the head of the ministry for social protection, Phyllis Kandie.[71] Stephen and I made presentations on universal lifecycle social protection to both of them, and others. We discussed the cost and how a gradual expansion might be financed, in part, from a gradual increase in tax revenues, which, other things being equal, tend to rise with economic growth. 'There was one critical moment', Stephen says.

> We got onto the political economy of poverty targeting and the Cabinet Secretary said she had been to a community where a lot of people were receiving the older persons cash transfer. She expected a big welcome but instead got complaints about the targeting system. I said, of course poverty-targeted schemes are often unpopular given the size of the targeting errors. I said I have never understood why politicians don't support universal programmes more than they do, given that politicians should want to be popular. I asked them if the reception in the community would have been different if the scheme had been universal.

After the meeting, Susan Mochache mentioned to Stephen the possibility of developing a universal pension as part of the government's campaign for the general election the following summer. Stephen said, 'Whatever you need, I'll help you, we'll do whatever you want.' Back in Nairobi a little while later, Stephen was asked to meet the Minister of Finance Henry Rotich.[72] Susan Mochache was there and David Kamau from WFP, with National Treasury officials. In the forty-five-minute meeting, Stephen presented how universal pensions contribute to economic growth and are politically popular. Henry Rotich asked questions about affordability. 'But he appeared to express no enthusiasm whatsoever', Stephen says.

Stephen heard nothing more until, on 30 March 2017, in his budget speech, Henry Rotich announced a new universal pension for everyone aged seventy years and over. It would be worth US$16 per month and raise government spending on tax-financed social protection from 0.3 to 0.4 per cent of GDP, taking a small but significant step towards universality.[73] Stephen received an email from Susan Mochache the same day.

> Dear Stephen, Let me extend my appreciation for your support, today Kenya adopted the over 70 years old universal older persons cash transfer. We are delighted as are all Kenyans. Many thanks and looking forward to further deliberations to strengthen our social protection. Best Regards, Principal Secretary Susan Mochache.

Kenyan citizens seventy years old and over were registered for the universal pension during the campaign for the August 2017 general election, which built on the existing poverty-targeted scheme. 'It was to show everyone the government was serious', Stephen says. The government won the election, and despite subsequent delays, because the registration during the election had been done quickly leading to mistakes in the registration data, the universal pension was introduced in January 2018.[74]

The World Bank's response

Inevitably, the World Bank was, again, not happy. It had loan conditions in place on using poverty targeting through proxy means testing.[75] 'It complained it hadn't been consulted', Stephen says. 'But what did they expect? The government kept it hidden so they could actually do it.'

Undeterred, the World Bank, with other donors including DFID, developed the Kenya Social and Economic Inclusion Project, including a US$250 million loan.[76] Around half the donor money in the project is for the poverty-targeted programme for vulnerable households in more arid parts of the country, housed in the National Drought Management Authority in the Ministry of Devolution and Planning.[77] The project was developed in consultation with government, or at least the friendly parts, and is mostly financed from the government's own resources. Other areas of spending include 'nutrition-sensitive' cash transfers, the enrolment of tax-financed social protection recipients onto the government's National Hospital Insurance Fund and improvements in aspects of social protection systems for cash transfer programmes, of which the universal pension is one. Given this, we can presumably say with confidence the programme is in line with government thinking. But the government is made up of diverse ministries with different interests. Stephen argues that the scheme was driven by the National Treasury wanting the World Bank's loan. What is clear is the World Bank was less supportive of the ministry that was in charge of social protection policy, the ministry for social protection. In the main project document for the new World Bank loan, the universal pension does not even merit a mention in the main text, only in a footnote.[78] So much for donors taking the lead from government: they effectively ignored the government's own flagship scheme.

There have been significant problems with the universal pension, which currently has 766,000 recipients.[79] Payments have been missed and there is no rolling registration for those passing seventy to get on the programme as there should have been. 'None of the donors, apart from David Kamau at the World Food Programme, got behind it', Stephen says. 'No one helped. It's like they wanted it to fail, but then it becomes a self-fulfilling prophecy.' A local source says the Kenya Social and Economic Inclusion Project, the focus of the new World Bank loan, has pulled government officials away from the universal pension. 'It has its own conditionalities. Government employees that gain something from the World Bank programme, including per diems, have a conflict of interest, as they're being pulled in another direction.' The source adds, 'The World Bank has had a huge influence. Nothing has moved forward. The World Bank have a clear agenda, it is still promoting poverty targeting.'

In a 2023 review the World Bank says, with an unmistakable air of satisfaction, 'After its first round of enrolment in 2018 . . . [the universal pension], which had been considered Kenya's flagship social protection program and the foundation of the country's vision of lifecycle social protection, was itself closed to new entrants. It continues to be closed to new entrants today.'[80] No mention is made of how the

World Bank did not support the universal pension, indeed tried to undermine it, nor of how it will support the government in getting its vision back on track.

Now, as elsewhere, COVID-19 and rising government debt have made things harder in terms of financing the universal pension. Donors will no doubt argue this shows that universality in Kenya is not affordable. But they would do better to turn a critical eye on themselves. The US$250 million World Bank loan for the Kenya Social and Economic Inclusion Project, with other donor funding, is sufficient to finance transfers for the universal pension for more than two years.[81] Given the government is already financing pension payments itself, those donor resources could also be invested in addressing the administrative issues mentioned as well as helping to expand the caseload. This looks like a pretty solid basis for a joint financing plan. So, it is about making choices, not affordability per se. What is more, hundreds of millions of dollars have been spent by donors and government on roulette wheel poverty-targeted schemes in the last two decades in Kenya.[82] The schemes will have done some good, as cash transfers do, and may have helped, at the outset, to introduce tax-financed social protection to Kenya. But how well do they now fit with the long-term development of a comprehensive social protection system? Achieving this requires alignment with local political reality and programme doability, and supporting the government's vision for social protection, not pulling another way. Given the government's introduction of a universal pension and the current consideration of a universal child benefit to further lay the foundations of a universal system, donors would do well to think about how they get behind that vision.[83]

In July 2019, Stephen helped the government draft a rebuttal to the World Bank's attack on the universal pension in that training room in Entebbe, as we have seen. The local source I speak to says, 'After the government responded, the World Bank pulled down their report attacking the universal pension. Then they wrote a letter of apology to the government.' But letter of apology or not, the World Bank, working from Washington and from its glass edifice in Nairobi, felt to me like an unaccountable alternative government during that period when the universal pension was under development and being introduced. Yes, you can point to World Bank and other donor achievements in Kenya, but the condition for support appears to be that policy is in the donors' own image, albeit in collaboration with parts of government outside the ministry of social protection. Where respect for institutions and for local politics and the autonomy of populations and governments fit into this is not clear. Kenya is not a perfect democracy.[84] But as in Nepal, this is all the more reason for donors including the World Bank to align behind decision-making and help strengthen, not cut across, lines of accountability between the population of Kenya and its government.

Chapter 12

AND THEN THINGS WENT SILLY

SOCIAL REGISTRIES

The beginning

What has been the World Bank's response to the ongoing challenges with poverty targeting? What has been its response to what it describes itself as the 'inbuilt statistical error' of proxy means testing in low- and middle-income countries?[1] In rare instances it has been to support universal programmes. More generally, and notwithstanding public commitments to universal social protection, it has been to double down on poverty targeting by encouraging governments to develop what are known as 'social registries'. And offering loans for them to do so.

Social registries are not to be confused with *single* registries. Richard Chirchir and Shez Farooq describe a *single* registry as 'a warehouse collecting information from all types of social protection programmes', whether poverty-targeted or universal based on individual entitlements.[2] This information may be on individuals or households in any scheme. A *social* registry, on the other hand, provides information on households 'to select the beneficiaries of poverty-targeted social assistance schemes'. Their purpose is to store data, ideally on every household in the population, to poverty target benefits – a range of benefits, not just one. Single registries are core to social protection systems. Social registries are optional.

The World Bank describes social registries as 'information systems that support outreach, intake, registration, and determination of potential eligibility for one or more social programs'.[3] They can be used to poverty target schemes outside social protection, for example, subsidies for healthcare insurance, scholarships and other education and training programs, legal services, housing benefits and utilities subsidies.[4] And the World Bank describes their strong intuitive appeal: 'social registries are efficient for programme administrators (who then do not have to collect the same information from the same people) and for clients (who do not have to provide the same information separately to multiple programs)'.[5] Furthermore, it says that social registries can link to multiple government systems such as 'ID platforms . . . civil registries . . . tax systems, housing and property registries, and systems related to social security contributions, pension benefits, health insurance, education, and vehicle administration, among others'. They enable 'a whole-of-government approach, allowing people to apply and be considered for programs through digital self-service windows in real time'.[6]

The World Bank goes further. 'Programmes can be layered together in ways that provide differentiated support for households across the income distribution.'[7] And some countries, such as Chile, Colombia and Costa Rica, have moved on to providing 'bundled services', where 'social workers help families to develop a plan of action, provide them with psycho-social support, help them to obtain basic paperwork (such as IDs), and access the programs for which the family qualify'. The intuitive appeal is compelling, on paper at least. And well-developed social registries cover a lot of programmes: for example, they are used to target fifty-two schemes in the Philippines, seventy programmes in Pakistan and eighty in Chile.[8] They inspire the World Bank to paint a picture of sunny uplands. 'From Guinea to Chile, Turkey, Djibouti, Pakistan, and Indonesia, social registries are helping connect people to a range of public services. These include social protection, health, and financial inclusion, based on the principle of "progressive universalism," expanding coverage, and in the process, prioritizing the poorest people.'[9]

Going back to origins Stephen says,

> The first real social registry was Cadastro Unico in Brazil, which started in 2001. Unusually, it's not based on the proxy means test. Brazil used something called the unverified means test, like in South Africa where you declare your income yourself. There is also the poor card in India, known as the Below Poverty Line (BPL) Card. It's the same concept and the current version started at roughly the same time as Cadastro Unico. It doesn't use the proxy means test either but an elaborate home-grown process. Then you have the Unified Database in Indonesia, which as we know started later, around 2011, that uses proxy means testing and helps to target both social protection programmes and health insurance.

Stephen reflects on how support for social registries emerged. 'I guess the World Bank thought, 'We've got a data base for targeting one programme using a proxy means test, which is great, so why don't we start using it to target all social programmes?" The initiative started relatively recently. 'Kathy Lindert and Philippe Leite in the World Bank became leading thinkers on the issue and a paper appeared in 2017', Stephen says.

> I met them both when I was in Indonesia a little before that. Kathy Lindert used to be in the World Bank's team in Brazil where she will have seen Cadastro Unico. After the 2017 paper it was suddenly all about social registries, which were now labelled as being at the heart of social protection systems. They started pushing social registries globally, essentially rebranding the proxy means test, which most social registries use. They had a new product to sell and connect to World Bank loans.[10]

And social registries spread fast. The World Bank says, 'As of 2013, 23 countries had social registries . . . but a more recent study found that this had increased to 60, though different definitions make it difficult to be precise.'[11]

Targeting errors

A key problem with social registries is the same as for the proxy means testing on which most social registries rely, namely targeting errors. We have seen the targeting errors associated with proxy means testing, and Stephen and colleagues Diloá Athias and Idil Mohamud do not hold back in describing how the issue transfers to social registries.

> Global evidence indicates that all social registries have failed abysmally in achieving their core purpose of accurately identifying the beneficiaries of social programmes. The targeting errors found in social registries are very high, as evidenced in the exclusion errors of programmes that use them. The lowest error found, to date, is 44 per cent but some social registries deliver errors above 90 per cent.[12]

To make matters worse, social registries spread the problem over a bigger canvas. Stephen and colleagues add, 'By using the same targeting methodology across a range of social programmes, social registries systematically exclude the majority of the poorest members of society from multiple schemes, causing significant harm.'

As discussed, difficulties with poverty targeting arise, in part, because levels of income can be similarly low across swathes of the population. Household characteristics, on which proxy means testing is based, can also change quickly. Stephen and colleagues describe how in Rwanda, '87 per cent of households changed in size [over two years] . . . Yet, this is only one of the "proxies" that would be used in a social registry algorithm when determining household wellbeing. When multiple proxies are considered, the changes in household characteristics over time are even greater.'[13] So social registries require continuous updating, but does this happen? Stephen and colleagues say, 'In most cases data is not updated for many years.' They point to gaps of at least six years in Indonesia and the Philippines and more than ten years in Pakistan and parts of Mexico. They add, 'However, there are a small number of countries that undertake registration more frequently: Vietnam, for example, does it annually while Rwanda re-classifies its population every two years.' They conclude that countries with social registries 'find that the information they hold is not only out of date but was often never of particularly good quality'. The World Bank recognizes the problem of time lags, saying, 'Risks of exclusion increase when social registries that are rarely updated are used.'[14]

Dynamic inclusion

Despite all of this, as ever, the World Bank is optimistic in its outlook. It explains that, 'the infrequent updating of registry data is often due to the use of time-consuming and costly survey sweeps.' It says, 'Such a practice is not inherent in [proxy means testing] and there is no reason the registry data cannot be updated more frequently using other approaches.'[15] One of these other approaches is 'dynamic inclusion'.[16] Daisy Sibun, describes how 'the Bank's Social Protection Department are now beginning to pursue an approach termed "dynamic inclusion", supporting countries to build on-demand registration and needs assessment systems'.[17]

Stephen and his colleagues are sceptical.

> The advocates of social registries . . . propose that, every time there is a change in a household, it should notify the social registry so that the information is kept up to date. This is clearly an impossible task: households are highly unlikely to make the effort to register even obvious changes, such as the number of people in the household, never mind changes in other proxies, such as whether they have a television or the number of animals they possess.[18]

This will surely be especially true for households living in remote areas with poor connectivity. Stephen adds,

> Fine, households can apply when they think they may be eligible and you can collect data on them straight away, but you still have the problem of data lags. You face having recent data on new recipients and old data on longstanding recipients. And we know how quickly people's circumstances change. Further, people are unlikely to update their data if it is likely to result in them being kicked off a programme.

The World Bank challenges this scepticism, arguing that registration in Chile and Brazil is fully dynamic.[19] It concedes that currently, 'Few social registries are designed to include . . . a [dynamic] data collection process.'[20] But it argues progress is being made. 'Colombia and Pakistan were early developers of large social registries and are both now moving away from periodic survey sweeps to more dynamic systems, supplementing the special-purpose gathering of data with data-matching from other government data sources.' But then the World Bank's optimism starts to stretch credibility. 'Dynamic inclusion . . . can be facilitated by creating a permanent and extensive network of local offices.' What is the likelihood of such a permanent and extensive network being put in place? For many, perhaps most countries, it would require a huge concentration of effort and resources, taking away from other vital priorities.

Total cost of social registries

There are clearly other costs associated with social registries, besides targeting errors and the small matter of creating a network of local offices. But here evidence is not always clear. We have seen the likely higher administrative costs associated with proxy means testing, because of the complexity of poverty targeting relative to universal programmes. The World Bank argues the administrative costs of social registries in determining the eligibility of households are hard to measure but 'range between US$1 and US$3 per household in most countries, or in the range of 1–3 percent of the value of benefits channelled through the system'.[21] In lower-income countries with start-up costs of newer systems this can go up to '7–8 percent'. Taken at face value, these look like reassuringly low costs and near levels we might expect for universal schemes.[22] Stephen and colleagues say the literature shows costs ranging 'from as low as US$1.27 per household in Colombia to as high as US$26 in northern Kenya'.[23]

In terms of total spending, a truly national social registry may cost, at the outset, in the region of US$50-US$100 million.[24] Against this, we would expect savings from targeting multiple programmes. The World Bank says savings have been generated by social registries being used by multiple programmes, for example US$248 million in Pakistan, US$157 million in South Africa and US$13 million in Guinea.[25] But there can also be waste. Bangladesh took a World Bank loan of US$87 million to do a proxy means test survey but the data was later found to be unusable.[26] Stephen and his colleagues say, 'Around 35 million households were surveyed in 2017 and 2018, amounting to almost the entire population. However, due to delays in developing the software for the social registry, it never became operational. It is now widely recognised that the information collected on households is out of date and no longer of any use.'[27]

But all of this published cost information is somewhat academic given issues with targeting errors. Would not the cost of moving targeting errors within acceptable bounds be significant, even huge? Especially if we bring the creation of an extensive network of local offices back into the equation. Even if we cannot answer this with any precision, we can surely say that the economic case for social registries has not been established. All the more so if we add in the other costs that we have seen with proxy means testing, including a lack of transparency and potential social discord, and a possible lack of political support and funding for poverty-targeted schemes, relative to universal programmes.

All of this should at least give the World Bank pause. Yet the World Bank's promotion of social registries continues with a vengeance. Kate O'Donnell, a PhD student at the International Institute of Social Studies (ISS) at Erasmus University in Rotterdam, is researching the development of social registries in sub-Saharan Africa. She says, 'Between 2010 and 2024, 46 countries in sub-Saharan Africa agreed a social protection loan with the World Bank. In all of these loans reference is made, either to plans to develop a social registry, or to a social registry that is already under development.'

Stephen says, 'The World Bank are pushing the proxy means test and social registries even when systems are weak, like in Rwanda and Uganda.' He adds, 'In fairness, Margaret Grosh has said administrative systems needs to be strong enough for social registries, but this gets ignored.'[28]

And the promotion of social registries is not just about the World Bank. Bilateral donors – from countries, incidentally, that would surely never allow social registries at home – have encouraged them elsewhere. Two examples are

Australia in Indonesia and the German Development Agency GIZ in Malawi.[29] 'DFID were into social registries too', Stephen says.

> I was in Pakistan in 2014 looking at reforming a scholarship scheme in one of the northern provinces. It was too dangerous to go there so we just interviewed people from the province in Islamabad. Richard Chirchir was with me. I presented our analysis of the proxy means test in Pakistan showing how bad the targeting was. DFID were there and said they'd just agreed to use the same proxy means test for a number of programmes they were helping to fund, and expressed concern that they hadn't realised the problems with it. The social registry idea had taken root, despite the dreadfully poor accuracy of the targeting.

Low coverage of social registries

An issue further undermining the case for social registries, if it needed it, is limited coverage. In most countries the majority of the population is excluded.[30] In its 2022 book on targeting, the World Bank says that coverage of social registries ranges 'from 75 percent of households or more in a quarter of the cases to less than 10 percent of households in another quarter of the cases'.[31] The median average coverage is just 21 per cent. In a 2021 blog Stephen's long-time collaborator Nicholas Freeland points out the resulting logical tangle:

> surely everyone is a potential beneficiary of social assistance? So, to have an authoritative list of all potential beneficiaries of social assistance, we would need a national registry of all individuals, not a social registry of only a subset of those individuals. We cannot choose the subset for the social registry unless we have a national registry in the first place.[32]

Stephen and colleagues say social registries 'have failed at the most basic level of including all households within their databases'.[33] They add, 'In some cases, it is because they are limited to specific areas of a country . . . in many other cases, it is a deliberate choice . . . . Usually, this is done to reduce costs . . . . For example, Indonesia deliberately restricted its social registry survey to 40 per cent of the population.' They point out that, as if to make it official, the World Bank 'have recently argued that it may be better to establish quotas for social registries so that only a minority of the population are surveyed. The rationale they use is that if all households were surveyed in contexts where poverty-targeted programmes are only able to reach a limited number of beneficiaries, it might raise expectations.'

Beyond this, Stephen and colleagues say social registries raise a significant issue on human rights and data privacy: 'donors . . . often employ much lower standards of data management when developing social registries across the Global South than they would use in their own countries.'[34] I say to Stephen that social registries represent a relabelling of the proxy means test and also their scaling up. And given they are for poverty targeting, and target by household, the whole process, by intent or accident, is designed to squeeze universal social protection programmes. He does not disagree. Stephen and colleagues point out that social registries cannot be used for tax-financed universal lifecycle social protection programmes, because they target by households not individuals.[35] The World Bank disputes this, but Richard Chirchir and Shez Farooq concur, arguing that social registries 'have the limited purpose of simplifying the targeting of household-based social assistance programmes'.[36] The clincher surely is that low coverage automatically precludes universality. But Stephen says,

> The World Bank still say you can use social registries for universal programmes. In the World Bank social registry paper from 2017 they make this claim that the social registry is used in Georgia to target the universal social pension. But that's not true: the social registry only covers 36 per cent of households in the country but around 50 per cent of households contain an older person. It's a nonsensical claim by the Bank, but it's all presented as so scientific and reasonable.[37]

Social registries can of course exist within a social protection system that contains universal programmes, but everything comes at a price. And they may make more sense in some contexts such as Brazil, if only because the government is already heavily invested, though this does not get away from the issue of large targeting errors.[38] But the case for the blanket promotion of social registries that is being seen in sub-Saharan Africa has clearly not been made. Stephen reflects, 'The idea of social registries has been out there and growing but is devoid of evidence.'

The battle for the future

Yet governments in low- and middle-income countries are agreeing to social registries. To the extent these governments represent the population, who are we to say that is wrong? Here, again, there is the issue of the leverage of donor resources. Daisy Sibun argues, 'in many cases World Bank financing . . . has a significant influence . . . on national governments' choices around their approach to programming.'[39] Loans are negotiated with governments needing resources and come with technical advice that social registries are a good thing to do. Among the countries in our story, Indonesia, Kenya, Malawi, Nepal and Tanzania *all* have social registries. In some countries, World Bank disbursements are made conditional on specific actions on social registries, in what are called Performance-Based Conditions, previously known as Disbursement Linked Indicators. This is the case in Kenya and Malawi.[40]

Yes, even Nepal is in the picture, as we have seen, a country where the government's commitment to tax-financed universal lifecycle social protection is so obvious. The World Bank says the government in Nepal 'has committed to establishing a social registry across the entire country, to be used by all [social protection] programmes'.[41] Stephen and his colleagues dispute this saying, 'in Nepal successive governments have felt little ownership of the social registry and have put it to limited use.'[42]

Stephen says of country government interactions with the World Bank on social registries,

> They are not being told what the evidence says. They are being told that they are getting this wonderful database that can be used for all kinds of wonderous things, including registering people for universal schemes. So, obviously they say yes. But, the World Bank don't tell them what social registries really are and the fact that they do not work and have never worked anywhere. It is like they are being conned by second-hand car salesmen from the World Bank who are selling them poor quality cars, but at a very high price. But, the car hardly gets out of the garage, while the World Bank walks away with its loan in place.

Might the World Bank concede that, even if we assume social registries with dynamic inclusion make sense in some middle-income countries with higher capacity – and given high targeting errors, there is little evidence for this – they may not be an appropriate destination for precious government resources and effort in *all* low- and middle-income countries? What is lacking here, as with poverty targeting, conditional cash transfers and workfare, is a process of standing back and assessing whether social registries make sense set against other options, in each unique context. Social registries are taken as inevitable, part of the natural order of things, the only question is how to try and improve them. Stephen laughs, 'In World Bank diagrams, social registries are placed at the centre of the whole system, rather than at the periphery, as one option for poor quality poverty targeting.'[43] He and his colleagues add,

> While advocates may interpret [low coverage of social registries across populations] . . . as a challenge to redouble their efforts, they would do well to reflect on whether the low coverage globally is, in fact, an indication of the weak support by governments . . . Angola is a good example of a failed social registry. Despite significant investment by the European Union in developing the software . . . the government of Angola has shown no interest in paying for the survey that would provide the information to populate the database.[44]

Stephen says, 'You have countries doing social registries that don't have identity cards or birth certificates for vast numbers of the population.' He and his colleagues argue that, 'it is questionable why countries would prioritise social registries over offering identity to their citizens. Surely, if funding is available to register people, priority should be given to offering birth certificates and national identity cards. With these, citizens would be visible to the state and better able to access public services.'[45] They add, 'A further significant benefit would be to facilitate their applications for individual, lifecycle social security entitlements, such as child benefits, old age pensions and disability benefits.' Human Rights Watch agree, suggesting in a 2023 paper on proxy means testing in Jordan that the World Bank should 'Focus financing and technical assistance on modernizing information systems that are critical to securing universal social protection, such as population registries and vital statistics databases, and ensure that such assistance is provided in a manner consistent with privacy and related human rights standards'.[46] Stephen says that, 'Countries would be better off building universal lifecycle systems with on-demand registration for individual entitlement programmes, using the civil registry, like they do in South Africa. There is no need for a social registry.'

Stephen and colleagues add that, 'the COVID-19 crisis has effectively blown apart the utility of all social registries, since relative household wellbeing across all societies has changed dramatically since early 2020. Any information collected by social registries before the pandemic is now virtually worthless.' They add, 'If countries were truly committed to social registries, they would completely renew their data post COVID-19 – undertaking mass national surveys – since the information they now hold is worthless. There are no signs of countries doing this.'[47] Stephen says, 'It's just a crazy ideological push.' He and his colleagues argue that the development of social registries is 'deeply political and influences the degree to which millions of men, women, girls and boys are included or excluded from social protection'.[48] Stephen concludes, 'It's all very sad. But we're not going away, we're going to keep challenging.'

Chapter 13

OTHER ARENAS IN ASIA AND THE ARABIAN PENINSULA

Mongolia, Kyrgyzstan and the IMF

In 2018, Stephen called out World Bank and IMF for their behaviour in Mongolia and Kyrgyzstan. The IMF are part of this story because the World Bank and IMF, by their own admission, 'collaborate closely on country assistance and policy issues that are relevant for both institutions'.[1] Governments can face constraints from both organizations. In 2017, 10 per cent of IMF loans included conditionalities linked to social protection.[2]

In Mongolia, a shadow boxing match affecting much of the population has taken place between the World Bank and IMF on one side and the government on the other. In 2006, the Mongolian government made its poverty-targeted child benefit universal, boosted at the time by high commodity prices including for minerals such as copper on which Mongolian exports depend.[3] It was supported in this by UNICEF, but opposed by the World Bank, IMF and the Asian Development Bank (ADB).[4] In 2010, following a *fall* in commodity prices, the government was obliged to abolish the child benefit as a condition for financial assistance from the IMF. But, in a sidestep, in the same year, it renewed its commitment to universal benefits by introducing an annual grant for every citizen, a form of universal basic income.[5] After further commodity price fluctuations the government was forced back on the ropes and agreed to poverty target its benefits again, in 2012.[6] But this was another feint. After a general election in July 2012, the new government refused to implement poverty targeting and instead abolished the annual grant for all citizens and reintroduced the universal child benefit, which now went to nearly 1 million children. But the World Bank and IMF were not done. After more falls in commodity prices, in collaboration with the ADB and Japan, they threatened to withhold loans unless the universal child benefit was targeted. Under pressure, the government agreed and introduced proxy means testing to target 60 per cent of children, in 2016.[7] But the government went back on this commitment in 2017 and made the child benefit universal again following an *increase* in government revenues, and finding that targeting had been unpopular with citizens.[8] The fight continued, and Stephen reflected in a blog twelve months later, 'For the past year or so, the IMF and its allies have, once again, been exerting considerable pressure on Mongolia to target the [universal child benefit], making targeting a condition

... for the disbursement of loans.'[9] The government agreed targeting would be reintroduced from 2018, with the compromise that it would reach 80 per cent of children, leaving the programme, ironically, nearly universal. The battle was apparently working its way to a draw and the IMF, ADB, World Bank and Japan released loan funds.[10] But it was not quite over. In response to COVID-19, the government increased the value of the benefit fivefold, to the equivalent of US$36 per month, and restored universality.[11]

The child benefit currently costs 3.7 per cent of GDP.[12] Ahead of COVID-19, when spending was much lower, the IMF's actions had been motivated by concerns over 'unsustainable public debt, falling international reserves, and lower growth'.[13] Yet the IMF itself also said, 'the savings from better targeting the [child benefit] will be used entirely to increase spending on the food stamp program for the most vulnerable.' There were to be no savings. So, what was the point of disrupting the programme? And what were two international financial institutions doing, picking a fight with a sovereign government over the granularity of domestic policy? Stephen writes, 'the IMF has meddled in internal social policy decisions which go well beyond its remit.'[14]

Meanwhile, in Kyrgyzstan, the IMF was at it again, supported once more by the World Bank. In June 2017, a law was passed to replace Kyrgyzstan's poverty-targeted programme for families with children, which used proxy means testing, with a universal child benefit, to start in January 2018.[15] Stephen reports that in Kyrgyzstan, as elsewhere, poverty targeting had been 'little better than random'.[16] He points out that ahead of the introduction of the universal child benefit, in late 2017, 'the IMF visited Kyrgyzstan to undertake a review of its loan programme ... In the IMF's own words: "The mission ... encouraged the authorities to explore ways to introduce targeting into the recently adopted universal child allowance law."'[17] Stephen continues: 'in a press release on 31st January 2018, the IMF triumphantly announced that the Government of Kyrgyzstan had agreed to "amend the law on universal child allowances to reintroduce targeting".' He adds, 'we know from informants that the targeting of the child benefits was supported by the World Bank.'

The IMF was concerned, among other things, about Kyrgyzstan's fiscal position. The poverty-targeted benefit had a budget of 0.6 per cent of GDP in 2015, and Stephen reported, 'the universal child benefits will require an investment of 1.3 per cent of GDP.'[18] So presumably things were getting out of control. Yet, according to the IMF's own press release, 'The 2017 fiscal deficit was *kept close to the 3.5 percent of GDP target*'[19] (My italics). Not only was it close to target, by way of comparison it was the same as the fiscal deficit of the United States for that year.[20] Even if the United States is not an appropriate standard, again, does the IMF have the right to intervene at this level of domestic policy?

Following events in Mongolia and Kyrgyzstan, Stephen reflected, 'So, what are the implications for the international community? It seems clear that the IMF and its partners are interfering in national policy discussions and using their power to influence decisions and subvert democracy.'[21] He adds in a 2018 paper for the Bretton Woods Project, 'There is a danger that [the IMF and World Bank] may, ultimately, undermine democracy while weakening ... national social cohesion, a dangerous tactic.' He continues, 'It is also worrying that the rest of the international community – including key UN agencies . . . appear to have remained silent.'[22]

The IMF's collaboration with the World Bank was getting it into hot water. In a 2018 blog Stephen refers to 'A recent IMF internal evaluation [which has] criticised the institution for its simplistic understanding of social protection and its reliance on the World Bank for technical advice.'[23] Stephen had made enough waves to be invited by the heads of the IMF in Mongolia and Kyrgyzstan to an online meeting. The discussion was amicable enough Stephen reports, and the two heads played down IMF expertise on social protection and recognized that they had reached beyond their remit. 'It was a friendly discussion but they didn't change what they were doing.' However, the IMF was conscious of how it was being perceived.

And the UN did speak up, despite being quiet on Mongolia and Kyrgyzstan. In 2017, seven senior UN experts wrote to Christine Lagarde, managing director of the IMF, saying, 'we are concerned about the general approach of the IMF to social security reforms that has sometimes put fiscal objectives above the objective of ensuring respect for the right to social security as a human right as set out in international human rights law.'[24] Christine Lagarde wrote back the following month, conceding that there were issues and that the IMF internal evaluation to which Stephen had referred had included 'suggestions to do better'.[25] By way of improvement, Lagarde mentioned that a new IMF framework on social protection was in the pipeline. She added, 'We do need to recognize . . . that the ultimate responsibility for taxation and spending measures rests with national governments and legislatures, and there are limits to how much the IMF can influence decisions that belong to the realm of the sovereign.'

Meeting Margaret Grosh

In 2019, the BBC picked up on a leaked document Stephen mentioned in that 2018 paper for the Bretton Woods Project. He had reported, 'In a paper that was not published, World Bank staff admitted that "The historical . . . evidence suggests that the forces pushing for better targeting are more regularly motivated by cutting entitlement bills and ensuring financial sustainability than by helping the poor".'[26] On the 19 March 2019 edition of *Hardtalk* from the BBC, the host Stephen Sackur put World Bank vice president Kristalina Georgieva under pressure for opposing universal tax-financed social protection schemes. He said, 'There's a guy called Stephen Kidd who . . . points to a leaked document from World Bank staff that admitted that the policy you favoured in Kyrgyzstan, which was a targeted policy rather than a universal policy, was . . . designed not to help the poorest but actually to save the Kyrgyz government money.'[27] Kristalina Georgieva replied she had no knowledge of that case and said, 'Of course we learn from experience. I'm not saying the Bank knows it all and we are always right.' She adds, 'When we review our experience we always say: what is it that we have learned that we need to do better?' The World Bank's track record on social protection suggests something different, though the line of argument didn't appear to do Kristalina Georgieva any harm: she later moved to become managing director of the IMF.

The month before the BBC broadcast, in February 2019, Stephen went head-to-head with Margaret Grosh, key founder of the World Bank's approach to poverty targeting. This was at an international conference on universal child benefits at the ILO headquarters in Geneva.[28] The venue was a fifteen-minute walk from the Inter-Parliamentary Union building in Geneva where the original landmark meeting on Social Protection Floors had taken place.

On the first day of the conference, the governments of Mongolia and Kyrgyzstan were invited to share some of their experience working with the World Bank and IMF. State Secretary of the Ministry of Labour and Social Protection in Mongolia, Unurbayar Gombosuren, told the audience that his government had introduced the universal child benefit to help in the transition from a centrally planned to a market economy, presumably to help unify the nation and strengthen the social contract. He said targeting the benefit using proxy means testing, as negotiated with the IMF and World Bank, had been 'a struggle'. 'It . . . leads to tensions and stigmatisation on the ground while undermining social cohesion.'

After that, Nazgul Tashpaeva from the President's Office in Kyrgyzstan spoke. She said the World Bank and IMF had been 'actively influencing' plans for a universal child benefit in her country. She added that UNICEF had pushed hard in the opposite direction, for a universal approach. 'They suggested we invest in children because that would be an investment in the long-term future of our country and we understand that.' Nazgul Tashpaeva said that switching to poverty targeting in 2017 'was pushed through', and she regretted that it 'wasn't based properly on the facts . . . or a full analysis of the situation'.

On day two, Margaret Grosh and Stephen spoke from their opposing positions on poverty targeting and universality. They sat on the podium to the left and right of chair Francesca Bastagli, from the Overseas Development Institute in London.[29] Margaret Grosh spoke first and referred to there being a small number of universal child benefits around and a larger number of universal pensions, but 'flagship programme after flagship programme of a poverty-targeted nature launched around the world'. She referred to the process of universal schemes leading to larger budgets through political popularity seeming to be 'not yet realised'.

When Stephen spoke, he said that it is ironic that poverty-targeted programmes benefit the rich, in that they are generally cheaper and use less tax revenue. He said that the main beneficiaries of universal programmes were the poor, despite universality, because they attract bigger budgets and transfer values and because benefits to the wealthy can be clawed back through taxes. Stephen also referred to one of Margaret Grosh's flagship poverty-targeted programmes, perhaps the greatest flagship, the PROSPERA programme in Mexico - the 'Model from Mexico for the World' - and how its recent demise demonstrated such programmes are vulnerable to a lack of political support.[30] Stephen said the idea there is a fixed group of poor children to target 'is a fictional construct'. He mentioned the 'massive' targeting errors in poverty-targeted programmes and the World Bank's continuous attempts to improve them. Stephen added, 'One definition of madness is you try to do the same thing over and over again and expect a different result.' He said, 'We need to reconceptualise social protection, get back to the rights perspective. Get back to the Universal Declaration of Human Rights . . . Social protection is for citizens, for everybody.'

Among the conference speakers that came after Margaret and Stephen was Olli Kangas, a professor at the University of Turku in Finland. In a defence of how universality in social policy can promote social cohesion, he said the issue for Finland after the 1918 civil war was how to unify the country, the 'reds' and the 'whites'. Universal education and universal school feeding were introduced, along with social insurance. 'It created a unified country. Children of red and white families were sitting side by side in the same schools and eating the same food. And they felt sameness.' He said that later there was a discussion on how to introduce a child benefit, whether to target it or not. Universality won out and a universal child benefit was introduced after the Second World War, at a time when the country was still relatively poor and recovering from war with the Soviet Union.

After Olli Kangas, Kumar Phuyal, a member of the National Planning Commission in the Government of Nepal, told the story of how his country, which only thirteen years previously had ended a ten-year civil war, was becoming middle-income and developing a vision to become high-income, with universal social protection schemes a central part of this development.

Universality and social cohesion

The speakers at the conference in Geneva had raised again the issue of how universal social protection, and universal social policy more generally, can be of central importance to national unity and development, as part of course of a wider range of government services.

Had there been speakers from places such as Mauritius, post-apartheid South Africa and post-Second World War Western Europe, they could no doubt have told a similar story. Yet the track record of the international community supporting social protection programmes and systems in low- and middle-income countries with a wide or universal coverage, to help reduce conflict and increase cohesion, gives cause for concern. Just in this story, we have heard that, in post-civil war Nepal, the World Bank put pressure on the government to poverty target universal benefits. And a recent study on donors more generally argues, 'social protection policy discourses are often characterised by a large degree of conflict blindness.'[31]

Stephen says,

> When you do poverty-targeted programmes in Kenya, Somalia, Burkina Faso or wherever it is fragile, you further undermine trust in government and social

cohesion. You *increase* fragility. Donors are doing completely the opposite of what they should be doing, not learning from how Europe moved from fragility to stability after the Second World War through the provision of universal public services. Or how a country like Nepal has doubled its tax revenues since 2000 and is the only country in South Asia with a universal social protection programme. With all the problems in Nepal and all the politics, they're building a more cohesive society.

Stephen writes, with Gunnel Axelsson Nycander from Act Church of Sweden and colleagues at Development Pathways, 'A national old age pension and/or child benefit in countries such as Afghanistan, Iraq, Myanmar, Somalia, South Sudan and Yemen could be a game-changer in building national social contracts and in signalling to everyone that they are part of the nation-state.'[32] They add, 'Yet, time and again, the support provided by development partners . . . defaults to [poverty-targeted programmes].' But is their analysis too optimistic? Is it over optimistic to argue that tax-financed social protection programmes with a wide or universal coverage *could* be important in stabilizing countries at risk of conflict? I don't believe it is.

Afghanistan and Syria

One interview among many I did with Stephen for this book took place a couple of months after the Taliban takeover of Afghanistan. He had to break off from our discussion for an online meeting with Abdallah Abdel Razzaq Al Dardarian, the United Nations Development Program's (UNDP) Resident Representative in Kabul. Stephen says,

> I wrote a vision for social security in Afghanistan in late 2020 that the UN were going to present to the government. I said, you're doing everything wrong in Afghanistan. Things are getting worse and worse, poverty rates are going up, the economy is collapsing. The problem is you're undermining the social contract in Afghanistan through the type of work you're doing. One way of rebuilding it is through universal programmes, universal cash benefits, that will give the government legitimacy.

He adds, 'This would contrast with the poverty-targeted conditional cash transfers the World Bank had implemented in Afghanistan, which the government showed no interest in scaling up. These stopped, and workfare programmes were then introduced, which the donors all loved but which nonetheless continued to undermine social cohesion.'

Exploring Stephen's argument further, a universal pension in Afghanistan of say US$15 per month, to everyone sixty-five and over, could have been delivered for less than a quarter of the US$4.2 billion in aid that went to Afghanistan in 2020, the last full year before the Taliban takeover.³³ And this is before we touch on the military spending there which has greatly exceeded aid. Stephen says,

> I wrote that vision in late 2020 so the UN could apply for massive funding from the international community to support universal benefits. But it didn't happen. Nothing was being learned from history about how you build strong, cohesive and effective nation states using universal public services and how universal cash benefits is often the best way of getting it started.

Abdallah Abdel Razzaq Al Dardarian, the UNDP Resident Representative in Kabul, knew well the value of universality and building the social contract. He was born in Syria, where a dreadful civil war was recently fought for so many years. He is the son of a Major General and holds a Master's in international political economy from the University of Southern California, from where he went on to do postgraduate research at the London School of Economics. He held the post of Deputy Prime Minister of Economic Affairs in Syria between 2005 and 2011, the year of the start of the civil war, when he was removed from his job for falling out with a cousin of president Bashar Assad. Al Dardarian has relayed to Stephen that the withdrawal of universal programmes was an underlying cause of the national collapse in Syria. Needless to say, the Global North including the World Bank and IMF had a role in this. In fact, the run-up to the civil war in Syria looks like a case study in the Global North doing more harm than good.

First of all, there is the role of the Global North in the climate crisis and its impact on Syria. According to an article published in a journal of the American National Academy of Sciences (NAS), 'There is evidence that the 2007–2010 drought contributed to the conflict in Syria . . . causing widespread crop failure and a mass migration of farming families to urban centres . . . human influences on the climate system are implicated in the current Syrian conflict.'³⁴ The resulting mass migration to urban centres came on top of the second factor influenced by the Global North, the arrival in Syria of Iraqi refugees after the 2003 Iraq War. In 2007, these were estimated at between 1.2 and 1.5 million.³⁵

Daisy Sibun describes the third factor that had been noted by Al Dardarian, the withdrawal of universal programmes. She points out how 'the Government removed a fuel subsidy overnight in 2008, raising the price of diesel . . . by 257 per cent'.³⁶ It was encouraged in this by the IMF.³⁷ It introduced a proxy means test to identify recipients for poverty-targeted benefits, intended to compensate for the universal fuel subsidy, supported by the World Bank.³⁸ Sibun says,

> In 2011, the National Social Assistance Fund (NSAF) aimed to cover the 6 per cent of the Syrian population then considered as 'ultrapoor', overlooking the widespread nature of vulnerability in the country and the political importance of investing in those on middle (but still insecure) incomes . . . The removal of universal subsidies in 2008 and the introduction of small and narrowly targeted cash transfers, that were entirely inappropriate for the universal nature of the

problem, is likely to have poured petrol onto the fire of an already desperate situation.

Removing fuel subsidies was not the wrong thing to do per se, in that such subsidies often benefit the better off more, where they are using more fuel. But, the narrow targeting of the compensation package was.

We will never know how much it would have helped in Syria if universal benefits had been introduced. Or will we? Subsidies are a common form of government support in Middle Eastern countries and how to change to a different system of support is a regional issue. Around the same time as events in Syria, Iran removed its own massive fuel subsidy. The government considered also targeting the compensating cash transfer at the poorest. But, according to IMF staff, 'it became clear that it would be administratively difficult to identify . . . recipients. Also, denying support for the upper income groups risked triggering public discontent.'[39] So, a universal benefit was introduced, in effect a universal basic income given that 'everyone was allowed to apply for the compensatory transfers, which were made equal for all applicants'. As a result, protests and conflict were avoided.[40]

There have been challenges for Iran since, on funding and a declining transfer value for the scheme, not helped by international sanctions on exports. In addition, as Stephen points out, the IMF, despite the earlier approval of staff for the scheme, 'persuaded the government to introduce targeting . . . contributing to the protests in December 2017.'[41] But the core of the benefit has stayed in place. UNICEF reports less than 10 per cent of households being excluded from the benefit. Professor Massoud Karshenas and academic Hamid Tabatabai describe it as having 'remarkable staying power' and UNICEF gives its own support concluding the scheme is 'the most rational and practical means of ensuring public support for a fundamental transformation of an outdated system of price subsidies'.[42]

Hope in the Arabian Peninsula

Development Pathways, the British-Kenyan consultancy company which Stephen heads, has recently set up the Inclusive Social Security Policy Forum, which focuses on the Middle East and North Africa and has been funded by the Ford Foundation. The Forum publishes online critiques of the World Bank and IMF's role in the region, arguing, 'without a serious shift in institutional approach, the two . . . will hinder governments' attempts to develop inclusive, modern social security systems.'[43] One country where this has *not* happened is Oman, which has kept the World Bank at bay. The ILO, led by Luca Pellerano, Senior ILO Social Protection Specialist for the Arab States, has been providing assistance to the government, along with UNICEF. This has included, as part of wider support, commissioning Development Pathways and a team comprising Tareq Abuelhaj and Shea McClanahan to support the development of a new social protection system, to run alongside economic reform.

Tareq Abuelhaj is originally from Jerusalem. When I speak to him on a link to New York, he tells me that the government in Oman has been considering major economic reform including the reduction of subsidies for electricity and water for a number of years. 'And it has recognised that social protection, and specifically social assistance, would be a good tool to smooth the road.' In considering reform options for tax-financed social protection, the government had approached the World Bank for advice a decade before. 'It gave them similar proposals to those they would give any fiscally constrained lower-income country, but the Oman government was looking for global best practice from high income countries', Tareq says. Oman declined the World Bank's advice and instead moved towards universality.

On 20 July 2023, the ILO announced, 'Far-reaching reforms in Oman set new benchmark for social protection in the region.'[44] It said that along with reforms to contributory schemes, a new law 'introduces government-funded universal social protection benefits, including a cash benefit for all children under the age of 18, a universal old age pension for senior citizens over the age of 60, and a universal disability allowance'.[45] The first payments were made in January 2024.

Oman provides important lessons on economic reform and universal support for countries in the Middle East and elsewhere, because the government has stayed in control. This contrasts with Syria and with another country in the region, Jordan. Tareq says, 'In Jordan, the World Bank has tried since 2007 to get the main social assistance programme, the National Aid Fund, to use proxy means testing.' The programme was already being means tested, but using declared income. The government in Jordan felt that future reform of the National Aid Fund should involve building a programme data base linked to tax records, to allow means testing to be done more effectively. This would also encourage further formalization of the labour market. But the World Bank argued that the fact that around a third of workers were still in the informal sector meant proxy means testing was needed. 'But why?' Tareq says. 'If you want to end up with direct means testing, why go off course and divert to proxy means testing?' He adds, 'The National Aid Fund held off pressure from the World Bank, year after year, for over a decade. But then COVID-19 hit and the government was short of money. The World Bank basically said, here's $350 million, but a condition of the loan is introducing proxy means testing.'[46] And that was that. In June 2023, Human Rights Watch said the switch to proxy means testing in Jordan is the switch to 'a crude ranking that pits one household against another, fuelling social tension and perceptions of unfairness'.[47]

Oman is clearly a different country to Syria and Jordan. It is high-income and oil-rich and has less, if any, demand for the resources of the World Bank. The World Bank has less leverage as a result. But universal programmes are still an option for less wealthy countries such as Syria and Jordan, if that is their preference. They can be introduced gradually, for example, by starting with a higher age for pensions or a lower age for a child benefit.[48] To put it in historical context, the expansion of universal social policy in Finland started when it was less wealthy, in terms of GDP per capita, than both Syria, as it was before the civil war, and Jordan.[49]

Stephen concludes, 'A new universal lifecycle social security system in Oman will be a radically new alternative system for the Arab world', Tareq concurs. 'I think Oman might influence other countries in the region. Gulf Cooperation Council countries look at each other. And I hope Iraq can be influenced too.' The Gulf Cooperation Council includes Bahrain, Kuwait, Qatar, Saudi Arabia and the United Arab Emirates. Tareq adds, 'The social contract in many Arab states has been built on universal subsidies, for food and fuel. But fiscal pressure followed by the influence of international institutions has led to universal subsidies being replaced by narrowly targeted programmes, as happened in Syria, and as is happening in Jordan now. I hope things in Iraq, and elsewhere, can be different.'

Chapter 14

IT'S FULL OF INTELLIGENT PEOPLE, SO WHY DOES THE WORLD BANK DO IT?

What the World Bank has done well

Why does the World Bank do what it does on tax-financed social protection? In answering this, it is important to acknowledge that the World Bank has done a lot of things on social protection, specifically tax-financed social protection, that are good. According to Professors Sam Hickey and Jeremy Seekings, of Manchester University and Cape Town University, the World Bank's support for modest safety nets in the 1990s 'marked an important break from the emphasis on contributory programmes that had dominated the social protection agenda for more than fifty years'.[1] This is the agenda for donors, not the agenda for high-income countries, which had been building tax-financed benefits for many decades. As we have seen, those 'safety nets' have raised much controversy, and in terms of accelerating the development of universal systems for the long term may have done more harm than good. Nevertheless, to give credit where it is due, as Hickey and Seekings say, in the early 2000s, 'The World Bank promoted (cash transfers) through workshops, conferences, publications, technical assistance and generous funding.' Other donors including DFID did too, but later and on a smaller scale.

Between 2004 and 2010, World Bank support to funding tax-financed social protection took off, partly in response to the 2008 global financial and economic crisis. Its loan commitments for 'safety nets' grew as we have seen from less than US$0.5 billion to US$2.5 billion.[2] The World Bank has expanded support further, through a period when other donors were reducing it, to the point where it now has a 'portfolio of almost US$29.5 billion in social protection financing, covering an estimated 880 million people' and 'provides social protection support in the form of lending, analytical work or both to over 118 countries'.[3] This growth has meant staff winning an internal battle for resources against other areas the World Bank supports such as health, education and infrastructure, when commitments first started to grow.

The World Bank has also done much work, with others, on the nuts and bolts of social protection systems, such as storing information on recipients or designing digital payment systems. This has been done in numerous countries. That said, this too has raised controversy, social registries being particularly contentious.

And the World Bank's work and programmes have inevitably had many positive impacts. We have seen that in Fiji and I have seen for myself how the World Bank helped to establish social protection in Kenya, as it did in Indonesia, although in both cases its promotion of poverty targeting, and, in Kenya, its opposition to the government's universal pension, again raises the question about the balance between harm and good over the long term. It has also started supporting system development for the government's universal programmes in Nepal. These are a few examples from this story and there will be many others.

Along with rising lending, there has been growth in World Bank staff working in the area. Stephen says, 'There has been a massive expansion of World Bank staff working on social protection. And they don't just work on loans, there are trust funds run by the World Bank that are funded by other donors.' What is more, pretty much every World Bank member of staff working on social protection that I have met appears committed and hard-working.

There is also a long-standing World Bank commitment to the collation of evidence on social protection which is presented on the World Bank's highly professional website. The source for this book, on rates of poverty, inequality, tax revenue as a proportion of GDP and many other things is all the World Bank. We like to complain about the organization while using its wonderfully accessible resources.

And access to information is prioritized by the World Bank. An example is the flow of emails from Ugo Gentilini, the former World Bank Global Lead for Social Assistance, which present the latest evidence on social protection, with useful summaries of the main messages.[4] When I ask Stephen what he thinks the World Bank have done well in social protection, he says, 'Ugo Gentilini's emails. He doesn't appear to censor stuff. They've been a really useful source of information.'

And the World Bank has always had a strong reputation for its technical ability. Michael Cichon, former Director of Social Protection at the ILO said, 'It is technically better than most agencies and has access to the best people money can buy.' I know from experience, if you work in a DFID country office, you must get on with the World Bank; it is one of your most important relationships. They have expertise in economics and governance, through staff or consultants, that few other organizations can match. And they are in countries for the long term, not blown about by political winds at home as bilateral donors can be. As the late Martin Ravallion, ex-head of research at the World Bank, has said, 'To its credit, the Bank does take a longer-term perspective on development than most other aid agencies; this is evident in the attention that the Bank has given to institutional development.'[5] So, the World Bank has plenty in the credit column, and the list could go on.

It's a bank – the incentive to agree loans

But why does the World Bank do what it does on tax-financed social protection? Why does it advocate for poverty targeting, often using proxy means testing,

14. It's full of intelligent people, so why does the World Bank do it?   151

across low- and middle-income countries? Why has it advocated for conditional cash transfers and workfare programmes, when there is so little evidence in their favour? The World Bank may have helped build some aspects of social protection systems, but it has helped less with the big-ticket items, the programmes themselves. Clearly these must be doable at a *national* scale, in environments with limited capacity, and popular enough to attract long-term funding. And they must be what representative governments want to do. This does not mean universal benefits in all cases, but the common choice for developed systems is a mixture of schemes, contributory and tax-financed, and for the latter, a mixture of universal schemes and those targeted at those on lower incomes.[6] Why is the default position to exclude universal schemes?

The starting point in answering this question is the fact that the World Bank is a bank, which means staff have an incentive to arrange loans to governments. Martin Ravallion says, 'the Bank's "lending culture" rewards operational staff for the volume of their lending.'[7] And, 'The pressure to lend influences the Bank's ability to deliver objective policy advice to client countries.' He adds, 'The managers/directors of the country teams have an incentive to push a high volume of lending to satisfy their bosses and ensure a decent budget for their unit, without giving sufficient consideration to the quality of that lending.'

The long-standing official I have spoken to at the ILO says that the World Bank's policies and priorities, shaped by its mandate to provide financing through loans, result in 'a particular focus on certain products to justify loans. This has shaped its focus on conditional cash transfers, and the more recent turn to social registries and digital technologies, which all require investment and loans.' Martin Ravallion adds, 'If something has not already been tried within the Bank, then it is often treated as risky.'[8] So hard-pressed World Bank staff inevitably reach for off-the-shelf instruments with a record of internal approval, supported by thinkers and a mountain of documentation in Washington DC. Stephen adds, 'There's no getting away from the fact that many World Bank staff – especially working in country programmes – don't really understand the complexities of social security and so they just repeat the simple mantras that they have been told.' The process of stepping back and looking at each unique context is curtailed.

To add to things, the World Bank may then use conditions for loan disbursements, known as Performance-Based Conditions, or at least agreed targets for what the government should deliver.[9] Conditions for disbursement and targets are defensible in systems with relatively weak checks and balances. But they can easily be misused. Stephen says, 'Conditions distort the policy process. The government, with its limited capacity, focuses on delivering on them. If they're poor quality conditions, the whole policy making process is distorted.'

It may be the case that what the World Bank is offering and building into conditions and targets coincides with what populations and their representative governments would want to do anyway, but it may not. To find out, a transparent and open consultation needs to take place on big decisions involving the World Bank. But Isabel Ortiz does not see this happening.

> Decisions about expenditure allocations and financing sources are taken behind closed doors by a few technocrats in the Ministry of Finance, often with the help of staff from IMF and the World Bank. This is bad governance. These decisions affect the lives of millions of people and must be done in national social dialogue with representative trade unions, employer federations, CSOs and parliamentarians.[10]

Why do governments allow this to happen? In part because they need the resources the World Bank can provide. And the World Bank makes sure it works closely with those at the centre of power. Stephen says, 'They find allies in ministries of finance.' Michael Cichon added, 'It has the ear of political players in most countries. It has huge credibility in ministries of finance, and it has support from the IMF on policy positions.' And, everywhere, there are differences of opinion within government to exploit, as we have seen in Kenya. Hickey and Seekings also point to the examples of Zambia and Uganda: 'one group of government officials was more closely aligned with the preferences of the World Bank . . . whilst a separate group shared many of the preferences of the European and UN development agencies.'[11] In all countries, including high-income countries, different ministries have different agendas.

Too much technical, not enough political

A second reason the World Bank does what it does is that it tends to think technically, rather than politically. International expert Marion Ouma and Professor Jimi Adesina's analysis of the development of social protection policies in Kenya concludes that the policy agenda there has been controlled by external actors, through a process of depoliticizing discussion.[12] They say that donors' de-politicization is driven by fear of political capture and interference. While fear of, for example, corruption is legitimate and requires proportionate controls, wanting to keep things under control because politics is unpredictable is not. Ouma and Adesina add, 'de-politicisation weakens democratic processes, compromises ownership and limits popular discussions on policies.' Mkandawire says that with the inflow of donor aid into low- and middle-income countries,

> the tendency has been to conduct the discussion on poverty in a 'non-political' or technocratic way . . . much of the time it concentrates on the problem of disbursing external resources (aid), and not on that of generating the resources required for the task . . . such an approach does not deal with the relationship between targeting and the political economy of domestic resource mobilization.[13]

So, the connection between programme design and long-term funding from tax revenues can get lost.

This critique can be applied to donors more generally, not just to the World Bank. According to Hickey and Seekings, 'The technical approach . . . is evident for most international organisations.'[14] In my own experience, donors have a habit of supporting the design of technically demanding, ever more complicated tax-financed social protection schemes which address multiple agendas – nutrition, early childhood development, health, education, livelihoods, infrastructure, economic growth, the localized impact of conflict, food insecurity, the climate crisis and on and on. Designing such programmes and finding supporters across different ministries may tick boxes for senior management in donor organizations but it can, unfortunately, blur the boundaries between sectors and distort sectors' institutional integrity. To take three examples from our story:[15]

- In Uganda, the World Bank's northern Uganda programme – delivering workfare, as well as support to income generation and community infrastructure rehabilitation – has been based in the Office of the Prime Minister, where support to northern Uganda is coordinated, not the ministry for social protection;
- In Ethiopia, as Stephen pointed out, the donor and government funded Productive Safety Net Programme (PSNP) – delivering, in the most food-insecure districts, workfare, unconditional transfers and livelihoods support, plus shock-responsive emergency support – is based in the Ministry of Agriculture, not the ministry for tax-financed social protection; and
- In Kenya, the programme for more arid parts of the country, originally funded by DFID and now including support from the World Bank and government – providing poverty-targeted cash transfers as well as shock-responsive emergency support – is based in the National Drought Management Authority in the Ministry of Devolution and Planning, not in the ministry for tax-financed social protection.

The primary objective of donors is, or should be, to help governments develop programmes that are simple enough to deliver on a national scale and that operate within clearly defined government sectors and ministries. Unfortunately, donor staff – me included – can ride roughshod over this. On the other hand, programmes such as the government's universal pension in Kenya can meet the criteria of doability and institutional integrity well. And yet it is the latter which donors including the World Bank choose to attack.

But it is not always easy for donor staff. I know from my own time in DFID how senior management always want to be nimble and address those multiple agendas. They want to see change and innovation. So, donor staff get distracted by small-scale, over-ornate programme design. We create something we can defend through our own organizational approval layers, where incentives point to delivering a short-term impact, across multiple sectors, within a three to five-year programme cycle. This is added to by donors employing staff that are proven in academic pursuits, not in developing government systems. Challenges are often addressed around tables in Western capitals or in donor offices within countries and technical solutions are found to 'solve' the problem. Too often, as a result, governments are distracted from the long and unglamorous grind of building relatively simple, deliverable core national systems.

Donors including the World Bank *do* support aspects of system building, as I have said. But the larger picture is they are too often pushing their own agenda, which can blow things off course. The World Bank now contends that for tax-financed social protection, poverty targeting in the *short term* can be a step to universal social protection in the *long term*.[16] The trouble is that, in government, as mentioned in the context of conditional cash transfers, the short-term becomes the long-term. Programmes take a rough minimum of three years to set up. And, if a complex design is being used, such as proxy means testing, especially social registries, government resources and capacity get drawn in this direction. We saw staff being pulled away from the universal pension in Kenya. Daisy Sibun says, universal and poverty-targeted schemes 'require practitioners to build different systems and infrastructure'.[17] And far too easily, progress on building relatively simple, deliverable core national systems is delayed. Mkandawire argues,

> we should bear in mind that, often, initial choices map out the path that countries eventually take . . . Choices made in the formative years can determine the future course of policies and practices (path dependence). Such choices entail institutions toward which interest will gravitate, severely restricting room for other options – including those that may have been universally accepted as desirable in the foreseeable future, though not feasible in the short run.[18]

Social protection programmes and systems can make good use of complexity and innovation, and are often helped by donors in this, for example using digital technology in paying benefits through mobile phones and developing digital management information systems. However, the core principles of programme design, deciding who should get support and how much, should prioritize delivering on a national scale in relatively low capacity environments and be relatively straightforward and transparent.

But donors' innovation and overcomplication are relentless. A 2021 World Bank blog considered the use of lotteries in allocating benefits in tax-financed social protection schemes.[19] The World Bank's 2022 book on targeting says, 'Non-administrative big data – such as from satellite imagery, mobile phones, and social media – and machine learning are expanding the data and techniques for [measuring proxies of welfare] at a dizzying pace.'[20] Great, there is scope for making proxy means testing even more complicated, with no evidence that this will improve accuracy. The World Bank goes on: 'Different statistical modelling techniques to inform proxy means testing can vary the weights given to observations in different parts of the income distribution or to errors of exclusion versus errors of inclusion.' There is no stopping it: 'better results might be obtained from a little more complexity . . . having a simple national model may be less accurate than having a suite of models for different areas . . . or administrative units.' Risks of complexity and ever-greater lack of transparency are, in fairness, acknowledged; 'the increase in opacity – a black box on top of a black box – may concern policy makers in some countries.' Not to mention the potential recipients of benefits, one might add. And, 'Some systems are designed in a way that requires greater capacity than the program or country can muster and might be better simplified.' But the World Bank concludes, 'It is expected that as more and bigger data become available on which to train machine learning, the combination will soon become increasingly common.'

There is a clear and urgent need for restraint and a wider perspective. Human Rights Watch, in its 2023 paper on the use of a proxy means testing algorithm in Jordan, warns that, 'This veneer of statistical objectivity masks a more complicated reality: the economic pressures that people endure and the ways they struggle to get by are frequently invisible to the algorithm.'[21] Nicholas Freeland, Stephen's long-time collaborator, adds to this in a satirical blog which refers to the future the World Bank is describing as a 'a dystopian fantasy world' in which the human race 'do not come across as having individual characters or any degree of agency. They accept their destiny with a kind of resigned fatalism.'[22] In this world, 'the system encourages [human beings] to deceive, imposes stigma on them, deprives them of dignity, creates perverse incentives, corrodes public morality, undermines social cohesion and sets one person against another to survive.'

Economists and their politics

Another reason that the World Bank does what it does, it must be said, is the presence of economists. The World Bank has many of them. And speaking as an economist, they *can* be a bit arrogant. All the more so when they are told to go out and help solve the world's problems. Stephen argues that economists have deep-seated political views, an ironic state of affairs given their – our – supposedly objective outlook.

> They're brain-washed into a neo-liberal viewpoint. They come out of universities having learned the same thing. It's not just the World Bank. They are taught that low taxes and small states are good. Many economists don't believe in human rights. They don't adequately challenge each other and they dismiss other thinking. All those World Bank staff working on social protection, none of them challenges the accepted paradigm.

Stephen acknowledges that there *are* progressive and open-minded economists. A prime example is the late Thandika Mkandawire. He also acknowledges that there are some free thinkers in the World Bank itself, though more on the research side. But he holds to his line on the majority of economists. And I have to say, as a graduate of the London School of Economics, I pretty much agree with Stephen's critique. I remember a lot of the teaching at university, at least on the macroeconomics side, being oddly narrow, at the same time highly technical and simplistic. There never seemed to be an acknowledgement of the uncertainties, of the wider picture. And I didn't hear alternative views set out, or challenging discussions from different viewpoints.

This lack of challenge within the world of economics probably contributes to a collective arrogance. I remember being taught a hard lesson by social development advisers and livelihoods advisers in DFID: that economists do not know best, that the world is more complicated than is assumed and that decisions are best made collectively. It was a painful process but one all Western economists should experience. Economics has an important role, yes. But it is only one piece of the pie and economists need to change how they interact with the outside world. They need to become more humble and open-minded, as the global campaign *Rethinking Economics* argues.[23] Kate Raworth, author of *Doughnut Economics*, concurs: 'now is a great moment for unlearning and relearning the fundamentals of economics.'[24]

The too-narrow world view coming out of the macroeconomics taught in Western universities is reflected in the thinking of the World Bank as a whole. Daisy Sibun looks at the development of that thinking over the decades. 'In the early 1980s, the World Bank published . . . the Berg Report, which . . . defined the "development problem" as a failure of state interventionism and proposed that the solution was paying attention to macroeconomics and "getting the prices right". Soon after, the Berg Report established what became known as "the Washington Consensus".'[25] This approach is described by Martin Ravallion as, 'fiscal discipline, cutting generalized subsidies, tax reforms, market interest rates, liberalizing trade and foreign direct investment, privatizing state-owned enterprises, de-regulation to encourage competition, and assuring legal security for property rights.'[26] The World Bank went on to provide loans to countries, with the IMF, attaching conditions as part of 'structural adjustment' that would draw on the Washington Consensus. Structural adjustment aimed to stabilize heavily indebted economies. Martin Ravallion says, 'There were clearly specific contexts where the policies made sense.'[27] And he adds, 'the poor have an interest in macroeconomic stability.'

But as we have seen, there followed a sequence of events that was to accelerate the promotion of poverty-targeted social protection schemes. Martin Ravallion says, 'programs for "structural adjustment" paid too little attention to the implications for poverty reduction and human development.'[28] As a result, by the late 1980s, 'Add-on programs to "compensate the losers from adjustment" were becoming common.' Daisy Sibun says what emerged was an approach labelled 'structural adjustment with a human face' where 'cash transfers targeted at the poorest [were used] as a countermeasure to "mop up" the inevitable negative impacts of economic restructuring.'[29] But this was a 'residual approach to social protection'. In this, 'responsibility for welfare rests on the individual with support reserved only for the "poor and needy" who are unable to help themselves through the market. This is in contrast to an institutional approach, which is "preventative" rather than "curative", providing support for the population as a whole to give each person equal opportunity.'

There is always an alternative

When I was at university, I got a clear message that there is no alternative to the macroeconomics taught there. But there was, there always is. Why? Because, as those social development and livelihoods advisers in DFID taught me, the world is complicated. The extent of this complexity was described in a special project in 2008 set up to explain why some countries grow faster and are more successful than others. Today, we are much more interested in what supports low-carbon growth, but the findings are still relevant. Known as the 'Growth Commission', and including two Nobel prize-winning economists, the project concluded, 'no generic formula exists. Each country has specific characteristics and historical experiences that must be reflected in its growth strategy.'[30] Of the Washington Consensus, it said, 'we believe this prescription defines the role of government too narrowly.' Policies 'should ... be country- and context-specific.' Governments 'will succeed only if their promises are credible and *inclusive*' (My italics). Social protection is argued for in the Growth Commission's report, along with 'access to basic services.'[31] Otherwise, 'popular support for a growth strategy will quickly erode.'[32] As we have seen, this aligns with Peter Lindert's research that finds that countries that are now wealthy invested significantly in 'social transfers' – tax-financed social protection, health spending and housing subsidies – as they moved through stages of development.[33]

World Bank staff may argue they have moved on from the Washington Consensus. What is more, some of the fast-growing countries in the Growth Commission report have collaborated closely with the World Bank, such as Indonesia. However, in promoting standard instruments for tax-financed social protection, often negotiated behind closed doors, the World Bank is not fitting the country-specific, credible and inclusive paradigm the Growth Commission describes. And to the extent that those instruments – poverty targeting, conditional cash transfers, workfare and social registries – are embedded within the Washington Consensus ideology, the World Bank has not moved on.

Another of the fast-growing economies in the Growth Commission report, China, has followed what Martin Ravallion describes as the 'non-Washington Consensus route.'[34] Another writer, Joshua Cooper Ramo, argues China's approach 'is flexible enough that it is barely classifiable as a doctrine.'[35] The Growth Commission says, 'The policy makers who succeeded in sustaining high growth were prepared to try, fail, and learn ... Deng Xiaoping ... described his approach as crossing the river by feeling for the stones – an oft-repeated phrase in China.'[36] China obviously has significant issues that it can be challenged on, and it is not a model for many things, including its reliance on authoritarianism: it is down at 148 out of 167 in the Economist Intelligence Unit world democracy rankings.[37] But China does highlight the point that there are always alternatives, that every context is different and that an open mind is essential. It also, arguably, shows appropriate humility on the part of Deng Xiaoping in 'feeling for the stones', which economists emerging from Western universities might do well to learn from.

An apparent inability or unwillingness to learn lessons

I believe a lack of humility affects the World Bank as an institution. This manifests itself in an apparent inability or unwillingness to learn lessons, on tax-financed social protection system design and no doubt elsewhere. While it portrays itself as a technical, evidence-driven organization, the World Bank appears willing at times to use evidence selectively, or even to misrepresent it, to support its actions.

Where is the challenge function within the World Bank, the critical thinking? And why isn't critical thinking encouraged? It may exist in some parts of the World Bank, but on social protection there is a clear reluctance to step back and look broadly at the pros and cons of poverty targeting, conditional cash transfers, workfare and now social registries. The promotion of a corporate position seems to dominate. Stephen's long-time collaborator Bernie Wyler calls this 'obfuscation'. Stephen adds, 'They say we are about advocacy and they are about evidence. No, it's the other way around. They are running an advocacy campaign, a very well-funded one.'

Martin Ravallion is an important source on the subject of learning, given that he was head of research at the World Bank from 2007 to 2012. He says there is a lack of lesson learning where it might put World Bank loans to countries under threat. But if there is a lack of critical thinking, where is the systematic evaluation of World Bank loan projects? Is this not standard practice for academics and analysts, including economists? Ravallion says, 'Evaluation is generally weak and imbalanced.' This is a charge that can be widened to other donors, but those donors will be looking to the World Bank for technical leadership. Ravallion says, 'The Bank was once a leader in cost-benefit analysis, but this is no longer true.' In fairness, cost-benefit analysis – the quantifying and monetizing of the costs and benefits of programmes – is not straightforward. For example, in the case of supporting tax-financed social protection schemes, how do you quantify the positive impact of a particular design on increased political support for programmes over the long-term? How do you separate design from other factors affecting long-term support? Having said that, the *framework* of cost-benefit analysis, the mind-set, is critical to decision-making. It allows us to consider, systematically, all of the likely impacts, all of the pros and cons, even if we cannot quantify them. This is standing back and looking at the big picture. It seems that World Bank staff are not doing this as much as they should and, as a result, the dice are being loaded in favour of poverty-targeted programmes that deliver, on paper at least, quantifiable short-term impact. But it is the long-term that matters in the end.

Martin Ravallion argues what is needed is 'a quite fundamental change in the Bank's culture such that managerial and staff incentives are reoriented from lending to learning'.[38] But he says such views have been aired before.

> Concerns about the alignment of incentives in the Bank are not new . . . Organizational changes in 1987, 1996, and 2014 sought to improve incentives

for learning from lending. But with reference to the changes in 1987 and 1996, the Independent Evaluation Group concluded that: 'These changes have not led to a significant change in learning from lending because they touched neither the culture nor the incentives' . . . all indications are that the lending culture thrives today.

The latest iteration of this attempt at reform is the World Bank's stated aim of becoming a global Knowledge Bank.[39] But it remains unclear how internal incentives will be altered.

Part of the reason incentives are so locked in may be the fact that, as an organization, the World Bank engages in so many areas within countries. This includes work on fiscal consolidation and managing debt sustainability. Within country offices, this must create a natural pressure for World Bank staff working on social protection to cut spending and poverty target benefits. This pressure will stem from staff working on the macroeconomic and fiscal side, who may not appreciate all of the implications. Stephen says, 'When you're stuck in a paradigm which everyone in your circle is reinforcing, how are you going to get out of it? It's not about whether you're clever or not. You just can't shift.' He adds,

> It took me ages to get out of being pro-poverty targeting in DFID. I think in the past you could become a big star in the World Bank by challenging the paradigm. On pension reform Nick Barr challenged privatisation. And there were others. I don't know, maybe you still can to some extent. You get occasional useful papers out of the Bank.

When will challenging the paradigm be widely encouraged again in the World Bank? When will it be encouraged on social protection? World Bank staff should not have to wait until they are outside the organization, like Martin Ravallion, before having the confidence to come forward and say what they believe needs to change.

Holding the World Bank to account

If the World Bank is finding it hard to change itself, why do countries funding it not apply more pressure? For tax-financed social protection schemes, why don't funding countries insist the World Bank consider all of the design options before encouraging countries in a particular direction?[40] Those contributing the largest amounts to IDA, the part of the World Bank providing concessional loans and grants to lower-income countries, are currently the United States, Japan, the UK, Germany, France, China, Canada, the Netherlands and Sweden.[41] Why doesn't all or part of this group press harder for meaningful World Bank reform?

Leaving aside higher-level political relationships, bilateral donors have a complicated and interdependent relationship with the World Bank. They need it to deliver much of their own overseas aid programmes, both globally and locally. Also, as mentioned, their offices in low- and middle-income countries often draw on the World Bank to understand issues in depth. In fairness, bilateral donors have a challenging task. Spending money to the satisfaction of often sceptical voters and parliaments at home is not easy, especially when it is being done in unpredictable environments with weak systems. Putting money into World Bank programmes means you can shelter under the World Bank's reputation and the same safeguards it applies to its own programmes, for example on corruption. This interdependency is strengthened by the World Bank trust funds that donors support.[42]

The relationship between bilateral donors and the World Bank is also strengthened by something I witnessed while I worked for DFID, the 'results and value for money agenda'. This agenda, which I have been aware of for the last fifteen years or so, puts a greater emphasis on meeting measurable short-term targets to justify spending. To some extent, it coincides with increases in aid spending, at least in DFID, which needs to be defended. We have seen Mkandawire describing how the World Bank and other donors switched from 'development' to 'poverty alleviation' in the 1990s.[43] For its part, the World Bank focuses on extreme poverty of under US$2.15 per day.[44] For all donors, the focus on poverty lends itself nicely to measurable targets in monitoring and evaluation frameworks. For tax-financed social protection specifically, the results and value for money agenda means the World Bank's approach of targeting 'the poor' can be appealing to bilateral donors and their need to meet three- to five-year programme objectives.[45] And everything sits in the context of the global development goals.[46] Stephen's colleague and ally Charles Knox-Vydmanov says,

> One idea I found interesting was the evolution of proxy means testing from a method rooted in neo-liberalism to one that rode on the technocratic and management-based goals on poverty reduction, linked to the internationally agreed Millennium Development Goals and Sustainable Development Goals. I think it's use in the 1980s and 1990s Chile and Mexico was really part of a neo-liberal agenda, but latterly I think it's a lot messier. Hence all the well-meaning staff in a whole range of international organisations who get behind it.

Ironically, this results agenda can detract from a true assessment of value for money for tax-financed social protection, which would include all benefits, including increases in political support over the long term, which tend to be too hard to quantify to get equal status.

There are exceptions to the lack of pressure from funders of the World Bank. Sometimes bilateral donors have set up in opposition. DFID challenged the World Bank on social protection during Stephen's time as leader of the Social Protection Team in DFID headquarters in London, working with others in the German and Finnish governments, in the ILO and elsewhere, putting an emphasis on long-term system development. But too often, critical faculties are softened. Nor are other organizations immune, including the United Nations, notwithstanding the ILO's ongoing campaign for universality. Stephen says, 'UN agencies need money. One source of money is becoming an implementer of World Bank projects.' This draws those agencies into the World Bank's way of doing things.

Finally, a blockage to challenging the World Bank is that frankly, it is not an easy thing to do. It involves an awful lot of reading apart from anything else. And people rarely have time to read everything in detail. I am sitting at home in a town in southern England, properly reading key World Bank papers on social protection from the last two or three decades for the very first time. The lack of space to read means a lot is assumed, taken as read. And the World Bank keeps piling it on, building what Charles Knox-Vydmanov calls 'an intellectual wall'. In the recent past, World Bank headquarters' publications on social protection have included a 443-page book on social protection systems, the 136-page *Charting a Course Towards Universal Social Protection*, a 539-page book on targeting, and a 336-page book on social protection in South Asia.[47] Indeed, the World Bank has been relatively restrained with the 100 page *State of Social Protection Report 2025*.[48] I know these publications are mainly intended for reference, but they fortify the World Bank's position.

On the other side of things, by way of hope, there is a wide campaign for universality, from the ILO and other parts of the United Nations, from independent voices including the Bretton Woods Project, Human Rights Watch and members of the Global Coalition for Social Protection Floors including Act Church of Sweden, among many others, and from Stephen himself and Development Pathways. And now there is a group of more than ninety economic justice, human rights and faith-based organizations from all over the world that have joined forces to advocate for the right to social security.[49] Stephen also mentions that the Ford Foundation, Action Against Hunger in France, the Centre for Sciences, Research and Action in Lebanon, and a whole lot of organizations around the Middle East and North Africa in countries such as Tunisia and Jordan are helping to challenge the World Bank's approach. And there will be many others elsewhere carrying the fight, relying on small resources set against the funding behind the World Bank's endless research and output.

Most importantly, there are the governments in low- and middle-income countries themselves that are laying the building blocks of comprehensive systems and at times determinedly standing up to the World Bank on social protection.

But this in the end begs the question, why are those same countries not fighting for change from within the World Bank, an institution with 189 member countries? Here we come up against the reality of how decisions are made there. Martin Ravallion says, 'The United States... [has] considerable power at the Bank, including in selecting the Bank's president, its weight in formal voting at the Board and in (more subtle) policy positions, and even in project implementation.'[50] To quote academic Jason Hickel, commenting on both the World Bank and the IMF, 'voting power in these institutions is skewed heavily in favour of rich countries. The US has de facto veto power over all significant decisions, and together with the rest of the G7 and the European Union controls well over half of the vote in both agencies.'[51] Jason Hickel adds, 'There have long been calls by civil society and political leaders in the Global South to democratise the World Bank and the IMF.' Referring to the composition and voting rights in the boards of both institutions, the UN secretary-general António Guterres says, 'The legacy of colonialism still reverberates.'[52]

Chapter 15

WINNING THE BATTLE FOR UNIVERSALITY

Nearly half of the world's population cannot access social protection

Some very good news is that the groundbreaking efforts of governments in low- and middle-income countries, at times with the support of the international community including the World Bank, have achieved an increase in global social protection coverage. According to the ILO, 'For the first time, more than half of the world's population (52.4 per cent) are covered by at least one social protection benefit . . . increasing from 42.8 per cent in 2015.'[1] Stephen and colleagues add, 'multi-tiered, rights-based systems are the norm in most high-income countries . . . and are becoming more common in middle-income countries, such as in Brazil, Mauritius and Mongolia.'[2] This is significant and welcome progress, though the ILO also says that in low-income countries, 'coverage has barely moved' and 3.8 billion people still do not have access to social protection.[3]

Social protection is only one part of wider government strategies to reduce vulnerability and promote sustainable national development, but it is an important part. High-income countries know this. Government spending on social protection in high-income countries, including contributory and tax-financed benefits is commonly higher than spending on others public services at an average 16.2 per cent of GDP.[4] This compares with spending of 8.5 per cent for upper-middle-income countries, 4.2 per cent for lower-middle-income countries and 0.8 per cent for low-income countries, much of which is confined to contributory schemes in the formal part of the labour market and public sector pensions.

As we have seen, the ILO has demonstrated that high-income countries began developing their social protection systems in earnest when they were at a similar level of GDP per capita to developing countries now.[5] Minouche Shafiq, former president of Columbia University among other roles, was referring to William Beveridge, father of the welfare state in the UK, when she said in 2018, 'Developing countries are now in their Beveridge moment.'[6] Tax-financed social protection needs to expand significantly to move systems towards universality. Contributory schemes need to grow too, but they are to some extent constrained by persistent labour market informality. The formal labour market can be expanded, but even small gains can take time.[7]

In terms of what level of expenditure countries should be aiming at, Stephen argues that a good rule of thumb is, 'building spending over time to 2 to 3 per cent of GDP on tax-financed social security will probably get you a good set of universal benefits.' In some countries spending is already much higher. Yet total government spending for social protection *as a whole*, both contributory and tax-financed schemes, is 1 per cent or less in countries as populous as Bangladesh, Ethiopia and Nigeria.[8] 'Building spending over time' is an important concept, because of the fact that increased spending can be accommodated within tax revenues that rise with economic growth.[9] This means other sectors can grow at the same time.

And over time of course, social protection can itself contribute to economic growth and help strengthen the social contract, both of which can help to increase tax revenues. It can be a virtuous circle. It is not static, but a dynamic sequence of events which must be allowed to play out over time.

The global context

There is an urgency to countries further expanding social protection coverage. The United Nations says, 'Since 2015, global poverty reduction was already slowing down and the impacts of the COVID-19 pandemic reversed three decades of steady progress with the number of people living in extreme poverty increasing for the first time in a generation.'[10] Women have been hit particularly hard. According to the agency UN Women, 'the pandemic intensified unpaid care and domestic work. With children out of school, heightened care needs of older persons, and overwhelmed health services . . . this burden has fallen disproportionally on the shoulders of women.'[11] Mahamane Cisse-Gouro of UN Human Rights adds, 'The COVID-19 pandemic, climate emergencies and related emerging conflicts and increasing inequality have made the gender gap even worse.'[12]

Now, nine per cent of the world's population, or 700 million people, live on less than US $2.15 per person per day.[13] The UN says that, 'Recovery from the pandemic has been slow and uneven as the world is presently facing multiple geopolitical, socio-economic, and climatic risks.' The World Bank states, 'The pandemic has caused unprecedented reversals in poverty reduction that are exacerbated by rising inflation and the effects of the war in Ukraine.'[14] The WFP says 238 million people are food insecure, with acute food insecurity hotspots such as Gaza.[15] And, according to a recent report, 'Contemporary global inequalities are close to early 20th century levels, at the peak of Western imperialism.'[16]

Even assuming global reductions in poverty get back on track, remaining poverty and the risks from technological changes affecting work and from conflict maintain the urgency of expanding social protection coverage. And then there is vulnerability to what the ILO describes as the 'triple planetary crisis – climate change, pollution and biodiversity loss'.[17] A series of actions is needed, at a global level, to mitigate and adapt to the crisis, one of which is to develop social protection systems everywhere with wide coverage. This will help adaptation and surviving climate-related shocks, help reduce the need for damaging behaviours such as over-exploiting natural resources, and support the transition to sustainable economic activity.

Added to this mix is migration and the rights of migrants. Development Pathways says, 'In 2022, the number of forcibly displaced people globally passed 100 million people for the first time in history.'[18] The situation has been worsened by conflicts in Syria, Sudan and Ukraine, by events in Afghanistan, the South Sudan emergency and the crisis in Venezuela. To forcibly displaced people can be added those moving for economic reasons. This interacts of course with the climate crisis, which is expected to lead to increasingly high migration from vulnerable regions.[19]

The World Bank and ILO-launched Global Partnership for Universal Social Protection to Achieve the Sustainable Development Goals argues that migrants should be included in social protection systems.[20] The EU has granted Ukrainian refugees the right to jobs, health, education and housing as well as social protection, for up to three years.[21] The ILO advocates for the 'implementation of bilateral and multilateral social security agreements ensuring equality of treatment' for migrant workers, refugees and their families.[22] Against this is the question of resources. For the most affected low- and middle-income countries, there remain huge economic challenges to realize the ILO's vision, aside from tough domestic political debates. Significant external funding may be needed, as it is, for example, for the more than one million refugees in Uganda and the more than three million Syrian refugees in Turkey.[23]

The World Bank and IMF have moved a bit, under pressure

Comprehensive social protection systems must ultimately be financed and controlled by those living within countries and their representative governments. Each country faces its own challenges and competition for resources and must make its own decisions. What might be the role of the World Bank on social protection going forward? It is still, arguably, the flagship of the Global North's support to development in low- and middle-income countries. Also, as mentioned, it provides more social protection financing than all other donors combined.[24] Working with the IMF, it has a potentially important role in future, but it must significantly change its behaviour to be deserving of it.

The IMF and World Bank have, as discussed, already started to inch down the road to reform, albeit under pressure. The IMF published a policy on social protection in 2022, which Stephen and others were asked to advise on. It says, 'The appropriate approach to targeting of transfers will depend on how governments balance the various costs and benefits associated with different targeting options.'[25] In other words, do not rule out universal tax-financed social protection schemes. We have seen the World Bank be similarly open in headquarters strategies and publications including in its 2022 publication *Charting a Course Towards Universal Social Protection*.[26] I have also heard World Bank staff say, off the record, that there need to be changes. So has Stephen's long-time collaborator Bernie Wyler. 'I think if you talk to the World Bank privately, they will concur there are huge issues around the models of social protection the World Bank has been promoting.' But look deeper into its publications, such as the *State of Social Protection Report 2025*, and you will still find a strong steer towards poverty targeting.[27] And this is reflected in the World Bank's behaviour within countries, where poverty targeting and social registries are still commonly promoted, attached to loans that governments cannot do without.

But even in practice things have started to change, a little bit. As well as the mentioned support to the system delivering universal lifecycle programmes in Nepal, in Papua New Guinea, the World Bank has supported a universal child grant with the Australian government, and there is a small pension the World Bank designed in the Maldives.[28] And Daisy Sibun points to Sudan where the World Bank has 'provided financing support for a temporary basic income scheme implemented by the Government that aims to reach around 80 per cent of its population of 43 million with monthly US$5 cash transfers'.[29] The Sudanese finance minister, Ibrahim al-Badawi, had recognized removing fuel subsidies would affect the vast majority of the population and, following the Iranian rather than the Syrian model, promised a high-coverage cash transfer to mitigate the impact. Sadly this could not play a role in preventing the descent into civil war. Stephen says the World Bank also helped to bring in a universal pension in Kosovo, in the 1990s. 'There have been some individuals in the World Bank who have understood the importance of social cohesion and state building post-conflict in contexts such as Kosovo.'[30] As we have seen, this is a pension funded by government, as is the new near-universal pension the World Bank supported in Fiji.

These examples offer a modicum of encouragement. The World Bank has also taken seriously the idea of a universal basic income, in particular in a book published in 2020.[31] A universal basic income (UBI) provided by governments – funded, in theory, by adjustments in the tax system – is an idea that has been campaigned for by organizations such as the Basic Income Earth Network and is supported by prominent figures as diverse as the UN secretary-general, the late Pope Francis and Elon Musk.[32] In South Africa, a successful campaign for a universal basic income has led to a recent commitment from the ruling party, the African National Congress, to deliver one within two years.[33] Elsewhere, the World Bank correctly points out that, despite numerous pilots across the world, the existence of a national universal basic income has so far been limited to countries such as Iran and, for a brief period, Mongolia.[34] It also mentions ongoing basic design issues: 'The debate on [universal basic income] is often chaotic and without precise definitional contours.'[35] It adds, 'systemwide issues are largely left unanswered, such as the relationship to the minimum wage.'[36] But it has not dismissed the idea of a universal basic income out of hand. This is another small piece of progress. And yet incentives within the World Bank, to promote poverty targeting and social registries, remain in place.

Learning from COVID-19

Those within the World Bank that oppose reform would do well to look at the lessons the World Bank itself draws from COVID-19. The pandemic was a huge test of global social protection systems. According to the United Nations, 'In response to the COVID-19 crisis, more than 1,700 social protection measures . . . were announced by 209 countries and territories.'[37] Donor support increased too, with the World Bank tripling financing to US$4 billion per year.[38]

The World Bank closely monitored responses to the COVID-19 pandemic and drew lessons for future crises in a report by Ugo Gentilini, then Global Lead for Social Assistance at the World Bank.[39] The report says that cash transfers – which include social protection schemes and humanitarian programmes – reached 'unprecedented levels of coverage'. That said spending was, predictably, much greater in high-income countries and systems in low- and middle-income countries were usually not up to the job of scaling up effectively. They were 'often unable to reach people at the middle or so of the income distribution'. The report adds that, in response to COVID-19, cash transfers 'were mostly unconditional, and eligibility was simplified'. Why? Because the speed of assistance was crucial. The endorsement of simple, unconditional and universal programmes is hard to ignore.[40] The ILO says, 'Crucially, [COVID-19] has made the case for universal social protection irrefutable. The weakness of limited safety-net approaches, typically characterized by narrow targeting and tightly monitored conditionalities, has become glaringly apparent.'[41] Another UN report talks of 'a renewed appreciation of universal social protection and the need for sustainable systems; and the indispensability of such systems as a cornerstone of all socially-just, healthy and well-functioning societies has become more self-evident'.[42]

The World Bank also reports on the successful response to COVID-19 in Mongolia, built – notwithstanding the efforts of the World Bank itself and others – on universality. There the government quintupled payments in its near-universal child benefit, which the World Bank refers to as 'one of the larger crisis response programs in the world'.[43] The World Bank adds, 'As part of its COVID-19 Crisis Response Program, Bolivia doubled the benefits of its universal social pension programme'. And Daisy Sibun points to the case of Morocco, where 'the large boost in social protection spending (2 per cent of GDP) that was administered . . . was apparently so popular and effective that the country has announced that it will increase its old age pension coverage and universalise the . . . child benefit'.[44]

Examples like these should be inscribed on the heart of all those interested in meeting future challenges, including the climate crisis. The World Bank talks about the 'inevitable shocks of the future, which climate change will only heighten in frequency and intensity'.[45] But the truth is, instead of learning lessons, we see donors including the World Bank focusing time and again on scaling up relatively small, over-complicated and narrowly targeted programmes, with high targeting errors. An example worth returning to is the Kenya Social and Economic Inclusion Project with the World Bank's US $250 million loan.[46] Part of this project is to improve the shock-responsiveness of the poverty-targeted programme for more arid parts of Kenya, by improving the triggering mechanism and developing a financing plan for emergency cash transfers. The programme was hailed in a recent book for being ready to respond to future disasters by providing 'an insurance policy', so that 'when the rains fail and the harvest is bad . . . [people] can afford to buy inputs and food for their families'.[47] What could be better? The problem is, this is in a country where government attempts to widen tax-financed social protection coverage towards universality, through the universal pension, in line with the subsequent lessons from COVID-19, have been opposed by the very same donor, the World Bank. There is no perspective. Using technology and innovative design in triggering mechanisms to scale up programmes *may* be defensible in specific circumstances. But without systems with at least a degree of national coverage already in place, this is putting the cart before the horse.

The promotion by donors of programmes with complex proxy means testing and triggering mechanisms is often justified by the term 'shock-responsive social protection'.[48] This refers to schemes that can scale up by increasing transfer values or by increasing recipients, when shocks hit. The term sounds impressive, but it ignores the fact that, as Nicholas Freeland points out, social protection schemes are already shock-responsive even before scaling up, in that they cushion people from the impact of lifecycle and broader shocks.[49] Furthermore, the example of Kenya shows us that the sort of programmes promoted under shock-responsive social protection too often detract from work on the sort of core system building that will do most of the heavy lifting when shocks hit. Another term that raises similar issues is 'adaptive social protection', which refers to tools to build the resilience of poor and vulnerable households to widespread shocks and clearly overlaps with 'shock-responsive social protection'.[50] It all appears to be a rebadging of poverty targeting and social registries, which are mentioned forty-two times in a recent World Bank paper on adaptive social protection.[51] For a regional take from elsewhere we can return to our local UN source in Fiji. They argue that adaptive, or shock-responsive, social protection requires a universal social protection approach in small islands states, using systems of national identification. Everyone is vulnerable to the climate crisis in Fiji and the Pacific, and universal schemes are popular with governments there as we have seen.[52]

> With COVID people have realised that universal programmes are a much more efficient way of reaching the population when there is a shock at scale. In the pandemic there was no way to do elaborate targeting for small islands states governments. I believe the World Bank and others will have to align with governments as they try to build adaptive and shock-responsive systems to protect and support every citizen.

The changing world of international development

The world of international development is changing. Alongside traditionally large bilateral donors such as the USA, Germany, Japan, the UK and France, China is becoming increasingly important.[53] In 2017, China adopted the Belt and Road Initiative which plans to reach '68 countries with an . . . investment as high as $8 trillion for a vast network of transportation, energy, and telecommunications infrastructure linking Europe, Africa, and Asia'.[54] It also makes rescue loans to Belt and Road Initiative countries, worth 20 per cent of total IMF lending over the past decade.[55] Development banks are changing too. In addition to the World Bank and existing regional development banks such as the Inter-American Development Bank, the ADB and the African Development Bank, there is the Asian Infrastructure Investment Bank that China has taken a lead in developing and the New Development Bank created by Brazil, Russia, India, China and South Africa.[56] There are also organizations such as the Ford Foundation and Alwaleed Philanthropies, and more recently, the Bill and Melinda Gates Foundation. This all has implications for the level and route of resources going to low- and middle-income countries. As do recent cuts in overseas aid from high-income countries which, according to the European Network on Debt and Development, 'risks increasing countries' dependence on the World Bank and IMF.' And there are other changes. For example, an agreement was made at COP27, reinforced at COP28 and COP29, for the payment of 'loss and damage' from wealthier nations to the rest of the world.[57] COP29 confirmed the commitment to a figure of US $300 billion per year, to be achieved by 2035, though it remains to be seen how much of this commitment is met.[58]

In this altering context, there are choices to be made about how resources flow from wealthy to less wealthy countries. These should be informed by how things have worked out to date. I speak to an international expert on social protection from Kenya on the subject, who is forthright. 'You need to dismantle the whole aid enterprise, especially for social protection.' They point to a general lack of government investment in sub-Saharan African countries as evidence that social protection has been promoted by international organizations rather than emerging organically, as the European welfare state did. In Europe, social protection developed out of a democratic process, and it was also part of wider social policy rather than being promoted on its own according to the expert. Democratic processes are what must be allowed to flourish in Africa. Things have been too top-down, and governments, on behalf of those voting them in, must determine spending decisions.

This is all indisputable, though it is not always easy. The level of democracy in countries varies hugely and while outside organizations should support democracy, care must be taken not to support autocratic regimes that work against citizens and simply look to minimize welfare bills. How much low investment in social protection in sub-Saharan Africa is a result of a *lack* of voter power?[59]

But the key point the expert is making is that each country is unique and has its own history and way of doing things and others must respect and support that. Countries in this story have a diverse history including ethnic divisions and military coups in Fiji, mass killings in the 1960s in Indonesia, dictatorship and conflict in Uganda and civil war in Nepal. The development of comprehensive, multi-tiered social protection systems is so often affected by crisis and conflict, but in particular ways in different countries. Even without conflict there will be a political battle. Peter Lindert says, 'the whole history of debate over social programmes is just a shifting back and forth between two poles of self-interest . . . There will always be a political tug-of-war between those who are more likely to benefit from redistribution and those who would be taxed by it.'[60] That battle is unique to each context and countries must follow their own path and let political dynamics play out. The unenviable challenge for donors is judging whether countries to which they offer support are moving in a positive direction.

The World Bank can cut across domestic politics in an unhelpful way, but so can other donors. 'Demonising the World Band is okay', the expert says. 'But I don't see any difference with DFID, UNICEF and everyone else. It's all variations of what the World Bank is doing.' I do not entirely agree. DFID and UNICEF have, at times, provided active opposition to the World Bank on social protection. For countries mentioned in this story, there is DFID in Uganda, DFID and UNICEF in Nepal, and UNICEF in Mongolia and Kyrgyzstan. Often, this opposition is down to particular individuals working in countries. Though there are also plenty of examples, even in this story, of DFID and UNICEF allying with the World Bank, as I did during that visit to Tanzania.

The challenge of capacity building

The international expert delves further into donors distorting the picture. 'Look at training courses and international study tours in social protection.' Funded by donors, these are used to show government officials how things are done in other countries, to influence them. 'We want to think it's all benign', the expert says. 'But it comes from a position of power. It can't be a benign exercise.' Again, I can think of exceptions. I would defend the training course Stephen and I did in Kenya for the government, funded by the World Food Programme, which helped ministers and officials push back against the domination of the World Bank and DFID. Then there is the important study tour for Zanzibar government officials and politicians to see the universal pension in Mauritius, partly paid for by Irish Aid and SIDA. But you cannot help thinking the expert is right most of the time. Think of the World Bank 'pilgrimage' to the poverty-targeted and conditional – and ill-fated – PROSPERA in Mexico in the early 2000s.[61] Stephen also remembers the donor study tours to the poverty-targeted and conditional Bolsa Familia programme in Brazil, and the fact that the much larger near-universal pension, the Previdencia Social, was ignored.

Study tours are part of a wider area donors get involved in, known as 'capacity building'. This is the process of helping to strengthen governments' capacity to design and deliver policies and programmes, so that they can do without external support. It is the area David Tumwesigye in Uganda wished had been done better. It involves investing in people and institutions in different ways, including training and mentoring. However, the expert says, 'No one needs more capacity building!' And here again they have a point, because so often it is something of an afterthought and does not work, or even sends things into reverse. These reverses can arise from donors recruiting the most able local people for themselves and leaving governments depleted. The expert says, 'I really don't see any capacity building at all. There are still no Kenyans, Ghanaians or Zambians who are regarded as experts on social protection within their countries.' Again, I can think of exceptions, such as Stephen's co-director at Development Pathways Richard Chirchir from Kenya, David Tumwesigwe from Uganda and Marion Ouma from Kenya who, with Professor Jimi Adesina from Nigeria, has been so critical of donor support to social protection there.[62] But the point still has great validity.

We should spare a thought for government staff, especially in the lowest-income countries, who work under considerable pressure. They are likely paid significantly less than their friends working for donors and international organizations and have a lack of resources in the face of their country's great need. They also have well-paid and confident donor staff constantly approaching them, asking for things to be done their way. Donors also compete among themselves by offering generous daily allowances to staff to participate in their programmes rather than those of another organization. It makes you wonder how officials do anything of the normal business of government at all.

And government staff have to watch while donors and consultants fly in, telling them that if they accumulate enough evidence from pilots, randomized control trials and various other surveys and research, their problems can be solved. Perhaps they see through it, but hold off saying anything because of the availability of donor resources. The expert does not hold back. 'Donors and the consultants they employ have got rich as they write papers and get promoted. Some consultants' rates are mind-boggling. That's the way development is structured.'

The strange world of consultancy has occurred to me before, including on my own work trips: the oddness of largely white people flying to countries with largely non-white populations. There are local staff in the offices of the World Bank and other donors within countries, but, in my experience, they are usually in relatively junior positions. Stephen of course is one of those white people, as am I. And we are very well paid when set against the government officials we work with, perhaps me all the more so as a freelance consultant rather than, as Stephen is, a paid member of Development Pathways' staff. But there is a distinction to be made. On the one hand, there are consultants and organizations invited in by governments the world over, including in wealthy countries, to provide technical support to decision-makers. We all like to criticize technical support from outside, but sometimes it is genuinely useful. On the other hand, there are donors including the World Bank that provide technical support but also have major resources attached to their advice which can be used to encourage policy in a particular direction it would not otherwise have gone in. This is not the same thing. So, a central issue may be whether technical advice is or is not attached to resources.

Before going further on that, another word on the issue of race. The international expert says the whole international aid industry is about race, from its genesis onwards, and that social protection epitomizes that. Stephen concurs with this, saying, 'we need to ask why some donor institutions believe that a [proxy means test] is an appropriate instrument to use among Africans (and, of course, Asians) but not among the comfortable, educated majority-white populations in their home countries.'[63] Sarah Champion, Member of Parliament in the UK and chair of the House of Commons' International Development Committee, says, 'the structure of the aid sector is beset by a fundamental power imbalance. Too often, decisions about funding and policy are taken in the offices of large, white-led organisations in the Global North though most aid programmes are delivered in low-income countries in the Global South . . . these power structures are remnants of colonialism.'[64] And Themrise Khan, an independent researcher from Pakistan with long experience working in international development says, 'no-one has bothered to (officially) ask even one aid recipient – state or non-state, from any country – what they think about the sector and whether they truly think they benefit from it.'[65]

Supporting what people and the governments that represent them want

All this is not to say that international aid should be stopped. Nor is it to deny that external financing and support can take some of the credit for the global expansion of social protection coverage the ILO has reported. But it is to say aid should be done differently, for social protection and no doubt elsewhere. The impact of external financing and support, now and in the long term, could be so much greater, and less damaging, if donors were less blinkered in their policy prescriptions and how they support governments. Simple solutions to the current situation are not easy, taking account of the pressure on the World Bank and other donors to deliver results in often unpredictable environments. However, broad principles must be followed. The expert says, 'I don't know the answers. But national governments should feel it is their own development.'

But should donors leave the scene completely? I ask Stephen if he thinks the World Bank has a role going forward. He says,

> Why would you put a neoliberal institution in charge of support to low- and middle-income countries, just to distort policy making processes? It is relatively new to social security. There is no raison d'etre saying it must be the World Bank. Transfer flows (from wealthy to less wealthy countries) are not as simple as people think. Financing should come from countries themselves. Other things must be changed, such as unfair international trade rules, illicit financial flows

and the debt burden countries face. Rich countries take lots away, and then give a little bit of it back through aid. They must stop destroying these countries, stop authoritarian regimes flourishing. Countries can then invest in social security and other public services. The world is still set up for rich nations.

And all of this is before we recall the historic wrongs of many rich countries, some of which appear in this story and some of which are still playing out, such as slavery, indentured labour, colonialism more generally, resource extraction, the climate crisis and conflicts and proxy conflicts to protect the interests of the Global North.

To put what Stephen is saying in context, Amnesty International points out, 'the cost of offering basic social security protection in all [low- and middle-income] states is estimated at US $440.8 billion a year, according to the ILO . . . less than the US $500 billion the Tax Justice Network estimated is lost annually by states to tax havens around the world.'[66] Fixing illicit financial flows feels like a long-term project, though Shahra Razavi, Director of Social Protection at the ILO, argues that 'the war in Ukraine has shown the power of states, especially when they act in concert, to combat illicit finance'.[67]

Nor is reordering international trade easy to contemplate, especially in the context of high and unpredictable tariffs on imports. Nor a quick end to the issue of debt. The World Bank says 60 per cent of low-income countries are at high risk of debt distress, or are already in it.[68] Debt is increasingly owed to the private sector and China.[69] Part is owed, of course, to multilateral institutions themselves, including the World Bank and IMF, which account for one-third of external debt payments due between 2022 and 2028, according to Action for Southern Africa.[70] But high debt is an argument for debt restructuring.[71] It is certainly not an excuse to sideline social protection. Decisions on how to balance spending across government sectors are always made in the context of restricted resources. High debt may affect the speed of implementation in the short term, but it should not affect the direction of travel. Nor should it be used by the World Bank to promote poverty targeting to the exclusion of universal schemes.

Stephen rightly says resources for social protection, beyond contributions, should come from governments themselves, at least in the long-term; otherwise, countries risk becoming accountable to external organizations. But for now transfers from wealthy to less wealthy countries must continue, if only to help a just transition to a low-carbon and sustainable global economy, including through the expansion of social protection. This is assuming reform in other areas such as debt, trade and illicit financial flows, does not happen quickly enough to do the job. The ILO says, 'the most vulnerable populations who have contributed the least to global emissions live in regions most susceptible to the climate crisis. Yet they have the fewest resources to cope with and adapt to the increasingly frequent and intense extreme weather events and slow-onset changes.'[72] The latter include such things as sea level rises and loss of biodiversity. Resources flows must continue, and even increase, whether they are called international aid, or reparations for past behaviour or funding for a just transition. The challenge is that those resource flows must do no harm, encourage representative government and allow each countries unique development story to unfold.

Returning to the issue of separating financial support from technical advice, it is conceivable that this may be part of the way forward. In Uganda, I worked for DFID on general budget support, where money is passed straight to the country's exchequer, to be used on whatever the government sees fit. This may include increasing rates of government pay: David Tumwesigye mentioned low rates of government pay and a dependence on donor per diems as an obstacle to reform in Uganda. Hugo Slim, a Senior Research Fellow at the Institute of Ethics, Law and Armed Conflict at the Blavatnik School of Government at Oxford University in the UK, sees merit in the broad approach. He says, 'The call is growing to "decolonize aid" and have international aid given directly to national governments or local organisations in a way that ends the white rule of UN agencies and international NGOs.'[73]

Under such an approach, technical advice on the design of programmes and systems, in social protection and other sectors, can be provided separately. Advice can therefore take a longer view rather than focus on short-term results. The expert I speak to has witnessed donors and the 'result and value for money agenda'. 'I see the pressure and frustration if governments drag their feet. Donors need results. And it is when they don't get results that all their textbook international development and capacity building goes out of the window.' And if governments are free to select consultants, advice can be free of donor bias. Might this be a model for the future? Government systems need to have strong enough systems to receive the money, and there needs to be a sufficiently positive policy environment and a sufficient level of government legitimacy, otherwise the money passed on could do more harm than good. This last point, as mentioned, is hard to judge, and I do not know whether DFID got it right in Uganda. But with any international aid directed to governments, judgement must be made.[74]

The specifics of solutions are always hard, but broad principles to follow are not. The expert says there *is* space for support being provided by wealthier countries. But there must be boundaries, connected to the citizen-state relationship. It is the population that votes which matters, and democracy must be allowed to work. 'Otherwise, national voices will continue to be crowded out.' Themrise Khan says, 'Decisions about how aid should be "done" in developing countries, or whether aid stays or goes, should be taken by those at the receiving end of this assistance.'[75] This is right in itself, and it makes aid more effective. The expert agrees with me that donors must return to following the principles set out in the Paris Declaration on Aid Effectiveness, which more than 100 countries signed up to in 2005. The Declaration sets principles for donors and governments to live by, including *ownership* – meaning low- and middle-income countries set their own strategies – and *alignment* – meaning donors get behind those strategies.[76] The Paris Declaration was on everyone's lips when I worked for DFID in 2005, but it has been displaced by the 'results and value for money agenda' and its need for short-term results. It is worth raising its profile again.

In the end it is about human rights

The World Bank may have a role in supporting countries on social protection going forward, if it allows - and seeks to learn from - much greater internal and external challenge. A clear inventory of its support to tax-financed social protection across the world would be a good starting point if it is not in train already, so we can see how well it fits with World Bank rhetoric on universality.[77]

Above all, the World Bank, and other donors, must learn a greater respect for the rights of representative governments to do things their way. But it would be wrong to finish without repeating that it is also about individual human rights and dignity, an area Stephen learned so much about from the Enxet in Paraguay. Here, the World Bank and other donors have a mixed record, as we have seen. Daisy Sibun writes, 'the World Bank ... [has] made it clear that ... [its] mandate does not leave ... [it] accountable to considerations of human rights.'[78] And it is not alone. Mkandawire points out,

> The Organisation for Economic Co-operation and Development (OECD) Development Assistance Committee (DAC) Guidelines on Poverty Reduction ... clearly highlights rights, influence, freedom, status and dignity as important components of well-being. However, the practice by most donors has not paid much attention to the fundamental implications of such guidelines for social policies, or the institutions for implementing such policies. Instead they have insisted on forms of social assistance that were likely to be disempowering and even humiliating.[79]

Human dignity is too often forgotten in designing what we have seen are untransparent, poverty-targeted programmes with roulette wheel-like selection processes, in the rush to get programmes that deliver results on helping 'the poor'. But if entitlement is unclear, how can people understand and claim their rights? Stephen's former colleague at Development Pathways Alexandra Barrantes adds, 'why do we still have so many social protection schemes that treat 'the poor' and 'vulnerable' as if they were somehow different from the rest of us?'[80] Mkandawire argues, 'While the literature on welfare policies in developed countries pays considerable attention to issues of justice and dignity, this does not seem to be the case in the literature on developing countries.'[81]

I am duty bound to say that the human rights argument is one I have only recently appreciated. As an economist, I have always thought, 'If there is no money for the programme, what is the relevance of human rights? It's secondary.' But now this feels economically naïve. History shows that sustainable growth and development is about countries going forward together. Schemes that do not respect human rights and that cause division can clearly hinder this. The World Bank and other donors have shown, in the promotion of poverty-targeted benefits using proxy means testing, conditional cash transfers and workfare, that without a clear sense of human rights, you can quickly head off in the wrong direction.

In fairness, the World Bank *has*, as we have seen, begun to move on human rights and social protection, at least in its pronouncements. Its 2022 book on targeting recognizes the 'psychic' cost of stigmatizing recipients and says, 'Good delivery systems are important for compliance with several of the principles of the human right to social security.'[82] So again, there are more seeds of hope if not yet enough changes in practice. And human rights do not preclude means-tested programmes, properly designed and invested in and respecting those human rights.[83]

Above all, social protection must be thought about as people receiving their entitlement, not handouts for the 'needy'. Professor Ha-Joon Chang of the School of Oriental and African Studies in London says the very nature of social protection is misunderstood. 'The common misunderstanding [of a social protection system] is that its main function is to give . . . free stuff to poorer people . . . paid for by the taxes that richer people pay . . . In fact . . . welfare benefits are not free. Everyone pays for them.'[84] Apart from benefits financed by contributions, people pay tax across the income distribution taking account of indirect taxes such as VAT.

A member of parliament in Mauritius, F. S. Chadien, made an impassioned speech on whether to poverty target the pension there or make it universal. It was in 1957, so perhaps we can forgive the gender bias.[85]

> *The old age pensioner has throughout the years paid taxes on commodities he has consumed as everybody else has. He has paid taxes on tea, sugar, tobacco, matches, rice, pulses, dried fish, rum, calico, khaki, everything he has consumed and used to be able to live as a useful member of our society. One way or another he has contributed to the national budget. The Old Age Pension scheme being financed out of public funds is [thus] a contributory one. The applicant for Old Age Pension has already paid in his contributions.*

There are many other ways people, especially women, contribute, including raising children in challenging circumstances, so developing the labour force and supporting the economy.[86] The fight for universal social protection is the fight for people getting the rights to which they are already entitled. And it is to stop othering 'the poor' and 'the vulnerable', given we are all the same and all vulnerable at different points in our lives.[87]

Stephen's long-time collaborator Steve Barrett, says, 'The intellectual debate on universality has been won.' This may be true in global dialogue. But it is not reflected in so many of the actions of the World Bank and other donors, who must support social protection systems in a way that supports the inclusive development of nations and their systems of democracy – if invited – or leave the scene completely.

In the end this is a story about the autonomy and dignity of both individuals and nations. The best assurance for the future is that too much is not left to the good intentions of donors and the efforts of campaigners from the Global North.

There must be proper accountability of the Global North to the Global South. Power needs to be with those whose interests are at stake. Themrise Khan says that, 'Northern donors and aid practitioners can reimagine aid assistance all they want. But aid professionals from the Global South must *always* be prepared to question their intentions, challenge the course they are taking, and doubt that they know best. And we must particularly ask our governments to do the same.'[88]

AFTERWORD

In April 2024, I travelled to Washington DC to present the main messages from this book in a seminar at the World Bank's headquarters, mentioned in Chapter 10. I was participating in the World Bank and IMF annual Spring Meetings, in the Civil Society Policy Forum. It was a pretty intimidating experience, standing up there and challenging that institution, and also a frustrating one. I felt accommodated but, at the same time, ignored. That is nothing new I'm sure for people critiquing the World Bank, and we should expect institutions to defend themselves, to hold a line. But the calmness of it all also suggested to me a lack of proper accountability, a lack of concern that others may have a point. I don't blame individuals. It is the ethos of the World Bank, an organization that is under pressure to give consistent answers and do great things in this world. I worked for DFID for many years, an organization that was also supremely confident in itself, and no doubt others saw similar behaviour in me and some of my colleagues.

In any case, after the seminar I stood in a subway station on the way back to my hotel and, as well as feeling great frustration, I felt a deepening respect for Stephen Kidd, the main subject of this book, to add to the respect I have had for a long time. He has been doing what I had just done for the last two decades. In the years I have been collaborating with Stephen, I have been in a supporting role. Now I knew what putting your head properly above the parapet feels like.

The episode made me doubly determined to finish this book. So too did hearing from Stephen and his wife Sandra about their challenges in setting up the company Development Pathways, in 2010, with others including Richard Chirchir. 'We didn't really have a clue what we were doing', Sandra says. 'We were quite idealistic. I was doing the administration as well as teaching full-time in a local school in a deprived area.' But they ploughed on, through Sandra's dad being diagnosed with myeloma in October 2011 and dying three months later, through having three children at home including their daughter Rebecca, who has additional care needs, and through Stephen's constant travelling. Stephen says, 'It was all a bit of a mess that whole period. I was just travelling all the time. I was working 365 days a year, I had to say yes to every piece of work.' Stephen and Sandra both lost their mothers after that, as they continued to build the company. But they stuck at it, with others apart from Richard Chirchir, including Bjorn Gelders, Diloá Athias, Nayha Mansoor, Alexandra Barrantes and many more. Now, they have established Development Pathways, with its fifty-six staff including ten in its office in Kenya which Richard Chirchir manages, ten in Jordan and sixteen in Australia, as perhaps the most important independent global voice challenging the World Bank on social protection.

Stephen gave up being a missionary for the Anglican Church in Paraguay, but he became a different sort of missionary, with a sense of universal justice undimmed. Smart Daniel, who we saw worked closely with the government in Zanzibar on its universal pension, says of him, 'Apart from his knowledge, he has commitment. Some have the skills but just earn their salary. For him it is devotion and dedication.' David Tumwesigwe, who worked for all those years in the Ugandan government says, 'He has a reputation of taking the bull by the horns, I really admire him for that. So much money gets wasted on programmes that never move to scale. He's a crusader.'

Being a crusader, albeit one grounded in evidence, means Stephen has plenty of people that disagree with him and oppose his work, not least in the World Bank. But I have never heard his integrity being challenged, nor his resolution. Bernie Wyler, who is working with Development Pathways in Jordan, says, 'Stephen was one of the first to pull the curtains away that covered World Bank obfuscation of the evidence on social protection.' The late Philip White, co-author of the UK government's guidance on measuring value for money in tax-financed social protection programmes, said, 'He's been at the cutting edge, taking on orthodoxies that are still prevalent.'

As we have seen, Stephen has also been an important member of a much wider international collaboration. Isabel Ortiz, former Director of the Social Protection at the ILO, says, 'I always got along with Stephen. My experience working with him was always good. There was almost no need to talk when we sat with each other in a meeting, we knew we were on the same side.' And the late Michael Cichon, Isabel Ortiz's predecessor, said of Stephen, 'Our agendas coincided. We had no disagreement on any political issues. In that battle we were in with the World Bank he was one of the big battle horses you need to have. In every battle you have you need some people that go ahead no matter what.'

Stephen leads from the front and has worked in many other countries not included in this story, including Angola, Bangladesh, Cambodia, Kiribati, Laos, Malaysia, Pakistan, Papua New Guinea, Rwanda, Timor-Leste and Uzbekistan. All over the world, the same patterns of World Bank behaviour on social protection have emerged, which he, with others, has challenged with resilience. The last email I had from Stephen before sending in the final manuscript of this book read,

> Just coming back from Angola where it was good to see the Angolans subverting the World Bank and turning their supposedly poverty-targeted programme into a universal one. After initially trying out proxy means testing, the Angolans rejected it as they did not want to provoke conflicts in the community. Of course, the World Bank has not given up and, following the approval of a new loan, they are once again pushing for a proxy means test and a social registry.

Stephen and his collaborators in the ILO and elsewhere are not the most important people working on social protection within low- and middle-income countries, nor are donor staff, even those in as powerful an institution as the World Bank. By far the most important are those living within countries and their governments.

But Stephen's story and that of his collaborators throws a light, I hope, on what is going on, in social protection at least, in the name of wealthier countries that fund the World Bank. And also on what is required to take on that institution and on what can be achieved. The World Bank has got away with its behaviour on social protection without wider outcry because it operates in a largely hidden world. Its documents may be accessible, but information is presented on its own terms, and any arguments with governments are usually behind closed doors.

Stephen, with Sandra's support, has been on a mission to throw light on this world. So too have the late Michael Cichon and Isabel Ortiz, and campaigners in the Global Coalition for Social Protection Floors and the new grouping of more than ninety organizations from around the world advocating for the right to social security. So have *many* others, including all those interviewed for this book. And I know there are people in the World Bank seeking change. Then there are all the additional people out there, in governments, local governments and NGOs, implementing programmes in challenging circumstances, overcoming obstacles every day and building, step by step, systems for the future. A book could have been written about any of them.

Isabel Ortiz says, 'Putting things in perspective, the fight for universal social protection and the right to social security was started by our parents, by our grandparents. They started building universal social security systems. My grandfather fought in the Spanish Civil War for a welfare state and died for it. Now it is our generational duty to continue the fight.' She, Stephen and innumerable visionaries in governments and organizations in countries all around the world have done just that. They have taken on the World Bank where necessary and, with energy and optimism, continued the fight for universal social protection in the Global South.

ANNEX

Measuring the performance of proxy means testing and other targeting methods

To find out how proxy means testing was performing, David Coady, Margaret Grosh and John Hoddinott, in their 2004 paper *Targeting of transfers in developing countries: review of lessons and experience*, created a special measure of performance, an index.[1] This divided the share of benefits that went to the poor by the proportion of the poor in the total population. So, the higher the index the better. And anything better than '1' means benefits are going disproportionately to the poor, which is a good thing. The poor was defined as the bottom 40 per cent, where this information was available.

The index was used to compare a variety of targeting approaches. And the scores were, with the best at the top:[2]

- *self-targeting* – where benefit levels are set low enough to put off those on higher incomes – 1.9
- *means testing* – defined as where incomes are measured directly, often impossible in lower income environments (in this book it is defined more broadly, to include poverty targeting) – 1.6
- *proxy means testing* – where eligibility for benefits is predicted using non-income household characteristics – 1.5
- *demographic targeting of the young* – where targeting of children is by age, also known as universal targeting – 1.5
- *community targeting* – where community groups or leaders decide who should be eligible for help – 1.4
- *geographic targeting* – where levels of poverty or other variables are used to target by geographic area – 1.3
- *demographic targeting of the elderly* – where targeting of older people is by age, also known as universal targeting – 1.2

So proxy means testing is scored as the equal third best targeting method. The highest performer, self-targeting, has often been used in workfare programmes supported by the World Bank. The second highest performer, means testing, defined here as measuring incomes directly, we can leave to one side because it is so often not possible in low- and middle-income contexts.

Proxy means testing is scored equal to demographic targeting of the young and above demographic targeting of the elderly – both examples of universality – despite having a significantly more complex targeting process that is more prone to error. This is because the index considers only benefits going to the poor as having value. So, for example, universal benefits going to beneficiaries above the poverty line, even just above, are regarded as leakage, so of no value. This is despite universal programmes being specifically designed to go to all households that meet the eligibility criteria, regardless of income level; the fact that most people are poor in lower-income countries by any reasonable measure of poverty, and poverty lines are often being somewhat arbitrary; the dynamic nature of incomes regularly taking people above and below the poverty line; and the potential benefits in terms of social unity and political support deriving from universal benefits.

The approach of concentrating on the proportion of benefits going to the poor is called 'Benefit Incidence Analysis'. Stephen and his colleagues argue that this approach 'gives no information about the extent to which the intended target group is reached. As such, it does not capture the kind of information needed for a rights-based implementation of a programme.'[3] In addition, a median index for the proxy means test of 1.5 – as seen in the scores – means, for example, if 40 per cent of the population are in poverty, they receive just 60 per cent of the benefits of the programme, which is not great. And there is a wide variation around this average for proxy means testing. The best performing programme, with an index of 2.1, was the Subsidio Único Familiar in Chile. The worst, at 0.5, is the Subsidio Familiar in Colombia, where the poor got just half of what they would have got through a random distribution of benefits.

NOTES

Glossary and abbreviations

1 This reflects how terms are used in the book, but definitions can vary by organizations and countries. The website socialprotection.org has been used as a source for a number of terms.

Introduction

1 United Nations (2015). Article 22.
2 It may be more accurate to say it *should* step in, as there are too often gaps.
3 Buller A. M. et al. (2018), Munoz Boudet A. M. et al. (2018) and Kidd S., Athias D. and Tran A. (2021).
4 ILO (2024).
5 Manuel M. (2022).
6 World Bank (2022a).
7 See, for example, Leisering L. (2019).

Chapter 1

1 World Bank (2022a). Though this is somewhat contradicted by the World Bank saying in 2023 it has 'committed $26 billion . . . helping 267 million people covered by social protection systems'. World Bank (2023b). This perhaps highlights the need for an accurate rolling inventory of World Bank support to social protection.
2 DFID is now integrated into the Foreign, Commonwealth and Development Office (FCDO).
3 This was backed up later by Stephen's colleague Diloa Athias who uncovered that the World Bank had, in fact, used incorrect numbers.
4 Kidd S. and Athias D. (2020). The finding is for the Hunger Safety Net Programme (HSNP).
5 There are some exceptions as we will see, for example in Indonesia.
6 ILO (2024) and for high-income countries see, for example, Jacques O. and Noël A. (2021).
7 The team was called the Reaching the Very Poorest Team at the time. Its name was changed to the Social Protection Team in 2006.
8 Though this is still debated. In fact, there appear to be as many definitions of social protection as there are organizations working on social protection – see definition of social protection at the beginning of the book. The term 'social protection' may well have been brought into common use by the donor community itself, rather than

governments in low- and middle-income countries, which could be the root of the problem. Stephen believes the term social protection was first used in Karl Polanyi's classic work, *The Great Transformation*, about the development of the market economy in the nineteenth century, published in 1944. 'Social security', a term more conventionally used in high-income countries to refer to the benefit system, is a much clearer phrase.

9   The risk of corruption, by those administering social protection schemes, or of fraud by those claiming benefits, will vary by programme design. In general, it is better to keep things simple and transparent, which is a point in favour of universal schemes rather than relatively complex poverty targeting. See van Stolk C. and Tesliuc E. D. (2010).
10 IMF (2022a).
11 DFID (2005).
12 DFID (2006). White Papers are flagship government policy documents.
13 Independent Commission for Aid Impact (2017). In reality, this includes some food and other in-kind transfers, for example in Ethiopia and Bangladesh. This was out of a total DFID budget of £5.3 billion (DFID (2012)). The rise in spending was, arguably, partly a response to the 2008 global financial and economic crisis, though by 2008 spending was already established on an upward trend. Spending of £20m in 2004 and £300m in 2010 (approximate figures) have been converted using rates of 1.91 for 2004 and 1.55 for 2010 and rounded.
14 Assuming programme administrative costs are 20 per cent of transfer costs.
15 Assuming households contain five people on average.
16 Leisering (2019). This is as opposed to the terms being used within individual programmes.
17 Economist Intelligence Unit (2023). If the government does not have an appropriate level of legitimacy, other support routes may be needed apart from aid provided to governments, for example humanitarian aid and support to civil society organizations (CSOs).
18 See, for example, Centre for Public Impact (2017).
19 Hanlon J. et al. (2010).
20 Ravallion M. (2016). The purpose of the IMF was to manage currency payment imbalances, and the World Bank to channel longer-term development finance.
21 Ravallion M. (2016).
22 Independent Evaluation Group (2006) and Ortiz I. et al. (2018).
23 Holzmann R. and Jorgensen S. (2000).
24 World Bank (2012c). This rise was partly in response to the 2008 global financial and economic crisis, but not all of these commitments will have been disbursed. And Manuel M. (2022).
25 For a list of countries where DFID was helping to fund social protection, see Independent Commission for Aid Impact (2017). Some of this DFID support was provided in collaboration with the World Bank, for example in Ethiopia.
26 Hickey S. et al. (2020).
27 Leisering L. (2019).
28 Pruce K. (2019).
29 In a move to raise the eyebrows of World Bank critics, Robert Holzmann later became governor of Austria's central bank after being nominated by Austria's far-right Freedom Party. *Central Banking*, 30 January 2019, at https://www.centralbanking

Notes 187

.com/central-banks/governance/people/4002291/austrian-far-right-party-nominates-economist-for-governor .
30 Hickey S. et al. (2020).
31 OECD (2009).
32 ODI (2016).
33 See for example Buller A. M. et al. (2018), Kidd S., Athias D. and Tran A. (2021), Wollburg C. et al. (2023) and from the USA, Kovski N. et al. (2023).
34 ODI (2016). Extra costs for persons with disabilities are estimated at 8–158 per cent of income in China, 9–12 per cent in Vietnam, 20–58 per cent in India and 40 per cent in South Africa. Development Pathways staff.
35 ODI (2016).
36 IMF (2022a).
37 IMF (2022a).
38 See, for example, Grigoli F. and Robles A. (2017).
39 Mkandawire T. (2005).
40 African Studies Association of the UK at https://asauk.net/awards-prizes/lasting-legacy-award/professor-thandika-mkandawire/ .
41 Celebrating the life of Professor Thandika Mkandawire at the London School of Economics at https://www.lse.ac.uk/international-development/Assets/Documents/PDFs/events/Thandika-Memorial.pdf .
42 Kwame Sundaram J. (2020). For a discussion of the Swedish welfare state see, for example, Chapter 1 of Madhav Thakur S. et al. (2003).
43 Policies adopted during structural adjustment, often referred to as the 'Washington Consensus', included 'fiscal discipline, cutting generalized subsidies, tax reforms, market interest rates, liberalizing trade and foreign direct investment, privatizing state-owned enterprises, de-regulation to encourage competition, and assuring legal security for property rights'. Ravallion M. (2016).
44 Mkandawire T. (2005).
45 Korpi and Palme (1998).
46 Korpi and Palme's paradox of redistribution has been challenged by more recent evidence. For example, in Gugushvilia D. and Laenena T. (2021). Gugushvilia and Laenena conclude 'there are substantial reasons to cast doubt on the validity of the causal model', but also that 'the fact remains that more universalist countries tend to have better redistributional outcomes'.
47 Mkandawire T. (2005). Social policy includes health, education and social protection.
48 The course was called 'Designing and Implementing Social Transfer Programmes' and was organized by the Economic Policy Research Institute (EPRI) and supported over time by UNICEF, DFID and other organizations such as HelpAge International. Ouma M. and Adesina J. (2018).
49 Hickey et al. (2020).

Chapter 2

1 4 feet 8 inches is 142 cm.
2 A direct grant school is a private school partly paid for by central government. Fees were set according to parents' ability to pay.
3 Kidd S. (2021).

4   Walker H. (2015).
5   Stephen's pay with the SAMS had been £90 (US$120) per month when he started in Paraguay and £220 (US$295) per month when Sandra and he were married.
6   Kidd S. (1997).
7   United Nations Permanent Forum on Indigenous Issues (2009).
8   Stephen undertook a further visit to the Turks and Caicos Islands, where he produced another challenging report on human rights.
9   Inter-American Court of Human Rights (IACHR) (2005).
10 Kidd S. (2021).
11 Inter-American Commission on Human Rights, Organization of American States (2009).

Chapter 3

1   UK government guidance on measuring value for money in tax-financed social protection programmes says of proxy means tests, 'Based on a weighted formula of easily verifiable proxy indicators for poverty derived from regression analysis of household survey data, [proxy means tests] 'predict' poverty and thus eligibility.' White P. et al. (2013).
2   Kidd S. and Athias D. (2020).
3   Minority Rights Group at https://minorityrights.org/country/fiji-islands/ .
4   Wolf E. R. (2010).
5   *The Guardian*, 13th October 2007, at https://www.theguardian.com/uk/2007/oct/13/lifeandhealth.britishidentity .
6   Fiji church records at https://www.familysearch.org/en/wiki/Fiji_Church_Records .
7   Conciliation Resources at https://www.c-r.org/programme/pacific/fiji-conflict-focus .
8   Global voices at https://globalvoices.org/specialcoverage/2009-special-coverage/fiji-constitutional-challenge-2009/ . More recently, Fiji has been ranked 80 out of 167 in the Economist Intelligence Unit world democracy rankings. Economist Intelligence Unit (2023).
9   World Bank World Development Indicators, latest year available. This is measured in current US$, which does not take into account price differences between countries. Measuring average income using 2017 Purchasing Power Parity international $ does not affect Fiji's broad ranking.
10 World Bank World Development Indicators, latest year available. The US$3.65 poverty line is in 2017 Purchasing Power Parity terms, which takes into account price differences between countries. Inequality, measured using the Gini coefficient, is 30.7 (2019).
11 Stephen, working with local academics in Fiji, uncovered the fact that the squatter settlements were being underrepresented in the national household survey which informs much of government policy, resulting in artificially low poverty rates.
12 Narsey Lal P. et al. (2009).
13 Government of Fiji (2016).
14 The Guardian 5th March 2021 at https://www.theguardian.com/world/2021/mar/05/reef-revival-fijis-corals-bouncing-back-after-ruinous-cyclone .
15 World Bank (2011b). The benefit was paid to 'poor and disadvantaged households (elderly, disabled and chronically ill, widows and deserted spouses)' and the value

varied according to family circumstances. The Fijian dollar average transfer value has been converted using a market exchange rate of 0.45.
16. In addition to the Family Assistance Programme, there were small programmes giving transfers for vulnerable children and food vouchers. There was also a relatively low-coverage provident fund, the Fiji National Provident Fund, a type of contributory pension, but one making a single one-off payment on retirement. United Nations Department of Economic and Social Affairs (UNDESA) and ILO, and World Bank (2011b).
17. World Bank (2011a).
18. The social workers' assessments were investigated using qualitative rather than quantitative methods.
19. Stephen also argued that, ideally, the household assessments wouldn't be done by social workers, who have their day job to do. Special assessors should be appointed.
20. World Bank (2011b).
21. Mkandawire T. (2005).
22. Shamil (2024).
23. Development Pathways (2022a).
24. Office of the United Nations High Commissioner for Human Rights (2023).
25. ODI (2016). The ODI study looked mostly at poverty-targeted schemes because of a lack of evidence for universal schemes, which tend to be funded by the government rather than donors and therefore commonly lack evaluation evidence. Donors are often keen to fund evaluations for schemes they support to demonstrate impact.
26. UNICEF (2021) and Grown, C. and Gupta, G. R. (2005).
27. UN Women at https://www.unwomen.org/en/hq-complex-page/covid-19-rebuilding-for-resilience/social-protection .
28. Office of the United Nations High Commissioner for Human Rights.
29. World Bank (2011a). Though the World Bank also mentioned means testing as an option to control the cost of the pension.
30. For more on the World Bank project cycle see https://projects.worldbank.org/en/projects-operations/products-and-services/brief/projectcycle .
31. Ministry of Social Welfare, Women and Poverty Alleviation, Government of Fiji (2011).
32. The pension is known as the Social Pension Scheme.
33. United Nations Department of Economic and Social Affairs (UNDESA) and ILO. The provident fund is called the Fiji National Provident Fund.
34. Government of Fiji at https://www.fiji.gov.fj/Media-Centre/News/SOCIAL-PENSION-SCHEME-ASSISTS-MORE-THAN-45,134-SEN. The transfer value has been converted to US$ using a market exchange rate of 0.45. The proportion of those sixty-five years and over in receipt of the tax-financed pension has been estimated using a World Bank figure of 52,873 for the total population aged sixty-five years and over, for 2021.
35. Knox-Vydmanov C. et al. (2023). 2022 spending level is for the financial year 2021/22.
36. Mkandawire T. (2005).
37. Government of Fiji https://www.fiji.gov.fj/Media-Centre/News/9,400-RECIPIENTS-BENEFIT-FROM-DISABILITY-ALLOWANCE. The transfer value has been converted using a market exchange rate of 0.45.
38. Knox-Vydmanov C. et al. (2023). Figure is for 2021/22. The disability benefit is known as the Allowance for Persons with Disability.

39 World Bank (2011a).
40 The child benefit, worth F$100 per month, or US$45, is known as the Care and Protection Allowance. It is paid to children of single mothers, deserted spouses, widows and prisoners' dependents living in or on the verge of destitution and with no source of income, children under the care of the State, children in foster care or cared by a guardian. United Nations Department of Economic and Social Affairs (UNDESA) and ILO. There are around 9,000 children in receipt according to the local UN source.
41 The Australian government-funded programme is called P4SP.
42 Knox-Vydmanov C. et al. (2023). Figure is for 2021/22.
43 United Nations Department of Economic and Social Affairs (UNDESA) and ILO.
44 Sibun D. and Seglah H. (2024).

Chapter 4

1 Kidd S. et al. (2023).
2 World Bank at https://www.worldbank.org/en/who-we-are. Extreme poverty is defined as those living on less than US$2.15 per day, which is in 2017 Purchasing Power Parity terms, allowing for price differences between countries. World Bank at https://www.worldbank.org/en/news/factsheet/2022/05/02/fact-sheet-an-adjustment-to-global-poverty-lines .
3 World Bank (2024a).
4 Ravallion M. (2016). The World Bank is able to sell AAA-rated bonds in the global financial market, then re-lend these funds at higher interest rates through the IBRD.
5 An exception is IDA20, which happened after two years because of COVID-19.
6 World Bank at https://ida.worldbank.org/en/about/contributor-countries. The World Bank also receives income from donors for administering services, from 'client' countries for reimbursable services and from short-term trust funds. Ravallion M. (2016).
7 World Bank (2022a). Though this is somewhat contradicted by the World Bank saying in 2023 it has 'committed $26 billion . . . helping 267 million people covered by social protection systems.' World Bank (2023b). This perhaps highlights the need for an accurate rolling inventory of World Bank support to social protection.
8 Manuel M. (2022).
9 World Bank (2022a). FY2021 is July 1 2020 to June 30 2021. Not all commitments will have been disbursed.
10 Grosh M. E. and Baker J. L. (1995).
11 Poorer households targeted for benefits needed to contain children, persons with disabilities or older people to be eligible. The proxy means test was also used to target housing subsidies and water subsidies.
12 The 1995 paper also describes simulations of the proxy means test done for Jamaica, Bolivia and Peru. Results were in the same ballpark. For example, one among many of the permutations of the model used for Peru 'performs reasonably well for leakage, with 35.1 per cent of benefits leaking'. Leakage here means benefits going to the non-poor.
13 Coady D. et al. (2004).
14 World Bank Development Indicators, latest year available. The US$3.65 poverty line is in 2017 Purchasing Power Parity terms, which takes account of price differences between countries. And *The Guardian*, 26th January 2018, at

https://www.theguardian.com/global-development/2018/jan/26/full-of-beans-rwanda-wants-its-citizens-to-drink-more-coffee#:~:text=At%20a%20cafe%20in%20Kigali,according%20to%20the%20World%20Bank . The cost of a latte is converted to US$ using a market exchange rate of 787 Rwandan francs per dollar.
15 White P. et al. (2013).
16 Freeland N. (2019).
17 Grosh M. et al. (2008).
18 Also given approval was community-based selection. The World Bank, and other donors, often use community targeting in combination with proxy means testing, though this does not necessarily create accuracy. The DFID-supported Hunger Safety Net Programme (HSNP) in Kenya uses this combination, but Stephen and colleagues have shown targeting is little better than random. Kidd S. and Athias D. (2020). Demographic targeting of children is also given approval. Its relatively good performance is because households with children tend to be poorer. But this approval is apparently not translated into a global World Bank campaign to promote universal child benefits.
19 Kidd S. and Wylde E. (2011). Targeting errors may derive from the design and implementation of programmes. Here it was specifically the design errors that were estimated.
20 This is the 'exclusion error'. It is equivalent to the 'inclusion error', the proportion of recipients that are eligible, in these calculations which take into account the intended coverage of poverty-targeted programmes. See Kidd S. and Athias D. (2020) for further explanation.
21 Leite P. (2014). And del Ninno C. and Mills B. (2015).
22 Brown C. et al. (2018).
23 Ravallion M. (2016).
24 Kidd S. et al. (2017).
25 See for example del Ninno C. and Mills B. (2015).
26 Kidd S. and Athias D. (2020). The quote refers to the 'exclusion error'. It is equivalent to the 'inclusion error', the proportion of recipients that are eligible, in these calculations which take into account the intended coverage of poverty-targeted programmes.
27 Grosh M. et al. (2022).
28 World Bank (2022a).
29 Leon Solano R. et al. (2024).
30 World Bank (2025).
31 Grosh M. et al. (2022). Figure 5.9. The title of Figure 5.9 is 'Inclusion and Exclusion Errors'. No mention is made in the chart of the fact the error being measured assumes only benefits reaching the poor have value, even for universal programmes designed to reach all in a population category regardless of income.
32 This approach, of looking at the proportion of benefits going to the poor, is called 'Benefit Incidence Analysis'. Stephen and his colleagues argue that Benefit Incidence Analysis 'gives no information about the extent to which the intended target group is reached. As such, it does not capture the kind of information needed for a rights-based implementation of a programme.' Kidd S., Axelsson Nycander G. and Seglah H. (2023). The World Bank also says, 'Instead of focusing only on errors of exclusion or inclusion, it is important to consider a fuller distributional analysis in evaluating the outcomes of social assistance programming.' In other words, worry more about people on lower incomes when looking at targeting errors. Stephen argues he and

colleagues had already shown where those excluded and included are ranked by level of household expenditure. See Kidd S. and Athias D. (2020).
33   This is leaving aside other costs common to programmes, poverty-targeted or not, such as enrolment and payment. The costs associated with programmes for persons living with disabilities will depend on the approach used to test eligibility.
34   Grosh M. et al. (2008). Though the book also says, 'the extra costs are generally balanced by the more accurate (sic) targeting achieved.'
35   White P. et al. (2013).
36   Administrative costs can be hard to measure accurately for a number of reasons including programmes often drawing on government resources, such as staff time, accommodation and equipment, the cost of which may appear under other government programmes.
37   Grosh M. et al. (2022).
38   Adato M. and Roopnaraine T. (2004).
39   White P. et al. (2013).
40   Camacho L. A. (2014).
41   Grosh M. et al. (2022). Community-based targeting, often used in combination with proxy means testing, can also incur social costs. It can lead to elite capture, a form of corruption benefitting those of higher standing in the community, and social exclusion. One example is Somalia, where displaced Bantu groups and Somalis of the 'wrong' clan were excluded from in-kind transfers. Howson K. (2023).
42   Yoshino C. A. et al. (2023). Programmes in the study are not necessarily poverty-targeted programmes.
43   Kidd S. (2019).
44   Yoshino C. A. et al. (2023).
45   ILO (2024). However, there is some instability in estimates, and some definitional issues. Figures for tax-financed benefits from ILO (2024) are as follows, with figures from the previous iteration of the publication, ILO (2021d), in brackets. Family and child benefits: means tested 58 (45), universal or near-universal 58 (38). This is for countries with statutory periodic child/family benefits only. Disability benefits: means tested 64 (38), universal or near universal 17 (32). This is for countries with statutory disability benefits only. Pensions: means tested 85 (85) countries, universal or near universal 42 (21). However, for pensions, the means tested estimate from ILO (2021d) is defined differently as it includes pension-tested benefits that may be near universal.
46   UK Office for Budget Responsibility at https://obr.uk/forecasts-in-depth/tax-by-tax-spend-by-spend/welfare-spending-pensioner-benefits/ .
47   Razavi S. et al. (2022).
48   Mkandawire T. (2005).
49   Gugushvilia D. and Laenena T. (2021).
50   Dadap-Cantal E. et al. (2021).
51   Ministry of Labour and Social Protection, Government of Kenya (2017).
52   Sibun D. and Seglah H. (2024).
53   It is reasonable to assume these programmes are tax-financed because donors don't generally finance universal programmes. DFID supporting the universal pension in Uganda is a rare exception. According to www.worlddata.info there are currently 152 low- and middle-income countries in the world. In its 2022 book, the World Bank argues that 'fully universal . . . child allowances exist in only 21 countries . . . and universal . . . social pensions in 19 countries', which it believes shows they are not politically popular. Grosh M. et al. (2022). Daisy Sibun and Holly Seglah get a lower

count for child benefits, a higher count for social pensions, and a significantly higher overall country count, which may be explained in part by Development Pathways including benefit-tested, near-universal programmes.

54   Pritchett L. (2005).
55   Coady D. et al. (2004). The same point is made in Fiszbein A. and Schady N. (2009).
56   Grosh M. et al. (2022). See 'Essay 9'.
57   Razavi S. et al. (2022).
58   Freeland N. (2018).
59   ILO (2021d).
60   World Bank at https://www.worldbank.org/en/news/feature/2014/11/19/un-modelo-de-mexico-para-el-mundo .
61   Associated Press at https://whyy.org/articles/mexico-gets-1st-leftist-leader-after-32-years-of-technocrats/
62   Bonthuis B. (2024).
63   Los Angeles Times at https://www.latimes.com/world-nation/story/2022-12-19/why-is-mexicos-amlo-one-of-the-worlds-most-popular-politicians-we-took-a-road-trip-to-find-out .
64   Kidd S. (2018c).
65   Kidd S. and Huda K. (2013).
66   Kidd S., Axelsson Nycander G. and Seglah H. (2023). A reasonable level of democracy is defined as scoring at least five on the democracy index developed by the Economist Intelligence Unit. See Economist Intelligence Unit (2023).
67   Razavi S. et al. (2022).
68   And some on low incomes may miss out if you are making, say, only pensioners and children eligible for benefits. Though you are reaching a large proportion of the population with programmes that actually work as you build towards a comprehensive system, and benefits do get shared within households.
69   While it is obvious that government legitimacy must be borne in mind, actually measuring government legitimacy is always challenging, as mentioned in Chapter 1. But it is a challenge donors must face.
70   Although programmes often have second and third phases so can last longer than three to five years.
71   Author's estimate. Excludes programme pilots, but includes countries where proxy means testing is under development by governments though not yet implemented.
72   Cortes A. (2020).
73   Milanovic B. (2019).
74   BBC, 19th October 2020, at https://www.bbc.co.uk/news/world-latin-america-54594707 .
75   Milanovic B. (2019).
76   Luis Fiori J. (2019).
77   Gammage S. et al. (2014).
78   Casey B. H. and Mustafa A. (2022).
79   Ortiz I. et al. (2018).
80   Milanovic B. (2019).
81   *Time* at https://time.com/6209552/gabriel-boric-chile-constitution-interview/ .
82   International Social Security Association (2023).
83   Reuters at https://www.reuters.com/world/americas/former-protest-leader-boric-seeks-bury-chiles-neoliberal-past-2021-11-17/ .

Chapter 5

1. Ashcroft V. (2015). This equates to a similar amount in US dollars.
2. The National Team for the Acceleration of Poverty Reduction is known as TNP2K. At that time, Palladium had a different name, GRM International, which was subsequently combined with six other companies to form Palladium.
3. The programme was called the Bantuan Langsung Tunai (BLT) Temporary Unconditional Cash Transfer. World Bank (2012a). The cut in fuel subsidies caused a doubling in the price of fuel.
4. Widjaja M. (2009).
5. Cameron L. and Shah M. (2011).
6. Though the conditions were not enforced initially. For a discussion of proxy means testing used in the programme, see Alatas V. et al. (2013). Older people and persons with disabilities were included in programme recipients from 2017. Mulyani Indrawati S. et al. (2022).
7. Office of the Vice President of the Government of Indonesia (2015). From 2011, information that had been used to proxy means test tax-financed social protection programmes was put on the Unified Database.
8. World Bank (2012a).
9. World Bank (2017a).
10. The approach is called 'Benefit Incidence Analysis'. See Box 3 in Kidd S., Axelsson Nycander G. and Seglah H. (2023) for a more detailed critique. See also annex to this book.
11. Exclusion errors are equivalent to inclusion errors where the coverage of poverty-targeted programmes is factored in in estimating targeting errors. Kidd S. and Athias D. (2020).
12. Kidd S. and Athias D. (2020).
13. This is the coverage in 2017, the year the data on which the estimate is based was collected.
14. Alatas V. et al. (2016). 93 per cent of PKH's target population was estimated to be excluded.
15. Office of the Vice President of the Government of Indonesia (2018).
16. Office of the Vice President of the Government of Indonesia (2018).
17. See for example McGregor K. E. (2009).
18. See for example *The Guardian*, 17th October 2021, at https://www.theguardian.com/world/2021/oct/17/slaughter-in-indonesia-britains-secret-propaganda-war and Bevins V. (2017).
19. World Bank at https://www.worldbank.org/en/archive/history/past-presidents/robert-strange-mcnamara .
20. World Bank World Development Indicators, latest year available. This is measured in current US$, which does not take into account price differences between countries. Measuring average income using 2017 Purchasing Power Parity international $ raises Indonesia's position to 60 per cent down the scale from richest to poorest.
21. World Bank Development Indicators, latest year available. The US$3.65 poverty line is in 2017 Purchasing Power Parity terms, which takes account of price differences between countries. Poverty under the national poverty line is estimated at 9 per cent (2023), and the Gini coefficient is 38.3 (2023) compared to 30.7 in Fiji (2019) and 43 in Chile (2022).

22 Office of the Vice President of the Government of Indonesia (2018). Stunting means height for age is significantly lower than it should be.
23 World Bank at https://www.worldbank.org/en/country/indonesia/publication/access-to-childcare-can-improve-womens-labor-market-outcomes-in-indonesia .
24 OECD at https://web-archive.oecd.org/temp/2024-02-06/475118-womens-economic-empowerment.htm .
25 OECD at https://www.oecd.org/dac/gender-development/investinginwomenandgirls.htm .
26 World Bank and Asian Development Bank (2021).
27 World Bank at https://www.worldbank.org/en/country/indonesia/brief/world-bank-and-environment-in-indonesia .
28 Office of the Vice President of the Government of Indonesia (2015).
29 Stephen mentions that 'the government had a tiny universal pension, but that was only reaching a few thousand people'.
30 World Bank (2017d).
31 World Bank (2011c), Cahyadi N. et al. (2018) and Microsave Consulting (2019). One of these costs is likely to be higher spending on administration. The 2011 World Bank evaluation argues that PKH is efficient in terms of administrative costs in relation to other conditional cash transfer programme, but does not make a comparison with, for example, universal unconditional programmes.
32 World Bank (2017d).
33 Mulyani Indrawati S. et al. (2022).
34 After 2018, the Social Assistance Working Group became the Social Protection Policy Team. In July 2022, Dyah Larasati took over as head. Sri Kusumastuti Rahayu remained in the team as an adviser until early 2023, funded by *Mahkota*.
35 Office of the Vice President of the Government of Indonesia (2018).
36 The Indonesian government also considered providing access to jobs as part of the future social protection system, though it was not included in the 2018 strategy. The new law was to have three pillars: tax-financed social protection, social insurance and access to jobs. The universal pension would be limited to those that do not receive a pension from elsewhere. It is not clear from the strategy whether it is the intention to retain conditions for poverty-targeted support to school-age children. Office of the Vice President of the Government of Indonesia (2018).
37 World Bank (2014) and World Bank (2021c).
38 World Bank World Development Indicators. 10 per cent is pre-COVID-19. The pandemic significantly disrupted tax revenues.
39 Kidd S. et al. (2020).
40 World Bank (2020b).
41 Mulyani Indrawati S. et al. (2022). Other programmes include Program Indonesia Pintar (PIP), poverty-targeted support for school students' education expenses, Kartu Indonesia Pintar (KIP) Kuliah, support to the expenses of students in tertiary education – which are both, arguably, part of the education sector rather than tax-financed social protection – and two relatively small programmes for older people and people living with disabilities.
42 Office of the Vice President of the Government of Indonesia (2018).
43 World Bank at https://www.worldbank.org/en/country/indonesia/publication/investing-in-people-social-protection-for-indonesia-2045-vision .
44 Mulyani Indrawati S. et al. (2022).

45 In terms of government legitimacy, Indonesia is 56 out of 167 in the Economist Intelligence Unit world democracy rankings. Economist Intelligence Unit (2023).
46 And Stephen's connection with Indonesia continues. The company of which he is CEO, Development Pathways, is working in Indonesia, through UNICEF, for Bappenas, the Ministry of National Development Planning.

Chapter 6

1. Conversation with Michael Cichon 12 May 2022.
2. World Bank (2022a)).
3. Holzmann R. and Jorgensen S. (2000)
4. World Bank at https://www.worldbank.org/en/news/feature/2014/11/19/un-modelo-de-mexico-para-el-mundo .
5. Hickey S. et al. (2020). Quotes are from Peck J. and Theodore N. (2015).
6. Leisering L. (2019).
7. Leisering L. (2019).
8. The international conference was sponsored by the World Bank and the Turkish government and attended by more than 300 people. For more background on the conference, see World Bank (2006).
9. Fiszbein A. and Schady N. (2009).
10. Özler B. et al. (2010).
11. Baird S. et al. (2011).
12. Kidd S. and Calder R. (2012).
13. Özler B. and Ferreira F. (2011a).
14. 'Quasi-experimental' means having to create a non-random control group, for example through regression discontinuity design, propensity score matching or difference-in-difference estimation. 'Experimental' means having a random control group.
15. Freeland N. (2013).
16. Özler B. and Ferreira F. (2011b).
17. Kidd S. and Huda K. (2013). Previdencia Social spending includes government-financed and contribution-financed spending.
18. The cited study is International Social Security Association (2013).
19. Freeland N. (2013).
20. Benhassine N. et al. (2013).
21. The earlier version of the report was dated 4 December 2012.
22. Baird, S. et al. (2014). The review also says the positive effect of conditions widens where they are strictly enforced.
23. Loeser J. et al. (2021).
24. ODI (2016).
25. Richterman A. et al. (2023).
26. Wollburg C. et al. (2023).
27. Bryan G. et al. (2023).
28. Özler B. and Ferreira F. (2011b).
29. Wollburg C. et al. (2023).
30. Wollburg C. et al. (2023).
31. Development Pathways (2022a).

32 Prencipe L. et al. (2021).
33 Bryan G. et al. (2023).
34 Kidd S. (2018c).
35 Özler B. and Ferreira F. (2011b).
36 Kidd S. (2018c).
37 Orton I. (2014). Orton also articulates the argument that conditional cash transfers can promote human rights, by encouraging public authorities to provide services and by encouraging recipients to demand them.
38 World Bank (2017c).
39 Özler B. and Ferreira F. (2011a).
40 Kidd S. and Calder R. (2012).
41 *The Guardian*, 30 September 2016, at https://www.theguardian.com/global-development/2016/sep/30/world-bank-name-and-shame-countries-fail-stunted-children .
42 Fiszbein A. and Schady N. (2009).
43 Bryan G. et al. (2023).
44 World Bank (2022a). This is based on the World Bank's ASPIRE data base.
45 For East Asia and the Pacific, South Asia and sub-Saharan Africa, spending is estimated at 2–6 per cent but earlier estimates, for 2018, are 5 per cent in South Asia, 12 per cent in East Asia and the Pacific and nearly a fifth in sub-Saharan Africa. World Bank (2022a) and World Bank (2018b). These are not included because of the instability of estimates. Current spending in the Middle East and North Africa is estimated at around 2 per cent and small or zero in Europe and Central Asia.
46 Ravallion M. (2016).
47 Presentation to International Conference on Universal Child Grants in Geneva, 2019. Social protection.org at https://socialprotection.org/international-conference-universal-child-grants.

Chapter 7

1 Stephen and Steve drafted the technical part of the bid and Maxwell Stamp staff drafted other parts.
2 *The Irish Times*, 15 October 2004, at https://www.irishtimes.com/news/local-ugandan-king-goes-to-court-over-uk-land-crimes-1.1162032
3 Armitage C. (2015).
4 I am not aware of any responsibility being accepted and any compensation being paid to date. In 2013, the *EastAfrican* website reported a disputed claim that the UK government paid an out-of-court settlement of £700 million to the Ugandan government, in 2007, which was not passed on to the Bunyoro. *The East African*, 18 May 2013, at https://www.theeastafrican.co.ke/tea/news/east-africa/bunyoro-in-fresh-push-for-compensation-amid-claims-uk-paid-700m--1316570 .
5 Jørgensen J. J. (1981).
6 Economist Intelligence Unit (2023). Quote from Economist Intelligence Unit (2021).
7 Gourevitch P. (2000).
8 Milton Obote was president after independence in 1962 until Amin took over in a coup in 1971. Obote's re-election in 1980 was disputed by Museveni and others. According to Human Rights Watch, 'Hundreds of thousands of civilians lost

their lives during the military dictatorship of Idi Amin (1971–79) and the second administration of Milton Obote (1980-85).' Human Rights Watch at https://www.hrw.org/reports/2001/africa/uganda/uganda.html .
9. The LRA started among ethnic Acholi communities, which had borne the brunt of the suffering. Human Rights Watch at https://www.hrw.org/news/2012/03/21/qa-joseph-kony-and-lords-resistance-army .
10. DFID were paying Maxwell Stamp to deliver the programme in Uganda. HelpAge International had helped Maxwell Stamp win the bid but left the contract.
11. Richard manages the Development Pathways office in Nairobi, Kenya. There are also offices in the UK, Australia and Jordan.
12. The programme was the DFID-supported Hunger Safety Net Programme (HSNP) in northern Kenya.
13. DFID were trying to do the same thing, part-funding first with a view to government taking over, in other African countries including Ethiopia, Ghana, Kenya and Tanzania, with varying success.
14. The pilot was proposed by the Chronic Poverty Research Centre, a project within the Overseas Development Institute (ODI) in London.
15. The ministry's full title is the Ministry of Finance, Planning and Economic Development (MFPED).
16. The full name of the ministry is the Ministry of Gender, Labour and Social Development, which also has wider responsibilities.
17. World Bank World Development Indicators, latest year available. Uganda is placed at 187 out of 207 for which data is available. This is measured in current US$, which does not take into account price differences between countries. Measuring average income using 2017 Purchasing Power Parity international $ changes Uganda's position to 178 out of 194 countries for which data was available.
18. World Bank Development Indicators, latest year available. The US$3.65 poverty line is in 2017 Purchasing Power Parity terms, which takes account of price differences between countries. Poverty under the national poverty line is 20 per cent (2019). The Gini coefficient is 42.7 (2019), compared to 43 in Chile (2022).
19. Ministry of Gender, Labour and Social Development, Government of Uganda (2019).
20. Ministry of Gender, Labour and Social Development, Government of Uganda (2019).
21. One in six boys also experience sexual violence during childhood.
22. This is not special to Uganda: one in three women and girls globally experience physical and/or sexual violence by an intimate partner. Buller A. M. et al. (2018).
23. See for example Buller A. M. et al. (2018). The study emphasizes, for some of the effects, that programme design is important for the impact to be positive.
24. Ministry of Gender, Labour and Social Development, Government of Uganda (2019).
25. Concern at https://www.concern.org.uk/news/these-12-countries-hosted-most-refugees-2023 .
26. Ministry of Gender, Labour and Social Development, Government of Uganda (2019).
27. Ministry of Gender, Labour and Social Development, Government of Uganda (2019).
28. The two parts were the Senior Citizens' Grant (SCG) and the Vulnerable Families Support Grant (VFSG). The VFSG was targeted using households' dependency ratio, a proxy for poverty. Dependency ratios were calculated by dividing the total number of vulnerable people, including older people and persons with disabilities, by the number of people that were able bodied of working age.

29 The conflict, involving pastoralists – mobile populations that move livestock in pursuit of grazing and water, has multiple sources including competition for pasture and water and cattle rustling. Food and Agriculture Organization et al. (2023).
30 The DFID programme, co-funded by the government and Irish AID, would be called Expanding Social Protection. US$80m is the initial budget DFID of £51.5m from the programme business case, available from the Foreign, Commonwealth and Development Office, Government of the United Kingdom at https://devtracker.fcdo.gov.uk/projects/GB-1-200349/documents, converted at an exchange rate of 1.61 and rounded up.
31 Stephen Kasaija took over after the first leader of the programme left following a corruption scandal. In addition, the start of the programme was delayed for a year because of a dispute over government staff pay.
32 2015 marked the beginning of the second phase of the programme. Development Pathways won the bid as official implementing partners with Maxwell Stamp. Bernie Wyler replaced Steve Barrett as head of the DFID programme, Juliet Attenborough arrived as a social protection specialist in 2016, for a year, Philip White was brought in to analyse the efficiency and effectiveness of the universal pension, and Bjorn Gelders and Diloa Athias supported building the evidence.
33 Ministry of Gender, Labour and Social Development, Government of Uganda (2019). The US$7 value is 25,000 Ugandan shillings converted at a market exchange rate of 3,794 shillings per dollar. The initial value was set at US$11. US$7 is equivalent to $19 per month in Uganda, if we allow for lower prices in Uganda compared to the USA. The Purchasing Power Parity exchange rate used is 1,310 for 2021 (from World Bank).
34 In fact, the government's contribution would surpass 60 per cent of spending in 2018. Though total government and donor spending on the universal pension as a proportion of GDP was just 0.07 per cent of GDP in 2017/18. Ministry of Gender, Labour and Social Development, Government of Uganda (2019).
35 The minister of finance, Syda Bumba, had moved elsewhere in May 2011.
36 David originally joined the programme as an economist, but this evolved to a role in advocacy.
37 Barrantes A. (2017).
38 Presentation by the IMF Resident Representative, December 2017. Data is for 2014 or latest year available in each country over the period 2009-2014.
39 World Bank World Development Indicators, latest year available. This is measured in current US$, which does not take into account price differences between countries. Measuring average income using 2017 Purchasing Power Parity international $ changes the rankings to Kenya 152, Tanzania 172, Uganda 178.
40 Ministry of Gender, Labour and Social Development, Government of Uganda (2019) and Gelders B. and Athias D. (2019).
41 ODI (2016).
42 The programme was called the Northern Uganda Social Action Fund (NUSAF). The second phase, NUSAF2, which started in 2009, contained support to income generation, community infrastructure rehabilitation and institutional development, as well as workfare.
43 The World Bank also worked in other areas of social protection in Uganda over time, such as contributory schemes.

44 The ministry for social protection drafted the first social protection policy for Uganda, complete with the then pilot universal pension, which was approved in 2015. Ministry of Gender, Labour and Social Development, Government of Uganda (2015).
45 The draft World Bank report, dated June 2019, was entitled *Uganda Social Protection Public Expenditure Review*. The author was not able to find a final version of the report online.
46 In this instance, a poverty-targeted child benefit was recommended.
47 Perhaps unsurprisingly, the 2019 review endorsed universality being at the heart of the social protection system. Ministry of Gender, Labour and Social Development, Government of Uganda (2019).
48 Development Pathways were in a bid led by Adam Smith International. The contract was awarded to DAI and Oxford Policy Management.
49 Foreign Commonwealth and Development Office, Government of United Kingdom (2022).
50 Steve Ashley also led the 2019 review of the social protection sector in Uganda.
51 World Bank (2023d).

Chapter 8

1 Subbarao K. et al. (2013).
2 Lindert P. H. (2004).
3 William Senior N. and Chadwick E. (1834).
4 For further information see Government of the United Kingdom National Archives at https://www.nationalarchives.gov.uk/education/resources/1834-poor-law/ .
5 McCord A. et al. (2021).
6 Government of the United Kingdom National Archives at https://www.nationalarchives.gov.uk/education/resources/1834-poor-law/ .
7 James Gardner, author of *A History of the Brighton Workhouses* (2012), speaking on BBC programme *Who Do You Think You Are?* 11th June 2022.
8 Nally D. P. (2008).
9 McCord A. et al. (2021).
10 McCord A. (2008) and McCord A. et al. (2021).
11 McCord A. (2008). Days of employment for workfare from Subbarao K. et al. (2013) and Berhane G. et al. (2017).
12 World Bank (2022a). This is based on the World Bank's ASPIRE data base. It is spending for 'public works' which are assumed to be workfare given they are presented as a part of social assistance. Spending on 'public works' in South Asia is not quoted due to the instability of estimates, which are 7 per cent currently but 25 per cent in 2018. World Bank (2018b). In Latin America and the Caribbean and Europe and Central Asia, spending is currently estimated at 3 per cent and is too small a figure to be quoted in East Asia and the Pacific.
13 The Governance and Social Development Resource Centre (GSDRC) at https://gsdrc.org/topic-guides/social-protection/global-issues-and-debates-2/public-works-programmes/. The GSDRC is a UK-based research centre set up by DFID.
14 Subbarao K. et al. (2013).
15 World Bank presentation, *Public Works Perspectives from International Experience*, at https://www.worldbank.org/content/dam/Worldbank/Event/safetynets/1.

%20Andrews_Public%20Works%20International%20Experience.pdf. More up-to-date numbers have not been found.
16. Carruth L. and Freeman S. (2021).
17. GIZ and University of Passau (2018).
18. Singh, R. K. (2017).
19. University of Sussex (2018). The quality of implementation has varied across states in India. For a discussion of issues around the implementation of MGNREGS in Bihar see Dutta P. et al. (2014).
20. McCord A. (2008), MGNREGS stands for Mahatma Gandhi National Rural Employment Guarantee Scheme. Maharashtra is a state in India.
21. In Rwanda, the programme is called the Vision 2020 Umurenge Programme (VUP). It provides around twenty days of labour a year for households with labour capacity.
22. The programme in Rwanda funded by DFID in support of the social protection system was jointly run by Mott McDonald and Development Pathways.
23. McCord A. and Slater R. (2009).
24. Subbarao K. et al. (2013). There is a discussion of some of the components that go to make up value for money, such as the cost to transfer US$1 of benefits to the poor. But as DFID guidance on value for money for tax-financed social protection schemes points out, workfare tends to be much more expensive than simple cash transfer programmes in delivering US$1 of benefits, so this does not help in the decision of whether to invest in workfare. White P. et al. (2013).
25. I discussed this with a group of global experts on workfare from the World Bank, the World Food Programme and the ILO at the Overseas Development Institute in London some time ago. They conceded that the fundamental economic case for workfare has not been made, and efforts are spent only on doing workfare as well as possible.
26. GIZ and University of Passau (2018).
27. Kidd S. and Athias D. (2020).
28. Berhane G. et al. (2017).
29. Tafere, Y. and Woldehanna E. (2012).
30. World Bank (2019a).
31. Ministry of Economic Planning and Development, Government of Malawi (2022).
32. Sengupta A. (2019). The scope of the blog includes India's Mahatma Gandhi National Rural Employment Guarantee Scheme (MGNREGS).
33. Foreign, Commonwealth and Development Office, Government of United Kingdom (2020).
34. GIZ and University of Passau (2018). In fairness, social protection programmes generally are not good at measuring impact after people have left programmes. But this is more concerning for workfare schemes because they invest so heavily in asset creation, as well as people's productivity, and need sustained impact to justify the cost.
35. Sabates-Wheeler R. et al. (2020).
36. World Bank Development Indicators, latest year available. The US$3.65 poverty line is in 2017 Purchasing Power Parity terms, which takes account of price differences between countries.
37. ILO (2021b). Apart from the PSNP, the Urban Productive Safety Net Project (UPSNP) provides transfers to 604,000 beneficiaries.
38. Economist Intelligence Unit (2023).
39. Foreign, Commonwealth and Development Office, Government of United Kingdom (2020).

40 World Food Programme at https://www.wfp.org/food-assistance-for-assets .
41 World Bank (2012c).
42 Mvukiyehe E. (2018).
43 World Bank (2012c). The strategy also includes an objective to do the same for cash transfers.

Chapter 9

1 ILO at https://webapps.ilo.org/public/english/protection/about/brochure/brochure2.htm
2 Comprehensive medical care for all is also a target. The ILO includes healthcare in its definition of social protection.
3 Kidd S., Axelsson Nycander G. and Seglah H. (2023).
4 United Nations (2015), Article 22. And United Nations at https://www.un.org/en/about-us/udhr/history-of-the-declaration .
5 The Convention's official title is C102 – Social Security (Minimum Standards) Convention, 1952 (No. 102). ILO at https://normlex.ilo.org/dyn/normlex/en/f?p=NORMLEXPUB:12100:0::NO::P12100_INSTRUMENT_ID:312247.
6 United Nations (1967).
7 Over this period, when the Social Security Department became the Social Protection Department, it expanded its interest beyond contributory social insurance to include tax-financed benefits.
8 For a discussion of the role this costing work played as an initial milestone in the later development of the concept of the Social Protection Floor, see ILO et al. (2022).
9 Mkandawire T. (2005). This list of attendees is according to ILO records, though it is not clear that everyone attended. Other attendees listed include Katja Hujo and Yusuf Bangura from UNRISD, Rachel Slater from the Overseas Development Institute (ODI) in London, Armando Barrientos from the Institute for Development Studies at Sussex University, Bea Cantillon from the University of Antwerp, Assia Bandrup from the German development organizations GIZ, a representative from the International Social Security Association (ISSA), Raymond Wagener from the Inspection Générale de la Sécurité Sociale and Viroj Tangcharoensathien from the International Health Policy Programme, Thailand.
10 The meeting was one of a series of regular meetings of UN agency heads known as the United Nations System Chief Executives Board for Coordination (UNCEB).
11 Sepúlveda Carmona M. (2009). Social security and human rights were discussed by Magdalena Sepulveda Carmona at a meeting in Geneva at around the same time, which Stephen and others attended.
12 The full list of agencies from a 2009 meeting in Turin included WHO, FAO, OHCHR, UN Regional Commissions, UNAIDS, UN-DESA, UNDP, UNESCO, UNFPA, UN-HABITAT, UNHCR, UNICEF, UNODC, UNRWA, WFP and the WMO. ILO and World Health Organization (2009).
13 ILO and World Health Organization (2009).
14 ILO (2011a).
15 Quoted in Sibun D. (2022a).
16 ILO (2011b).

17 ILO at https://normlex.ilo.org/dyn/normlex/en/f?p=NORMLEXPUB:12100:0::NO::P12100_INSTRUMENT_ID:312247.
18 Stephen argues, convincingly, that social security is a distinct public service alongside other public services including health, education and social services, and that mixing health or anything else belonging to another sector with social security can cause confusion.
19 Isabel Ortiz, who took over from Michael Cichon as Director of Social Protection at the ILO, believed part of the explanation for the World Bank's attitude to the Social Protection Floor was it believed it was equivalent to a poverty-targeted 'safety net'.
20 ILO (2012).
21 Sibun D. (2022a).
22 Sibun D. (2022a).
23 ILO (2024) and for high-income countries see, for example, Jacques O. and Noël A. (2021).
24 For Stephen's view, 'that not every social security scheme within a universal system should be universal', see Kidd S., Axelsson Nycander G. and Seglah H. (2023).
25 ILO and World Bank (2015).
26 The website for the initiative, known as USP30, is at www.usp2030.org.
27 Information is collected through the Social Security Enquiry. See information on progress towards SDG 1.3 from the ILO at https://www.social-protection.org/gimi/WSPDB.action?id=32.
28 See, for example, Ortiz I. et al. (2017) and Ortiz I. et al. (2019).
29 *The Guardian*, 30th September 2016, at https://www.theguardian.com/global-development/2016/sep/30/world-bank-name-and-shame-countries-fail-stunted-children.
30 Kidd S. (2016).
31 See, for example, Gentilini U. (2018). For later references see, for example, Grosh M. et al. (2022) and Leon Solano R. et al. (2024).
32 Sibun D. (2022a).
33 Foreign, Commonwealth and Development Office, Government of United Kingdom (2023).
34 Global Partnership for Universal Social Protection (2019).
35 Grosh M. et al. (2022).
36 For estimates of take-up rates of means-tested benefits in the UK see Department for Work and Pensions, Government of United Kingdom (2022).
37 Grosh M. et al. (2022). Targeting by age or other 'fairly easy-to-observe categories' is referred to as 'Demographic/categorical targeting'.
38 World Bank (2022a).
39 World Bank (2025).
40 For a summary of resolutions and conclusion on social protection agreed at the 2021 International Labour Conference see ILO (2021c).
41 The Coalition includes the Africa Platform for Social Protection, the Friends of the Disabled Association (FDA), the Women in Informal Employment: Globalising and Organising (WIEGO) and the Friedrich Ebert Foundation (FES) from Germany, among many others.
42 https://www.hrw.org/news/2024/04/15/letter-world-bank-and-imf-executive-directors-failings-promote-human-right-social.
43 https://www.socialprotectionfloorscoalition.org/campaigns/social-security-for-all-key-pillar-for-new-eco-social-contract/towards-the-right-to-social-security-for-all/.

44. United Nations (2021b). For the UN secretary-general's full policy brief see United Nations (2021a).
45. Federal Ministry of Labour and Social Affairs, Government of Germany (2022).
46. United Nations (2022).
47. United Nations at https://www.un.org/sustainabledevelopment/blog/2022/09/media-advisory-with-billions-of-people-facing-greatest-cost-of-living-crisis-in-a-generation-leaders-to-gather-at-un-to-address-solutions-for-job-growth-and-social-protection/.
48. United Nations Office of the High Representative for the Least Developed Countries, Landlocked Developing Countries and Small Island Developing States (2022).
49. Global Accelerator at https://www.unglobalaccelerator.org/un-and-world-bank-host-donor-meeting-accelerate-universal-social-protection-and-employment-through.
50. Townsend P. (2009).
51. For a more detailed discussion of the impact of the Recommendation, see ILO (2019b).
52. Juan Somavia said, 'I think the world does not lack the resources to eradicate poverty; it lacks the right priorities.' ILO (2009).

Chapter 10

1. BBC, 22nd September 2009, at http://news.bbc.co.uk/1/hi/8268651.stm.
2. Recipient numbers are from the Government of Nepal budget documents. The universal pension is called the Senior Citizen Allowance, and the benefit for widows and single women 60 years or over is called the Single Women and Widows Allowance. The disability benefit was divided into the Full Disability and Partial Disability Allowances in 2009. Those receiving a pension from the government, army or police are not eligible for these benefits. Palacios R. J. (2016).
3. World Bank (2021b). The age limit was lowered from seventy-five to seventy for the general population, but it was sixty for Dalits – previously known as 'untouchables' – along with residents of the poorest province in Nepal, Karnali.
4. Ministry of Labour and Employment, Government of Nepal and ILO (2017) and World Bank (2021b). Source for lowering the age limit to 68, in 2022, *Republica*, 29th May 2022, at https://myrepublica.nagariknetwork.com/news/govt-reduces-minimum-age-limit-for-elderly-allowance-to-68-from-70-years/.
5. World Bank (2021b) and Development Pathways staff. The conversion to US$ is at the market exchange rate of 131 rupees to the dollar. The value of the pension is US$118 per month if we use an exchange rate which allows for the fact things are much cheaper to buy in Nepal than in the USA. The Purchasing Power Parity rate used is 34 rupees to the dollar (from World Bank).
6. https://www.issa.int/node/195543?country=877 . The conversion to US$ is at the market exchange rate of 84 rupees to the dollar.
7. Palacios R. J. (2016), World Bank (2021b) and European Union and UNICEF (2022). The widows and single women benefit was partly expanded by a court ruling in 2010 to include widows of any age.
8. The programme is known as the Child Grant or child nutrition grant. Palacios R. J. (2016) and World Bank (2021b). An Endangered Ethnicity Allowance was also introduced with a relatively small number of recipients.

9   *The Rising Nepal*, 1st May 2024, at https://www.risingnepaldaily.com/news/42347.
10 World Bank (2021b).
11 World Bank (2021b). Total spending on social protection is 4.8 per cent of GDP. The remaining 0.1 per cent is 'Labour Market Programs' including skills training and the Prime Minister Employment Programme.
12 Spending for Indonesia is pre-COVID-19.
13 Data on GDP per capita from World Bank World Development Indicators, latest year available. Nepal is placed at 186 out of 207 for which data is available, Uganda is placed 187. This is measured in current US$, which does not take into account price differences between countries. Measuring average income using 2017 Purchasing Power Parity international $, Nepal's position is 161 out of 194 countries for which data was available and Uganda's 178.
14 For greater detail, see, for example, World Bank (2018a).
15 Letter from Baburam Bhattarai to the Prime Minister 4 February 1996, at https://www.satp.org/satporgtp/countries/nepal/document/papers/40points.htm .
16 Holmes R. and Upadhya S. (2009).
17 World Bank (2018a).
18 World Bank World Development Indicators. The US$3.65 poverty line is in 2017 Purchasing Power Parity terms, which takes account of price differences between countries. The proportion of the population below the national poverty line is 25 per cent (2010).
19 World Bank (2018a).
20 World Bank World Development Indicators, latest year available. The Gini coefficient is 32.8 (2010) compared to 30.7 in Fiji, 38.3 in Indonesia and 42.7 in Uganda.
21 The climate crisis also affects polar regions disproportionately. International Atomic Energy Agency at https://www.iaea.org/newscenter/news/climate-change-polar-and-mountainous-regions.
22 International Centre for Integrated Mountain Development, Global Facility for Disaster Reduction and Recovery and World Bank (2011).
23 United Nations Office for Disaster Risk Reduction at https://www.preventionweb.net/publication/nepal-flood-2017-post-flood-recovery-needs-assessment and World Bank (2018a).
24 World Vision at https://www.worldvision.org/disaster-relief-news-stories/2015-nepal-earthquake-facts.
25 World Bank (2018a).
26 See for example Bennett L. et al. (2008).
27 Reliefweb at https://reliefweb.int/report/nepal/nepal-gender-and-protection-brief.
28 Basnet Bista S. et al. (2022) and United Nations Development Programme (2020).
29 UNICEF at https://www.unicef.org/nepal/nutrition.
30 Drucza K. (2016a).
31 Stephen was invited by Rebecca Calder to work on the design of a United Nations Capital Development Fund (UNCDF) programme.
32 To help improve systems, Rebecca Calder brought in Stephen and his colleague at Development Pathways Richard Chirchir to support work on improving programme management information systems.
33 Drucza K. (2016a).
34 World Bank (2010).
35 For evidence of very low incomes, see, for example, Bhakta Paudel B. (2022).
36 Willmore L. (2007).

37 Greenslade M. (2018).
38 Drucza, K. (2016b).
39 Holmes R. and Upadhya S. (2009).
40 Prasad Adhikari T. et al. (2014). While the research was on the child grant, the authors state, 'we should keep in mind that, with most households in our sample receiving at least three other social protection transfers, often using the same delivery mechanism, it is difficult for respondents to isolate their perceptions of this particular transfer.'
41 World Bank World Development Indicators.
42 Kidd S. et al. (2020).
43 Kidd S. et al. (2011). Looking at proxy means testing and community-based targeting, the paper also highlights high targeting errors, the risk of community-based targeting being manipulated by local elites and the risks of stigmatizing recipients.
44 Kidd S. and Calder R. (2011).
45 World Bank (2016).
46 Sibun D. (2022a).
47 World Bank (2021b).
48 World Bank (2021b).
49 According to a recent article in the journal Economic Modelling, the absence of peace and cohesion can 'have long-lasting and devastating effects on a country's economic and social development', especially in lower-income contexts. Le T.-H. et al. (2022). In addition, were you still to argue for cutbacks in social protection, contributory benefits, which go to a relatively small part of the population but cost more than half of total spending, may be a more logical place to start than tax-financed schemes. For evidence on the impact of growth on poverty reduction, see Kharas H. and Dooley M. (2022).
50 Taxes on goods and services were 47.5 per cent of total tax revenue in 2019, the last year before COVID-19, according to the World Bank.
51 In fact, it is arguably the combined impact of all government services that should be measured, if that is possible, not just social protection schemes and taxation.
52 Kidd S. et al. (2022).
53 Perhaps this should not be a surprise given that the split between indirect taxes and direct taxes which we would expect to be more progressive, is similar in low and middle-income countries as a proportion of total tax revenue. This is, in fact, shown in the World Bank's own analysis. See World Bank (2022a). The split is also similar for high-income countries that are outside the OECD. There *is* a risk of the poor losing out in some countries. For example, Sean Higgins and Nora Lustig, writing in the *Journal of Development Economics*, describe the net impact of taxes, benefits and indirect subsidies as being to increase poverty in Ethiopia and Ghana. Higgins S. and Lustig N. (2016).
54 In any case, it is not a static picture because tax systems can be improved over time and become progressive as well as being improved in other ways, such as drawing in more in the informal sector to pay tax on incomes.
55 Economist Intelligence Unit (2023).
56 World Development Indicators. The average rate of growth is a simple average of rates of growth 2007-2019. National debt as a percentage of GDP is latest year available (2020 for Nepal).
57 *The Himalayan*, 4th July 2020, at https://thehimalayantimes.com/business/world-bank-elevates-nepal-to-lower-middle-income-economy. Though Nepal remains

relatively low on the ladder of richest to poorest countries, measured by GDP per capita.
58 We may say that where there is macroeconomic instability and unsustainable debt, institutions like the World Bank and IMF have a greater responsibility. Though even here they must be careful not to overstep the mark in terms of influencing the detail of domestic policy.
59 Sibun D. (2022a).
60 ILO (2024). Spending excludes health.
61 Lindert P. H. (2004).
62 United Nations Economic and Social Commission for Asia and the Pacific (ESCAP) and Development Pathways (2022).
63 ILO (2019a). GDP per capita comparisons allow for inflation over time.
64 Lindert points to one exception, Singapore. So, do we at last have at least one model of a country following the free market route? In fact, no, because the Singapore government owns 90 per cent of the land there. And more than 80 per cent of the population lives in housing constructed by Singapore's public housing agency. Bruenig M. (2018). It is hardly an unfettered free market. Myths permeate the social protection and wider social policy dialogue, and must be challenged with evidence.

Chapter 11

1 Willmore L. (2007).
2 BBC at https://www.bbc.co.uk/news/av/world-africa-36427814 . Zanzibar was a country separate to Tanzania before 1964, with a history of slavery and Portuguese, Arab and British rule.
3 Ministry of Labour Employment and Youth Development, Government of Tanzania in collaboration with HelpAge International (2010).
4 World Bank World Development Indicators, latest year available. This is measured in current US$, which does not take into account price differences between countries. Data is available for 207 countries. Measuring average income using 2017 Purchasing Power Parity international $ changes Tanzania's ranking to 172 out of 194 countries for which data was available.
5 World Bank Development Indicators, latest year available. And World Bank (2017e). The US$3.65 poverty line is in 2017 Purchasing Power Parity terms, which takes account of price differences between countries. The population under the national poverty line is 26.4 per cent (2018). The Gini coefficient is 40.5 (2018).
6 Ministry of Labour Employment and Youth Development, Government of Tanzania and HelpAge International (2010).
7 Seekings J. (2016).
8 Also, there were a member of the Zanzibar House of Representatives and officials from the ministry for social protection. The party of four from the Tanzania mainland included the Deputy Minister for Labour. Seekings J. (2016).
9 World Bank at https://www.worldbank.org/en/country/mauritius/overview.
10 Subramanian A. and Roy. D (2001).
11 Wolf E. R. (2010).
12 Meade J. (1961).
13 Subramanian A. and Roy. D (2001).

14 Interviews with government officials in HelpAge International film on the universal pension in Mauritius at https://www.youtube.com/watch?v=RyetLX-5OvU&t=1s. The official title of the pension is the Basic Retirement Pension (BRP).
15 World Bank (2004).
16 Universal pension cost from Willmore L. (2007). Civil service pension cost from Financial Services Commission Mauritius (2003). The World Bank misrepresented the cost of the universal pension according to Willmore. A 2001 study commissioned by the World Bank quoted the cost in 1998–99 at 3 per cent of GDP. The actual cost was at 1.7 per cent, estimated by Willmore, for 2003, using Mauritius Central Statistical Office data. Willmore points out a footnote in the 2004 World Bank paper which explains the discrepancy: to the universal pension cost has been added a number of transfers to those under 60 going to widows, persons with disabilities, orphans and inmates. 'The World Bank . . . used this flawed estimate to advocate reducing or targeting age pensions in Mauritius, with no mention of the qualifying footnote.'
17 Willmore L. (2007).
18 Sheilabai Bappoo, Minister of Social Security, National Solidarity and Senior Citizens Welfare and Reform Institutions, 2005 to 2010, speaking in HelpAge International film on the universal pension in Mauritius at https://www.youtube.com/watch?v=RyetLX-5OvU&t=1s.
19 Address by the President of Mauritius at https://www.humanrightsinitiative.org/programs/ai/rti/international/laws_papers/mauritius/president_address_mauritius.pdf.
20 Transfer value from Ministry of Social Integration, Social Security and National Solidarity, Government of Mauritius at https://socialsecurity.govmu.org/Pages/Department/PRESCRIBED-RATES-OF-BASIC-PENSIONS.aspx. The pension is worth 13,500 rupees per month for those aged 60 years of age and over and below 90. It increases to 21,210 at 90 and 26,210 at 100. The rate has been converted using a market exchange rate of 45 rupees per dollar. Cost is author's calculation. Cost in rupees, for June 2022, from Government of Mauritius at https://statsmauritius.govmu.org/Pages/Statistics/ESI/Soc_Sec/Soc_Sec_Yr21-Yr22.aspx . GDP for 2022 from Government of Mauritius at https://statsmauritius.govmu.org/Documents/Statistics/ESI/2022/EI1661/NAE_Jun22_300622.pdf.
21 For middle-income countries, cost is for universal pensions, from Development Pathways staff. For high-income countries, cost is public spending on old-age pensions, from Harker R. (2022). Figures are for latest year available (2017). Comparators are Pay-As-You-Go schemes, like the Mauritius universal pension, funded from current tax revenues rather than past contributions.
22 World Bank (2021a). The World Bank also makes recommendations on imminent changes to the contributory pension system: 'A number of implementation details on the recently introduced Contribution Social Généralisée (CSG) will be key, including setting the level and gradual increase of benefits in a fiscally sustainable manner.' Poverty targeting and alternative reforms are also mentioned, in IMF (2022b).
23 Mauritius Revenue Authority at https://www.mra.mu/index.php/eservices1/financial-assistance/csg-child-allowance#:~:text=The%20monthly%20CSG%20Child%20Allowance,July%202023%20to%20June%202024. The value of the child benefit, entitled the CSG Child Allowance, is 2,000 rupees per month in the first year and 2,500 rupees per month in the second year. It has been converted using a market exchange rate of 45 rupees per dollar.

Notes

24 Seekings J. (2016).
25 The universal pension is called the Zanzibar Universal Pension Scheme (ZUPS). Its value on local currency is 20,000 Tanzania shillings. This has been converted using a market exchange rate of 2,332 shillings per US dollar.
26 Seekings J. (2016).
27 Seekings J. (2016).
28 360 degrees Mozambique at https://360mozambique.com/world/africa/top-ten-african-countries-with-the-highest-GDP-per-capita-in-2025/.
29 Seekings J. (2016).
30 Seekings J. (2016).
31 Ulriksen M. S. (2016). The programme is called the Productive Social Safety Net (PSSN).
32 Tanzania Social Action Fund (2019).
33 Prencipe L. et al. (2021).
34 Kidd S. and Athias D. (2020).
35 Tanzania Social Action Fund (2019).
36 World Bank (2020a).
37 World Bank (2018b) and World Bank (2020a).
38 See for example, Tanzania Social Action Fund (2019).
39 World Bank (2012b).
40 Tanzania Social Action Fund (2019). On the accuracy of targeting, Stephen and his colleague at Development Pathways Diloa Athias argue there is 'little difference in the consumption of selected and non-selected households'. Kidd S. and Athias D. (2020).
41 Ulriksen M. S. (2016).
42 World Bank (2020a).
43 World Bank (2019c).
44 Ministry of Gender, Children, Disability and Social Welfare, Government of Malawi (2016).
45 World Bank World Development Indicators, latest year available. Malawi is placed at 204 out of 207 for which data is available. This is measured in current US$, which does not take account of price differences between countries. Measuring average income using 2017 Purchasing Power Parity international $ changes Malawi's position to 188 out of 194 countries for which data was available.
46 World Bank Development Indicators, latest year available. The US$3.65 poverty line is in 2017 Purchasing Power Parity terms, which takes account of price differences between countries. Poverty under the national poverty line is 50.7 per cent (2019). The Gini coefficient is 38.5 (2019).
47 Government of Malawi (2022). The programme is called the Social Cash Transfer Programme (SCTP) and is currently supported by the World Bank, the European Union, the German government's development bank KfW and Irish Aid.
48 Miller C. et al. (2008).
49 World Bank (2019e). See also World Bank (2019d).
50 Government of Malawi (2022).
51 ILO at https://www.social-protection.org/gimi/ResultAchieved.action;jsessionid=LEvHY9OyoC7JKfU2qelRY4l5yKZWFrbtPxt71yt8URY9ZJ9ZDcmt!-688150444?id=799&lang=FR.
52 The official title of the ministry for social protection was the Ministry of East African Community, Labour and Social Protection. The Social Protection Secretariat had a coordinating role for social protection policy across the Kenyan government.

53 Ministry of Labour and Social Protection, Government of Kenya (2017).
54 https://www.socialprotection.or.ke/single-registry.
55 Ministry of Labour and Social Protection, Government of Kenya (2017). The state contributory scheme is the National Social Security Fund, though this provides a lump sum on retirement not a pension. In addition, it is not social insurance in that resources are not pooled. There are also private pensions in Kenya for wealthier workers.
56 Reliefweb at https://reliefweb.int/report/ethiopia/horn-africa-drought-humanitarian-update-10-june-2022.
57 World Bank World Development Indicators, latest year available. GDP per capita is measured in current US$, which does not take account of price differences between countries. Kenya is 172 out of 2017 countries for which data is available. Measuring average income using 2017 Purchasing Power Parity international $, which takes account of price differences between countries, changes Kenya's ranking to 152 out of 194 countries for which data was available. The US$3.65 poverty line is in 2017 Purchasing Power Parity terms. The population under the national poverty line is 36.1 per cent (2015). In terms of inequality, the Gini coefficient is 38.7 (2021).
58 Ministry of Labour and Social Protection, Government of Kenya (2017).
59 Dowden R. (2008).
60 Elkins C. (2005).
61 Dowden R. (2008).
62 Elkins C. (2005).
63 *The Guardian*, 5th October 2012, at https://www.theguardian.com/world/2012/oct/05/mau-mau-veterans-win-torture-case. Al Jazeera, 6th October 2012, at https://www.aljazeera.com/features/2012/10/6/britains-brutal-rule-in-kenya-on-the-docks.
64 The core programmes were the Cash Transfer for Orphans and Vulnerable Children (CT-OVC), funded by donors and government, the Older Persons Cash Transfer (OPCT), funded by government, and the Hunger Safety Net Programme (HSNP) which was run out of a separate ministry, the Ministry of Devolution and Planning, and funded by donors (DFID) and government. There was also a relatively small Cash Transfer for Persons with Severe Disabilities (PWSD-CT), funded by government, school feeding and a programme called General Food Distribution, both funded by donors and government, and workfare programmes funded by donors.
65 Ministry of Labour and Social Protection, Government of Kenya (2017).
66 World Bank (2019b).
67 The team had also been asked to develop an Investment Plan for the future of social protection in Kenya.
68 DFID worked closely with the World Bank in Kenya, but the two organizations hadn't always been aligned. A decade or so before, Stephen says, the World Bank had tried to make the programme for orphans and vulnerable children a conditional cash transfer programme. The Cash Transfer for Orphans and Vulnerable Children (CT-OVC) started as a pilot in 2004, supporting orphans and vulnerable children facing poverty and dealing with the negative effects of HIV/AIDS epidemic. Working for DFID in London, Stephen helped the DFID office in Kenya to resist the World Bank's efforts.
69 Ouma M. and Adesina J. (2018).
70 Ministry of Labour and Social Protection, Government of Kenya (2017).
71 Cabinet Secretary is the title of government ministers that head departments in the Kenyan government. Susan Mochache and Phyllis Kandie, from the Ministry of

72 His official title was Cabinet Secretary for the National Treasury.
73 Ministry of Labour and Social Protection, Government of Kenya (2017). The universal pension is called the Inua Jamii Senior Citizens' Scheme. Its value on local currency is 2,000 Kenyan shillings. This has been converted to dollars using a market exchange rate of 122.4 shillings per US dollar.
74 The speed of registration, ahead of the election, meant rates of registration in some areas with lower capacity and higher poverty rates were lower than elsewhere. Porisky A. et al. (2023).
75 See World Bank (2017b).
76 World Bank (2019b). UNICEF also participated in the Kenya Social and Economic Inclusion Project.
77 This is the Hunger Safety Net Programme (HSNP). Part of the project's objectives was to strengthen the shock-responsiveness of the programme.
78 World Bank (2019b). See 'Sectoral and Institutional Context'.
79 World Bank (2023c). This includes those on the original Older Persons Cash Transfer (OPCT) for those sixty-five years of age and older.
80 World Bank (2023c).
81 Author's own calculations. Assuming 766,000 recipients. See World Bank (2023c).
82 Spending on such schemes in 2016/17, before the introduction of the universal pension, was around 0.3 per cent of GDP. GDP in 2017 was US$82.04 billion (from World Bank). The first poverty-targeted scheme, the Cash Transfer for Orphans and Vulnerable Children (CT-OVC), was introduced as a pilot in 2004 and as a programme in 2007. Spending has gradually increased on poverty-targeted programmes since.
83 World Bank (2023c). Stephen has been back to Kenya with Development Pathways to support the government on a universal child benefit, though this was interrupted by COVID-19 and hasn't yet come to fruition.
84 Kenya is 92 out of 167 in the Economist Intelligence Unit world democracy rankings. Economist Intelligence Unit (2023).

Chapter 12

1 Grosh M. et al. (2022).
2 Chirchir R. and Farooq S. (2016).
3 Leite P. et al. (2017).
4 Lindert K. et al. (eds) (2020). See also Grosh M. et al. (2022) on social registries being used for non-social protection programmes.
5 Lindert K. et al. (2020).
6 Lindert K. et al. (2020).
7 World Bank (2022a).
8 Kidd S., Athias D. and Mohamud I. (2021).
9 Lindert K. et al. (2020).
10 The 2017 paper is Leite P. et al. (2017).
11 World Bank (2022a).

12 Kidd S., Athias D. and Mohamud I. (2021). This is the 'exclusion error', that is, the proportion of those intended to be included in the programme that are in fact excluded. It is equivalent to the 'inclusion error', the proportion of recipients that are eligible, in these calculations, which take into account the intended coverage of poverty-targeted programmes. See Kidd S. and Athias D. (2020) for further explanation.
13 Kidd S., Athias D. and Mohamud I. (2021).
14 World Bank (2022a).
15 Grosh M. et al. (2022).
16 See Lindert K. et al. (2017).
17 Sibun D. (2022a).
18 Kidd S., Athias D. and Mohamud I. (2021).
19 Grosh M. et al. (2022).
20 World Bank (2022a).
21 Grosh M. et al. (2022).
22 Drawing on Grosh M. et al. (2008), UK government guidance on measuring value for money in tax-financed social protection programmes says the share of administrative costs in total programme costs clusters in the range of 5 to 15 per cent 'in well-executed cash and in-kind transfers'. White P. et al. (2013). This is a slightly different measure of cost efficiency from administrative costs as a proportion of the value of benefits, but provides broad guidance.
23 Kidd S., Athias D. and Mohamud I. (2021).
24 US$50–US$100 million assumes 10–20 million households and an average cost per household of US$5. The World Bank says costs 'range between US$1 and US$3 per household in most countries, or in the range of 1–3 percent of the value of benefits channelled through the system'. Grosh M. et al. (2022). But given it also says in lower income countries with start-up costs of newer systems this can go up to '7–8 percent', US$5 is used as a rough mid-point in the range.
25 Lindert K. (2020).
26 *The Daily Star*, 28th April 2021, at https://www.thedailystar.net/backpage/news/national-poverty-registry-project-delayed-data-obsolete-2085049.
27 Kidd S., Athias D. and Mohamud I. (2021).
28 See Grosh M. et al. (2008).
29 For GIZ's approach in Malawi see https://www.giz.de/en/worldwide/65183.html.
30 Kidd S., Athias D. and Mohamud I. (2021).
31 Grosh M. et al. (2022).
32 Freeland N. (2021a).
33 Kidd S., Athias D. and Mohamud I. (2021).
34 Kidd S., Athias D. and Mohamud I. (2021).
35 Kidd S., Athias D. and Mohamud I. (2021).
36 Chirchir R. and Farooq S. (2016).
37 See table 2 in Leite P. et al. (2017).
38 The conditional cash transfer programme Bolsa Familia, which uses the social registry Cadastro Unico, has an estimated exclusion error of 44 per cent. Kidd S. and Athias D. (2020).
39 Sibun D. (2022a).
40 For Kenya, see World Bank (2019b) and for Malawi, see World Bank (2019d).
41 World Bank (2021b).
42 Kidd S., Athias D. and Mohamud I. (2021).

43 The World Bank refers to the basics of building universal social protection systems as 'foundational IDs, *social registries*, beneficiary operations management systems, and (social protection] payment systems' (My italics). Lindert K. et al. (2020).
44 Kidd S. (2021).
45 Kidd S., Athias D. and Mohamud I. (2021).
46 Human Rights Watch (2023).
47 Kidd S., Athias D. and Mohamud I. (2021).
48 Kidd S., Athias D. and Mohamud I. (2021).

Chapter 13

1   IMF at https://www.imf.org/en/About/Factsheets/Sheets/2022/IMF-World-Bank-New.
2   Kidd S. (2018c).
3   UNICEF (2019b) and Kidd S. (2015). The child benefit is called the Child Money Programme (CMP). Export information from IMF (2017).
4   Kidd S. (2015).
5   This was called the Human Development Fund and was worth USD $90 per year in 2010. It was increased to USD $190 in 2011. Kidd S. (2015).
6   The government also introduced annual payments for retired people and persons with disabilities. These were worth USD $900 per year. Monthly payments of USD $50 for students were also introduced. Kidd S. (2015). Most pensions are paid through social insurance in Mongolia and the tax-financed pension is relatively small.
7   Sibun D. (2022a).
8   Kidd S. (2018b).
9   Kidd S. (2018b).
10 Sibun D. (2022a).
11 UNICEF at https://www.unicef.org/mongolia/stories/child-money-every-child.
12 Sibun D. and Seglah H. (2024).
13 IMF (2017).
14 Kidd S. (2018b).
15 UNICEF (2019c). The poverty-targeted programme was called the Monthly Benefit for Poor Families (MBPF).
16 Kidd S. (2018b).
17 IMF at https://www.imf.org/en/News/Articles/2017/11/09/pr17430-imf-staff-concludes-visit-to-the-kyrgyz-republic.
18 Kidd S. (2018a).
19 IMF at https://www.imf.org/en/News/Articles/2018/01/31/pr1834-imf-staff-concludes-visit-to-the-kyrgyz-republic.
20 USA Bureau of the Fiscal Service at https://www.fiscal.treasury.gov/reports-statements/financial-report/2017/government-financial-position-and-condition.html. By way of context in terms of debt sustainability, the stock of Kyrgyzstan central government debt as a proportion of GDP was 61 per cent in 2017 (from World Bank).
21 Kidd S. (2018b).
22 Kidd S. (2018c).

23 Kidd S. (2018b). The IMF internal evaluation is Independent Evaluation Office of the IMF (2017).
24 Letter from UN experts to Christine Lagarde, 21st December 2017, at https://www.ohchr.org/sites/default/files/Documents/Issues/Development/IEDebt/Open_Letter_IMF_21Dec2017.pdf. The UN experts were: Juan Pablo Bohoslavsky, Independent Expert on the effects of foreign debt, Hilal Elver, Special Rapporteur on the right to food, Catalina Devandas Aguilar, Special Rapporteur on the rights of persons with disabilities, Rosa Kornfeld-Matte, Independent Expert on the enjoyment of all human rights by older persons, Alda Facio, Chair of the Working Group on the issue of discrimination against women in law and in practice, Léo Heller, Special Rapporteur on the human rights to safe drinking water and sanitation and Maria Virginia Bras Gomes, Chair of the Committee on Economic, Social and Cultural Rights.
25 Letter from Christine Lagarde to UN experts, 31st January 2018, at https://www.ohchr.org/sites/default/files/Documents/Issues/Development/IEDebt/310118_IMF_response_open_letterSocialProtection.pdf.
26 Kidd S. (2018c).
27 See 1 minute 47 seconds in at https://www.youtube.com/watch?v=60m1jloFUIE.
28 Socialprotection.org at https://socialprotection.org/international-conference-universal-child-grants.
29 Margaret and Stephen were participating as part of a wider panel which included David Piachaud, Emeritus Professor of Social Policy, London School of Economics, Olli Kangas, Professor of Practice at the University of Turku and the Director of the Equal Society Research Programme at the Academy of Finland, Pau Vicent Mari Klose, Spanish High Commissioner on Child Poverty, Government of Spain and Kumar Phuyal, Member of National Planning Commission Government of Nepal. Socialprotection.org at https://socialprotection.org/international-conference-universal-child-grants.
30 World Bank at https://www.worldbank.org/en/news/feature/2014/11/19/un-modelo-de-mexico-para-el-mundo.
31 Harvey P. and Mohamed H. (2022).
32 Kidd S. et al. (2020).
33 This assumes 941,940 people 65 and over (from World Bank). It allows a generous 20 per cent additional costs for administration.
34 Kelley C. P. et al. (2015).
35 al-Khalidi A. et al. (2007).
36 Sibun D. (2022b).
37 IMF at https://www.imf.org/en/News/Articles/2015/09/28/04/52/mcs102908.
38 Harsch L. (2019).
39 Guillaume D. et al. (2011).
40 Baji Y. (2011).
41 Kidd S. (2018c). See also Public Services International at https://publicservices.international/resources/news/the-protests-in-iran-and-the-role-of-the-international-monetary-fund?id=7859&lang=en.
42 Karshenas M. and Tabatabai H. (2019) and UNICEF (2019a).
43 Inclusive Social Security Policy Forum at https://www.isspf-mena.com/. See, in particular, Kidd S. D. (2022).
44 ILO at https://www.ilo.org/resource/article/far-reaching-reforms-oman-set-new-benchmark-social-protection-region.

45 ILO at https://www.ilo.org/resource/news/ambitious-reforms-oman-pave-way-universal-social-protection.
46 See Performance Based Condition 2 on page 22 of World Bank (2022c).
47 Human Rights Watch (2023).
48 The pension can be expanded by reducing the age limit over time, and the child benefit can be expanded by, for example, allowing children to stay on the benefit as they increase in age.
49 ILO (2019).

Chapter 14

1 Hickey S. et al. (2020).
2 World Bank (2012c). Not all of these commitments will have been disbursed.
3 World Bank (2022a) and Manuel M. (2022). Total support from other major donors increased with COVID-19. The World Bank quote on its portfolio is somewhat contradicted by it saying in 2023 that it has 'committed $26 billion . . . helping 267 million people covered by social protection systems'. World Bank (2023b). This perhaps highlights the need for an accurate rolling inventory of World Bank support to social protection.
4 See also Ugo Gentilini on X, @Ugentilini.
5 Ravallion M. (2016).
6 ILO (2024) and for high-income countries see, for example, Jacques O. and Noël A. (2021).
7 Ravallion M. (2016).
8 Ravallion M. (2016).
9 They were previously known as Disbursement Linked Indicators.
10 Quoted in Sibun D. (2022a).
11 Hickey S. et al. (2020).
12 Ouma M. and Adesina J. (2018). Ouma and Adesina also argue that inserting technical experts and influencing through 'social learning' are important.
13 Mkandawire T. (2005).
14 Hickey S. et al. (2020).
15 The northern Uganda programme refers to the second phase of the World Bank's Northern Uganda Social Action Fund Project (NUSAF2), which started in 2009. The Kenya programme referred to is the Hunger Safety Net Programme (HSNP), supported by the Kenya Social and Economic Inclusion Project which includes a US$250 million World Bank loan.
16 See World Bank (2022a).
17 Sibun D. (2022a).
18 Mkandawire T. (2005).
19 Bance P. and Schnitzer P. (2021).
20 Grosh M. et al. (2022).
21 Human Rights Watch (2023).
22 Freeland N. (2022).
23 Rethinking Economics at https://www.rethinkeconomics.org/about/.
24 Raworth K. (2017).
25 Sibun D. (2022a).

26 Ravallion M. (2016).
27 Ravallion M. (2016).
28 Ravallion M. (2016).
29 Sibun D. (2022a).
30 Commission on Growth and Development (2008). The study looked at a specific group of thirteen countries – Botswana, Brazil, China, Hong Kong China, Indonesia, Japan, Republic of Korea, Republic of Malaysia, Malta, Oman, Singapore, Taiwan, China and Thailand – which in the last half century had grown 7 per cent a year or more for at least twenty-five years consecutive years.
31 Social protection is referred to as 'Social safety nets'.
32 There are many other recommendations including openness to trade, strong and effective government and greater investment in infrastructure.
33 Lindert P. H. (2004).
34 Ravallion M. (2016).
35 Cooper Ramo J. (2004).
36 Commission on Growth and Development (2008).
37 Economist Intelligence Unit (2023).
38 Ravallion M. (2016).
39 World Bank at https://www.worldbank.org/en/about/unit/brief/knowledge-bank.
40 As a starting point contributing countries could ask the World Bank to provide an accurate rolling inventory of tax-financed programmes it supports through financing, including the prevalence of social registries and poverty targeting through proxy means testing, as well as conditional cash transfers and workfare. This could be accompanied by properly facilitated discussions on how it all fits with World Bank rhetoric on universality. Perhaps this is in train already as part of the World Bank's plan to be a Knowledge Bank. It would be good to think so.
41 World Bank at https://ida.worldbank.org/en/about/contributor-countries.
42 World Bank trust funds are flexible pools of money that can be used for different activities within the remit of the fund. See World Bank at https://www.worldbank.org/en/programs/trust-funds-and-programs for more information.
43 Mkandawire T. (2005).
44 World Bank at https://www.worldbank.org/en/news/factsheet/2022/05/02/fact-sheet-an-adjustment-to-global-poverty-lines. US$2.15 per day is in 2017 Purchasing Power Parity terms that allows for price differences between countries.
45 This is at the programme design stage at least. During programme implementation, targeting errors may mean targets are harder to achieve.
46 United Nations at https://sdgs.un.org/goals.
47 Lindert K. et al. (2020), World Bank (2022a), Grosh M. et al. (2022) and World Bank (2024b).
48 World Bank (2025).
49 See the group's 2024 letter to World Bank and IMF Executive Directors at https://www.hrw.org/news/2024/04/15/letter-world-bank-and-imf-executive-directors-failings-promote-human-right-social.
50 Ravallion M. (2016).
51 Hickel J. (2020).
52 United Nations (2020).

Chapter 15

1. ILO (2024).
2. Kidd S., Axelsson Nycander G. and Seglah H. (2023). Though system design can vary significantly. For high-income countries, see, for example, Jacques O. and Noël A. (2021).
3. ILO (2024).
4. ILO (2024). Social protection spending excludes health.
5. ILO (2019). GDP per capita comparisons allow for inflation over time.
6. Greenslade M. (2018).
7. For a discussion of the difficulties of expanding the formal labour market, see for example Ridao-Cano C. et al. (2023). For a discussion of persistent labour market informality, see World Bank (2019f).
8. ILO (2024). Spending on social protection excluding health is Bangladesh 0.9 per cent of GDP, Ethiopia 1.0 and Nigeria 0.7.
9. Stephen's company Development Pathways has usefully illustrated how universal schemes can be gradually introduced, should countries wish to go down this route. See, for example, Kidd S., Mansoor N. and Barca A. (2023).
10. United Nations at https://sdgs.un.org/goals/goal1.
11. UN Women (2021).
12. Quoted by Office of the United Nations High Commissioner for Human Rights at https://www.ohchr.org/en/stories/2023/07/women-and-girls-deserve-full-access-social-security. Mahamane Cisse-Gouro is Director of the Human Rights Council and Treaty Mechanisms Division in UN Human Rights.
13. World Bank at https://www.worldbank.org/en/topic/poverty/overview. This is at 2017 Purchasing Power Parity. Purchasing Power Parity allows for differences in prices between countries.
14. World Bank at https://www.worldbank.org/en/topic/poverty.
15. World Food Programme at https://www.wfp.org/news/wfp-response-new-ipc-food-security-assessment-gaza.
16. Chancel L. et al. (2021).
17. ILO (2024).
18. Development Pathways (2022b).
19. See, for example, European Parliament (2022).
20. Global Partnership for Universal Social Protection to Achieve the Sustainable Development Goals, or USP2030, at https://usp2030.org/.
21. Council of the European Union at https://www.consilium.europa.eu/en/infographics/temporary-protection-displaced-persons/.
22. ILO (2021a).
23. Concern at https://www.concern.org.uk/news/these-12-countries-hosted-most-refugees-2023.
24. Manuel M. (2022).
25. IMF (2022a). This followed a 2019 strategy on social spending generally. IMF (2019).
26. World Bank (2022a).
27. World Bank (2025).
28. World Bank (2022b).

29 Sibun D. (2022a). Sudan received US$820 million for the Sudan Family Support Programme (SFSP) from the World Bank and other donors for the programme's first six months.
30 The Kosovo pension is funded by the government, like the near-universal pension in Fiji which the World Bank also supported.
31 Gentilini U. et al. (2020).
32 See Basic Income Earth Network at https://basicincome.org/, https://basicincome.org/news/2018/09/un-secretary-general-endorses-ubi/ and https://basicincome.org/news/2020/12/pope-francis-advocates-basic-income-in-new-book/. And World Governments Summit at https://www.worldgovernmentsummit.org/observer/articles/2017/detail/elon-musk-on-why-the-world-needs-a-universal-basic-income.
33 *The Guardian*, 8th June 2024, at https://www.theguardian.com/world/article/2024/jun/08/free-money-south-africa-floats-universal-basic-income-for-all . For information on the Universal Basic Income Coalition in South Africa see Black Sash at https://www.blacksash.org.za/universal-basic-income-coalition/.
34 Grosh M. et al. (2022).
35 Gentilini U. et al. (2020).
36 The issue is, if all households are guaranteed a basic income, will private firms be able to adjust wages down and still gain a sufficient supply of labour? And is this something a minimum wage can address?
37 United Nations at https://sdgs.un.org/goals/goal1.
38 Manuel M. (2022).
39 Gentilini U. (2022).
40 There was also an endorsement of social registries in helping to scale up programmes but, given their generally partial coverage and reliance on proxy means testing, it is not clear why. The World Bank concedes, 'even in some countries with comparatively mature systems, weaknesses in their social registries and payment systems undermined their ability to respond rapidly to the crisis, particularly in terms of covering new beneficiaries.' And the World Bank concedes elsewhere that proxy means testing is 'Insensitive to quick changes in well-being' Grosh M. et al. (2022).
41 ILO (2021d).
42 ILO et al. (2022).
43 Grosh M. et al. (2022).
44 Sibun D. (2022a).
45 Grosh M. et al. (2022).
46 World Bank (2019b).
47 Clarke D. J. and Dercon S. (2016).
48 See, for example, World Bank at https://www.worldbank.org/en/news/feature/2022/05/24/how-the-world-bank-supports-shock-responsive-social-protection-systems.
49 Freeland N. (2021b).
50 Bowen T. et al. (2020).
51 Bowen T. et al. (2020).
52 Sibun D. and Seglah H. (2024).
53 Mandon P. and Tesfaye Woldemichael M. (2023). For preliminary 2023 data on aid from OCED countries see OECD at https://www.oecd.org/en/topics/policy-issues/official-development-assistance-oda.html.
54 Hurley J. et al. (2018).
55 Horn S. et al. (2023).
56 Ravallion M. (2016).

57 United Nations Environment Fund at https://www.unep.org/news-and-stories/story/what-you-need-know-about-cop27-loss-and-damage-fund.
58 https://unfccc.int/news/cop29-un-climate-conference-agrees-to-triple-finance-to-developing-countries-protecting-lives-and
59 Lindert P. H. (2004). Lindert identifies income growth, population ageing and the fullness of democracy as the main determining factors for 'social transfer' spending levels for countries over time. 'Social transfers' are defined as tax-financed social protection plus health spending and housing subsidies.
60 Lindert P. H. (2004).
61 Hickey S. et al. (2020).
62 Ouma M. and Adesina J. (2018).
63 Kidd S. (2020). Stephen also considers conditional cash transfers, workfare and other aspects of social protection schemes supported by the World Bank and other donors as questionable on the grounds of race.
64 Chapter 5 in OECD (2023).
65 Khan T. (2020).
66 Amnesty International at https://www.amnesty.org/en/latest/news/2023/05/global-amnesty-international-calls-for-universal-social-protection-as-overlapping-crises-leave-hundreds-of-millions-facing-disaster/.
67 Razavi S. et al. (2022).
68 World Bank (2023a).
69 UN Trade and Development at https://sdgpulse.unctad.org/debt-sustainability/ and Guerrieri P. (2024).
70 Written evidence submitted to UK International Development Committee Inquiry into the issue of debt relief in low-income countries at https://committees.parliament.uk/writtenevidence/109449/html/.
71 On addressing debt see for example Fresnillo I. (2024).
72 ILO (2024).
73 Slim H. (2020).
74 If the government does not have an appropriate level of legitimacy, other support routes may be needed, for example humanitarian aid and support to civil society organizations (CSOs).
75 Khan T. (2020).
76 The full list of the five principles in the Paris Declaration is: *Ownership*: Developing countries set their own strategies for poverty reduction, to improve their institutions and tackle corruption. *Alignment*: Donor countries align behind these objectives and use local systems. *Harmonization*: Donor countries coordinate, simplify procedures and share information to avoid duplication. *Results*: Developing countries and donors shift focus to development results and results get measured. *Mutual accountability*: Donors and partners are accountable for development results. The Accra Agenda for Action in 2008 modified this list. OECD at https://www.oecd.org/dac/effectiveness/parisdeclarationandaccraagendaforaction.htm.
77 As a starting point contributing countries could ask the World Bank to provide an accurate rolling inventory of tax-financed programmes it supports through financing, including the prevalence of social registries and poverty targeting through proxy means testing, as well as conditional cash transfers and workfare. This could be accompanied by properly facilitated discussions on how it all fits with World Bank rhetoric on universality. Perhaps this is in train already as part of the World Bank's plan to be a Knowledge Bank. It would be good to think so.

78 Sibun D. (2022a). Daisy Sibun adds, 'Two UN Human Rights Council Special Procedures mandate holders suggested in 2012 that World Bank financing should support the human rights obligations of states. In a letter of response, the then General Counsel, Anne-Marie Leroy, and the Vice-President for the Africa Region, Makhtar Diop, stated that 'only economic considerations – meaning those that have a direct and obvious economic effect relevance to the Bank's work – can be taken into account in decisions by the Bank and its officers . . . in our view, your suggestion goes beyond the bounds of the Bank's institutional mandate'.
79 Mkandawire T. (2005).
80 Barrantes A. (2019).
81 Mkandawire T. (2005).
82 Grosh M. et al. (2022).
83 Stephen and colleagues give South Africa as an example of where targeting by income is done better through an unverified means test: 'whenever a person qualifies for a scheme, they can apply and be immediately selected, if eligible.' They point out, 'When individuals apply . . . they declare their income and the government believes that they are telling the truth . . . It is possible that some people could give a false income declaration and be accepted onto the scheme, but the evidence indicates that this is not a significant issue' Kidd S. et al. (2020). Stephen and his colleagues add, 'Brazil's Bolsa Família programme also uses an unverified means test but excludes 44 per cent of those who are eligible. This is because Brazil does not accept all of those who declare incomes below the income eligibility line and, instead, imposes quotas on each municipality.'
83 ILO (2011b).
84 Chang H. J. (2022). Narrated on the BBC, 20th October 2022.
85 F.S. Chadien, recorded in Debates of the Legislative Council of Mauritius, 25 June 1957. Quoted in Willmore L. (2003).
86 The UN estimates that if unpaid care work were assigned a monetary value, it would account for between 10 and 39 per cent of GDP, depending on the country. UNRISD (2010).
87 See Kidd S., Axelsson Nycander G. and Seglah H. (2023) for a discussion of the importance of using inclusive language when discussing social protection.
88 Khan T. (2020).

Annex

1 Coady D. et al. (2004).
2 Index results, which are the median average, are rounded to one decimal place. The review also looked at self-selection by take-up of food subsidies, which had a median index score of 1.0. In addition, the fact that the score for means testing isn't higher presumably reflects the difficulty of directly measuring incomes in lower-income environments.
3 Kidd S., Axelsson Nycander G. and Seglah H. (2023).

BIBLIOGRAPHY

Adato, M. and Roopnaraine, T. (2004). *A Social Analysis of the Red de Proteccion Social (RPS) in Nicaragua*. Washington DC: International Food Policy Research Institute.

Alatas, V., Banerjee, A., Hanna, R., Olken, B., A., Purnamasari, R. and Wai-Poi, M. (2013). *Self-targeting: Evidence from a Field Experiment in Indonesia*.

Alatas, V., Banerjee, A., Hanna, R., Olken, B. A., Purnamasari, R. and Wai-Poi, M. (2016). *Self Targeting: Evidence from a Field Experiment in Indonesia. Journal of Political Economy* 124 (2): 371–427.

al-Khalidi, A., Hoffmann, S. and Tanner, V. (2007). *Iraqi Refugees in the Syrian Arab Republic: A Field-Based Snapshot*. Washington DC: Brookings Institution.

Armitage, C. (2015). *The Residuals of Colonial Rule and Its Impact on the Process of Racialisation in Uganda*. Working paper. Centre for Ethnicity and Racism Studies, University of Leeds. Leeds, UK.

Ashcroft, V. (2015). *Poverty Reduction Support Facility: Independent Completion Report*.

Avram, S. and Popova, D. (2022). *Do Taxes and Transfers Reduce Gender Income Inequality? Evidence from Eight European Welfare States. Social Science Research* 102: 102644.

Baird, S., Ferreira, F., Özler, B. and Woolcock, M. (2014). *Conditional, Unconditional, and Everything in Between: A Systematic Review of the Effects of Cash Transfer Programmes on Schooling Outcomes. Journal of Development Effectiveness* 6 (1): 1–43.

Baird, S., Mcintosh, C. and Özler, B. (2011). *Cash or Condition? Evidence from a Cash Transfer Experiment. Quarterly Journal of Economics* 126 (4): 1709–53.

Baji, Y. (2011). *Muted Response to Iranian Subsidy Cuts. Institute for War and Peace Reporting*. 25 February 2011. London: Institute for War and Peace Reporting.

Bance, P. and Schnitzer, P. (2021). *Can the Luck of the Draw Improve Social Safety Nets?* World Bank Blog, 11 February 2021. Washington DC: World Bank.

Barrantes, A. (2017). *How Has National Ownership of Uganda's Senior Citizens' Grant Developed?* Development Pathways Blog, 5 December 2017. London: Development Pathways.

Barrantes, A. (2019). *The Golden Rule, Applied to Social Protection*. Development Pathways Blog. 10 October 2019. London: Development Pathways.

Basnet Bista, S., Standing, K., Parker, S. and Sharma, S. (2022). *Violence against Women and Girls in Humanitarian Crisis: Learning from the 2015 Nepal Earthquake. South Asian Journal of Law, Policy, and Social Research* 1 (2).

Benhassine, N., Devoto, S., Duflo, E., Dupas, P. and Pouliquen, V. (2013). *Turning a Shove into a Nudge? A 'Labelled Cash Transfer' for Education*. Cambridge: National Bureau of Economic Research.

Bennett, L., Ram Dahal, D. and Govindasamy, P. (2008). *Caste, Ethnic and Regional Identity in Nepal: Further Analysis of the 2006 Nepal Demographic and Health Survey*. Calverton: Macro International Inc.

Berhane, G., Hoddinott, J., Kumar, N. and Margolies, A. (2017). *The Productive Safety Net Programme in Ethiopia Impacts on Children's Schooling, Labour and Nutritional Status*.

Impact Evaluation Report 55. New Delhi: International Initiative for Impact Evaluation (3ie).

Bevins, V. (2017). *What the United States Did in Indonesia*. 20 October 2017. Washington DC: The Atlantic.

Bhakta Paudel, B. (2022). *Socio-Economic and Health Status of Elderly People in Nepal*. Journal of Development and Social Engineering 8 (2): 1–8.

Bonthuis, B. (2024). *An Assessment of the 2019 and 2020 Pension Reforms in Mexico*. IMF Working Paper 2024/53. Washington DC: International Monetary Fund.

Bowen, T., del Ninno, C., Andrews, C., Coll-Black, S., Gentilini, U., Johnson, K., Kawasoe, Y., Kryeziu, A., Maher, B. and Williams, A. (2020). *Adaptive Social Protection: Building Resilience to Shocks*. International Development in Focus. Washington DC: World Bank.

Brown, C., Ravallion, M. and van de Walle, D. (2018). *A Poor Means Test? Econometric Targeting in Africa*. Journal Of Development Economics 134: 109–24.

Bruenig, M. (2018). *How Capitalist Is Singapore Really?* People's Policy Project.

Bryan, G., Chowdhury, S., Mobarak, A. M., Morten, M. and Smits, J. (2023). *Encouragement and Distortionary Effects of Conditional Cash Transfers*. Journal of Public Economics 228: 105004.

Buller, A. M., Peterman, A., Ranganathan, M., Bleile, A., Hidrobo, M. and Heise, L. (2018). *A Mixed-Method Review of Cash Transfers and Intimate Partner Violence in Low- and Middle-Income Countries*. The World Bank Research Observer 33 (2): 218–58. Oxford: Oxford University Press.

Cahyadi, N., Hanna, R., Olken, B. A., Adi Prima, R., Satriawan, E. and Syamsulhakim, E. (2018). *Cumulative Impacts on Conditional Cash Transfer Programs: Experimental Evidence from Indonesia*. Cambridge: National Bureau of Economic Research.

Camacho, L. (2014). *The Effects of Conditional Cash Transfers on Social Engagement and Trust in Institutions: Evidence from Peru''s Juntos Programme*. Discussion Paper 24/2014. Bonn: German Development Institute.

Cameron, L. A. and Shah, M. (2011). *Can Mistargeting Destroy Social Capital and Stimulate Crime? Evidence from a Cash Transfer Program in Indonesia*. Discussion Paper 6736. Bonn: Institute for the Study of Labor (IZA).

Carruth, L. and Freeman, S. (2021). *Aid or Exploitation?: Food-for-work, Cash-for-work, and the Production of 'Beneficiary-workers' in Ethiopia and Haiti*. World Development 140: 105283.

Casey, B. H. and Mustafa, A. (2022). *COVID-19 Underlines the Problems of Savings-based Pensions: The Case of Kosovo and Chile*. London School of Economics Blog. 17 June 2022. London: London School of Economics.

Centre for Public Impact (2017). *What Drives Legitimacy in Government?* London: Centre for Public Impact.

Chancel, L., Piketty, T., Saez, E. and Zucman, G. (coordinators) (2021). *World Inequality Report 2022*. Paris: World Inequality Lab.

Chang, H. J. (2022). *Edible Economics: A Hungry Economist Explains the World*. London: Allen Lane.

Chirchir, R. and Farooq, S. (2016). *Single Registries and Social Registries: Clarifying the Terminological Confusion*. Pathways Perspectives 23. London: Development Pathways.

Clarke, D. J. and Dercon, S. (2016). *Dull Disasters? How Planning Ahead Will Make A Difference*. Oxford: Oxford University Press.

Coady, D., Grosh, M. and Hoddinott, J. (2004). *Targeting of Transfers in Developing Countries: Review of Lessons and Experience*. Washington DC: World Bank.

Commission on Growth and Development (2008). *The Growth Report: Strategies for Sustained Growth and Inclusive Development*. Washington DC: World Bank.

Cooper Ramo, J. (2004). *The Beijing Consensus*. London: The Foreign Policy Centre.

Cortes, A. (2020). *The Chilean October: Neoliberalism Was Born and will Die in Chile?* 23 January 2020. London: Open Democracy.

Dadap-Cantal, E., Fischer, A. and Ramos, C. (2021). *Targeting versus Social Protection in Cash Transfers in the Philippines: Reassessing a Celebrated Case of Social Protection. Critical Social Policy* 41 (3): 364–84.

del Ninno, C. and Mills, B. (2015). *Safety Nets in Africa: Effective Mechanisms to Reach the Poor and Most Vulnerable*. Washington DC: World Bank.

Department for International Development (DFID), Government of United Kingdom (2005). *Social Transfers and Chronic Poverty: Emerging Evidence and the Challenge Ahead*. DFID Practice Paper. London: Department for International Development (DFID), Government of UK.

Department for International Development (DFID), Government of United Kingdom (2006). *Eliminating World Poverty: Making Governance Work for the Poor*. DFID White Paper. London: Department for International Development (DFID), Government of UK.

Department for International Development (DFID), Government of United Kingdom (2007). *Development on the Record: DFID Annual Report 2007*. London: Department for International Development (DFID), Government of UK.

Department for International Development (DFID), Government of United Kingdom (2012). *DFID Annual Report and Accounts 2011–12*. London: Department for International Development (DFID), Government of UK.

Department for Work and Pensions, Government of United Kingdom (2022). *Income-related Benefits: Estimates of Take-up: Financial Year 2019 to 2020*. London: Department for Work and Pensions, Government of UK.

Deutsche Gesellschaft für Internationale Zusammenarbeit (GIZ) and University of Passau (2018). *Do Public Works Programmes Work? A Systematic Review of the Evidence in Africa and the MENA Region*. Bonn: Deutsche Gesellschaft für Internationale Zusammenarbeit (GIZ). Passau Germany: University of Passau. Policy brief from original paper by Beierl, S. and Grimm, M. (2017), University of Passau. Passau Germany: University of Passau.

Development Pathways (2022a). *Gender Equality and Human Rights*. London: Development Pathways.

Development Pathways (2022b). *Universal Social Security for the Realisation of Human Rights: A Collection of Briefs*. London: Development Pathways.

Dowden, R. (2008). *Africa: Altered States, Ordinary Miracles*. London: Portobello.

Drucza, K. (2016a). *Social Inclusion and Social Protection in Nepal*. PhD thesis, School of Humanities and Social Sciences. Melbourne: Deakin University.

Drucza, K. (2016b). *Social Inclusion in the Post-conflict State of Nepal: Donor Practice and the Political Settlement. Global Social Policy* 17 (1).

Dutta, P., Murgai, R., Ravallion, M. and van de Walle, D. (2014). *Right to Work? Assessing India's Employment Guarantee Scheme in Bihar. Equity and Development*. Equity and Development series. Washington DC: World Bank.

Economist Intelligence Unit (2021). *Democracy Index 2020: In Sickness and in Health?* London: Economist Intelligence Unit.

Economist Intelligence Unit (2023). *Democracy Index 2023: Age of Conflict*. London: Economist Intelligence Unit.

Elkins, C. (2005). *Imperial Reckoning: The Untold Story of Britain's Gulag in Kenya*. Austin: Holt McDougal.

European Parliament (2022). *The Future of Climate Migration*. Brussels: European Parliament.

European Union and UNICEF (2022). *Social Protection Budget Brief Update: FY 2022/23*. Kathmandu: UNICEF Nepal.

Federal Ministry of Labour and Social Affairs, Government of Germany (2022). *Just Transition: Make It Work Towards Decent and High Quality Work*. G7 Employment Ministerial Meeting Communiqué. Berlin: Federal Ministry of Labour and Social Affairs, Government of Germany.

Filmer, D., Friedman, J., Kandpal, E. and Onishi, J. (2018). *Cash Transfers, Food Prices, and Nutrition Impacts on Ineligible Children*. World Bank. Policy Research Working Paper 8377. Washington DC: World Bank.

Financial Services Commission, Mauritius (2003). *Annual Report*. Ebene: Financial Services Commission.

Fiszbein, A. and Schady, N. (2009). *Conditional Cash Transfers: reducing Present and Future Poverty*. Washington DC: World Bank.

Food and Agriculture Organization, Intergovernmental Authority on Development and Interpeace (2023). *Conflict, Climate Change, Food Security and Mobility in the Karamoja Cluster*. Rome: Food and Agriculture Organisation.

Foreign, Commonwealth and Development Office, Government of United Kingdom (2020). *Annual Review of Building Resilience in Ethiopia Programme*. London: Foreign, Commonwealth and Development Office, Government of the UK.

Foreign Commonwealth and Development Office, Government of United Kingdom (2022). *Annual Review of Expanding Social Protection Phase II*. London: Foreign, Commonwealth and Development Office, Government of the UK.

Foreign, Commonwealth and Development Office, Government of United Kingdom (2023). *International Development in a Contested World: Ending Extreme Poverty and Tackling Climate Change*. White Paper. London: Foreign, Commonwealth and Development Office, Government of the UK.

Freeland, N. (2013). *Mis-labelled Cash Transfers (MCTs)*. Pathways Perspectives 12. London: Development Pathways.

Freeland, N. (2018). *Poverty-targeting: The Social Protection Flaw?* Pathways Perspectives 26. London: Development Pathways.

Freeland, N. (2019). *Poor Targeting: A Response to Pathways' Paper on How Best to Reach Those in Poverty*. Development Pathways Blog. 19 March 2019. London: Development Pathways.

Freeland, N. (2021a). *Social Registry. . .or Regular Sophistry*. Development Pathways Blog. 23 June 2021. London: Development Pathways.

Freeland, N. (2021b). *The Pleonasm of Shock-responsive Social Protection*. Development Pathways Blog. 6 December 2021. London: Development Pathways.

Freeland, N. (2022). *Book Review: 'Revisiting Targeting in Social Assistance: A New Look at Old Dilemmas'*. Blog, 20 April 2022.

Fresnillo, I. (2024). *Debt Justice in 2024: Challenges and Prospects in a Full-blown Debt Crisis*. Brussels: European Network on Debt and Development (Eurodad).

Gammage, S., Alburquerque, T. and Durán, G. (2014). *Poverty, Inequality and Employment in Chile*. Conditions of Work and Employment series 46. Geneva: International Labour Organisation.

Gaspar, V., Poplawski-Ribeiro, M. and Yoo, J. (2023). *Global Debt Is Returning to Its Rising Trend*. International Monetary Fund Blog, 13 September 2023. Washington DC: International Monetary Fund.

Gelders, B. and Athias, D. (2019). *Quantitative Impact Analysis of Uganda's Senior Citizens Grant*. Kampala: Ministry of Gender, Labour and Social Development, Government of Uganda.

Gentilini, U. (2018). *What Lessons for Social Protection from Universal Health Coverage?* World Bank Blog. 22 August 2018. Washington DC: World Bank.

Gentilini, U. (2022). *Cash Transfers in Pandemic Times: Evidence, Practices, and Implications from the Largest Scale Up in History*. Washington DC: World Bank.

Gentilini, U., Grosh, M., Jamele Rigolini, J. and Yemtsov, R., eds. (2020). *Exploring Universal Basic Income: A Guide to Navigating Concepts, Evidence, and Practices*. Washington DC: World Bank.

Global Partnership for Universal Social Protection (2019). *Together to Achieve Universal Social Protection by 2030 (USP2030) – A Call to Action*. Global Partnership for Universal Social Protection.

Gourevitch, P. (2000). *We Wish to Inform You that Tomorrow We Will Be Killed With Our Families*. Picador.

Government of Fiji (2016). *Post-Disaster Needs Assessment: Tropical Cyclone Winston, February 20, 2016*. Suva: Government of Fiji.

Government of Malawi (2022). *Malawi Social Cash Transfer Programme Strategic Plan: 2022 – 2027*. Lilongwe: Government of Malawi.

Greenslade, M. (2018). *A Progressive Moment: Social Protection's Rationale Identified as Citizenship, not Charity at IMF/London School of Economics Event*. Development Pathways Blog. 8 November 2018. London: Development Pathways.

Grigoli, F. and Robles, A. (2017). *Inequality Overhang*. International Monetary Fund Working Paper 17/76. Washington DC: International Monetary Fund.

Grosh, M. E. and Baker, J. L. (1995). *Proxy Means Tests for Targeting Social Programs: Simulations and Speculation*. Living Standards Measurement Study Working Paper No. 118. Washington DC: World Bank.

Grosh, M., del Ninno, C., Tesliuc, E. and Ouerghi, A. (2008). *For Protection and Promotion: The Design and Implementation of Effective Safety Nets*. Washington DC: World Bank.

Grosh, M., Leite, P., Wai-Poi, M. and Tesliuc, E., eds. (2022). *Revisiting Targeting in Social Assistance: A New look at Old Dilemmas*. Washington DC: World Bank.

Grown, C. and Gupta, G. R. (2005). *Taking Action: Achieving Gender Equality and Empowering Women*. Task Force on Education and Gender Equality, UN Millennium Project.

Guerrieri, P. (2024). *Managing Debt in the Developing World*. 4 February 2024. Rome: Aspenia online.

Gugushvilia, D. and Laenena, T. (2021). *Two decades after Korpi and Palme's "paradox of redistribution": What have we learned so far and where do we take it from here? Journal of International and Comparative Social Policy* 37 (2): 112–27.

Guillaume, D., Zytek, R. and Reza Farzin, M. (2011). *Iran–The Chronicles of the Subsidy Reform*. International Monetary Fund Working Paper 11/167. Washington DC: International Monetary Fund.

Hanlon, J., Barrientos, A. and Hulme, D. (2010). *Just Give Money to the Poor*. Boulder: Kumarian Press.

Harker, R. (2022). *Pensions: International Comparisons*. UK House of Commons library. London: UK House of Commons.

Harsch, L. (2019). *Social Protection in the Syrian Arab Republic*. Beirut: United Nations Economic and Social Commission for Western Asia (UNESCWA).

Harvey, P. and Mohamed, H. (2022). *The Politics of Donor and Government Approaches to Social Protection and Humanitarian Policies for Assistance During Crises*. London: Department for International Development (DFID), Government of UK.

Hickel, J. (2020). *Apartheid in the World Bank and the IMF*. Al Jazeera Opinions. 26 November 2020. Doha: Al Jazeera.

Hickey, S., Lavers, T., Nino-Zarazua, M. and Seekings, J. (2020). *The Politics of Social Protection in Eastern and Southern Africa*. Oxford: Oxford University Press.

Higgins, S. and Lustig, N. (2016). *Can a Poverty-reducing and Progressive Tax and Transfer System Hurt the Poor? Journal of Development Economics* 122: 63–75.

Holmes, R. and Upadhya, S. (2009). *The Role of Cash Transfers in Post-Conflict Nepal*. London: Overseas Development Institute (ODI).

Holzmann, R. and Jorgensen, S. (2000). *Social Risk Management: A New Conceptual Framework for Social Protection and Beyond*. Washington DC: World Bank.

Horn, S., Parks, B. C., Reinhart, C. M. and Trebesch, C. (2023). *China as an International Lender of Last Resort*. Policy Research Working Paper 10380. Washington DC: World Bank.

Howson, K. (2023). *Three Reasons Community-based Targeting is a Threat to Social Stability*. Development Pathways Blog. 5 January 2023. London: Development Pathways.

Human Rights Watch (2023). *Automated Neglect: How The World Bank's Push to Allocate Cash Assistance Using Algorithms Threatens Rights*. New York: Human Rights Watch.

Hurley, J., Morris, S. and Portelance, G. (2018). *Examining the Debt Implications of the Belt and Road Initiative from a Policy Perspective*. Policy Paper 121. London: Centre for Global Development.

Independent Commission for Aid Impact, United Kingdom (2017). *The effects of DFID's cash transfer programmes on poverty and vulnerability*. London: Independent Commission for Aid Impact.

Independent Evaluation Group (2006). *Pension Reform and the Development of Pension Systems: An Evaluation of World Bank Assistance*. Washington DC: World Bank.

Independent Evaluation Office of the International Monetary Fund (2017). *The IMF and Social Protection*. Washington DC: International Monetary Fund.

Inter-American Commission on Human Rights, Organisation of American States (2009). *Indigenous and Tribal People's Rights Over Their Ancestral Lands and Natural Resources: Norms and Jurisprudence of the Inter-American Human Rights System*. Washington DC: Inter-American Commission on Human Rights.

Inter-American Court of Human Rights (IACHR) (2005). *Case of the Yakye Axa Indigenous Community v. Paraguay: Judgment of June 17, 2005*. San José Costa Rica: Inter-American Court of Human Rights.

International Centre for Integrated Mountain Development (ICIMOD), Global Facility for Disaster Reduction and Recovery and World Bank (2011). *Glacial Lakes and Glacial Lake Outburst Floods in Nepal*. Kathmandu: International Centre for Integrated Mountain Development (ICIMOD).

International Labour Organisation (2009). *Opening Address by Juan Somavia Director-General of the International Labour Office to the Tripartite Meeting of Experts on*

Strategies for the Extension of Social Security Coverage. Geneva: International Labour Organisation.
International Labour Organisation (2011a). *International Labour Conference, 100th Session, 2011 Report VI: Social Security for Social Justice and a Fair Globalization*. Geneva: International Labour Organisation.
International Labour Organisation (2011b). *Social Protection Floors for Social Justice and a Fair Globalization. Report IV (1)*. Geneva: International Labour Organisation.
International Labour Organisation (2012). *R202 Social Protection Floors Recommendation, 2012 (No. 202)*. Geneva: International Labour Organisation.
International Labour Organisation (2019a). *100 Years of Social Protection: The Road to Universal Social Protection Systems and Floors. Volume 1: 50 Country Cases*. Geneva: International Labour Organisation.
International Labour Organisation (2019b). *Universal Social Protection for Human Dignity, Social Justice and Sustainable Development*. Report on the General Survey on the implementation of the Social Protection Floors Recommendation, 2012 (No. 202). Geneva: International Labour Organisation.
International Labour Organisation (2021a). *Extending Social Protection to Migrant Workers, Refugees and Their Families: A Guide for Policymakers and Practitioners*. Geneva: International Labour Organisation.
International Labour Organisation (2021b). *Mapping of the National Social Protection System in Ethiopia, including Social Health Protection*. Geneva: International Labour Organisation.
International Labour Organisation (2021c). *Resolution Concerning the Second Recurrent Discussion on Social Protection (Social Cecurity)*. Geneva: International Labour Organisation.
International Labour Organisation (2021d). *World Social Protection Report 2020-2022: Social Protection at the Crossroads – in Pursuit of a Better Future*. Geneva: International Labour Organisation.
International Labour Organisation (2024). *World Social Protection Report 2024–26: Universal Social Protection for Climate Action and a Just Transition*. Geneva: International Labour Organisation.
International Labour Organisation and World Bank (2015). *Launch of the World Bank Group and ILO Universal Social Protection Initiative, Calling the Attention of World Leaders to the Importance of Universal Social Protection*. Geneva: International Labour Organisation.
International Labour Organisation and World Health Organisation (2009). *Social Protection Floor Initiative: The Sixth Initiative of the Ceb on the Global Financial and Economic Crisis and Its Impact on the Work of the UN System. Manual and Strategic Framework for Joint UN Country Operations*. Geneva: International Labour Organisation.
International Labour Organisation, Food and Agriculture Organisation and UNICEF (2022). *UN Collaboration on Social Protection: Reaching Consensus on How to Accelerate Social Protection Systems-Building*. Geneva: International Labour Organisation. Rome: Food and Agriculture Organisation. New York: UNICEF.
International Monetary Fund (IMF) (2017). *Mongolia: 2017 Article IV Consultation and Request for an Extended Arrangement Under the Extended Fund Facility*. Washington DC: International Monetary Fund.
International Monetary Fund (IMF) (2019). *A Strategy for IMF Engagement on Social Spending*. IMF Policy Paper 2019/016. Washington DC: International Monetary Fund.

International Monetary Fund (IMF) (2022a). *IMF Engagement on Social Safety Net Issues in Surveillance and Program Work.* Fiscal Affairs Department and Strategy, Policy, and Review Department. Washington DC: International Monetary Fund.

International Monetary Fund (IMF) (2022b). *Mauritius: Staff Report for the 2022 Article IV Consultation.* Washington DC: International Monetary Fund.

International Social Security Association (ISSA) (2013). *Social Security Coverage Extension in the BRICS: A Comparative Study on the Extension of Coverage in Brazil, the Russian Federation, India, China and South Africa.* Geneva: International Social Security Association (ISSA).

International Social Security Association (ISSA) (2023). *Social Pensions in the Americas: Recent Developments.* 19 October 2023. Geneva: International Social Security Association (ISSA).

Jacques, O. and Noël, A. (2021). *Targeting within Universalism. Journal of European Social Policy* 31 (1).

Jørgensen, J. J. (1981). *Uganda: A Modern History.* London: Routledge.

Karshenas, M. and Tabatabai, H. (2019). *Universal Basic Income by Default: Lessons from Iran's 'Cash Subsidy' Programme.* In M. Torry (ed.), *Palgrave International Handbook of Basic Income.* First edn. London: Palgrave Macmillan.

Kelley, C. P., Mohtadi, S., Canec, M. A., Seager, R. and Kushnir, Y. (2015). *Climate Change in the Fertile Crescent and Implications of the Recent Syrian Drought. Proceedings of the National Academy of Sciences (PNAS)* 112 (11): 3241–46.

Khan, T. (2020). *Who Speaks for the Global South Recipients of Aid?* 7 July 2020. Global Dashboard.

Kharas, H. and Dooley, M. (2022). *The Evolution of Global Poverty, 1990–2030.* Washington DC: Brookings Institution.

Kidd, S. (1997). *The Working Conditions of Indigenous People in the Chaco.* Published in Antislavery International (1996). *Enslaved Peoples in the 1990s: Indigenous Peoples, Debt Bondage and Human Rights.* London: Anti-slavery International. Copenhagen: International Work Group for Indigenous Affairs.

Kidd, S. (2015). *The Political Economy of 'Targeting' of Social Security Schemes.* Pathways Perspectives 19. London: Development Pathways.

Kidd, S. (2016). *Universal Social Protection: The ILO Attempt, Once More, to Persuade the World Bank to Commit to Inclusivity and the Right to Social Security for All.* Development Pathways Blog. 4 October 2016. London: Development Pathways.

Kidd, S. (2018a). *Free at Last! Kyrgyzstan's Liberation from Poor Relief, with Universal Social Security for Children.* Development Pathways Blog. 16 January 2018. London: Development Pathways.

Kidd, S. (2018b). *Mongolia and Kyrgyzstan Lose Out in Their Struggle with the IMF Over the Targeting of Child Benefits.* Development Pathways Blog. 21 February 2018. London: Development Pathways.

Kidd, S. (2018c). *Pro-poor or Anti-poor? The World Bank and IMF's Approach to Social Protection.* London: Bretton Woods Project.

Kidd, S. (2019). *The Demise of Mexico's Prospera Programme: A Tragedy Foretold.* Development Pathways Blog. 6 February 2019. London: Development Pathways.

Kidd, S. (2020). *Black Lives Matter – in Social Protection and International Development.* Development Pathways Blog. 25 June 2020. London: Development Pathways.

Kidd, S. (2021). *Love and Its Entanglements among the Enxet of Paraguay: Social and Kinship Relations within a Market Economy.* Lanham: Rowman and Littlefield.

Kidd, S. and Athias, D. (2020). *Hit and Miss: An Assessment of Targeting Effectiveness in Social Protection With Additional Analysis*. Working paper. London: Development Pathways. Uppsala: Act Church of Sweden.

Kidd, S., Athias, D. and Mohamud, I. (2021). *Social Registries: A Short History of Abject Failure*. Working paper. London: Development Pathways. Uppsala: Act Church of Sweden.

Kidd, S., Athias, D., Nastasi, S. and Pop, A. (2022). *Inequality and Social Security in the Asia-pacific Region*. New York: United Nations Development Programme (UNDP).

Kidd, S., Athias, D. and Tran, A. (2021). *Universal Child Benefits: Transforming the Lives of Children across South Asia*. Working Paper 2021-01. Kathmandu: UNICEF South Asia.

Kidd, S., Axelsson Nycander, G. and Seglah, H. (2023). *Advocating for Universal Social Security: How to Win Hearts and Minds*. London: Development Pathways. Uppsala: Act Church of Sweden.

Kidd, S., Axelsson Nycander, G., Tran, A. and Cretney, M. (2020). *The Social Contract and the Role of Universal Social Security in Building Trust in Government*. Working paper. London: Development Pathways. Uppsala: Act Church of Sweden.

Kidd, S. and Calder, R. (2011). *Conditional Cash Transfers: Their Relevance for Nepal*. London: Development Pathways. London: Department for International Development (DFID), Government of UK.

Kidd, S. and Calder, R. (2012). *The Zomba Conditional Cash Transfer Experiment: An Assessment of Its Methodology*. Pathways Perspectives 6. London: Development Pathways.

Kidd, S., Calder, R. and Wylde, E. (2011). *Assessing Targeting Options for Nepal's Social Grants: What Does the Evidence Tell Us?* London: Development Pathways. London: Department for International Development (DFID), Government of UK.

Kidd, S., Gelders, B. and Bailey-Athias, D. (2017). *Exclusion by Design: An Assessment of the Effectiveness of the Proxy Means Test Poverty Targeting Mechanism*. Social Protection Department. Geneva: International Labour Organisation.

Kidd, S. and Huda, K. (2013). *Bolsa Unfamiliar*. Pathways Perspectives 9. London: Development Pathways.

Kidd, S., Mansoor, N. and Barca, A. (2023). *An Affordable and Feasible Path to Universal Social Security using the Principle of Universality*. London: Development Pathways. Uppsala: Act Church of Sweden. London: Action Against Hunger.

Kidd, S. and Wylde, E. (2011). *Targeting the Poorest: An Assessment of the Proxy Means Test Methodology*. Canberra: Australian AID (AusAID).

Kidd, S. D. (2022). *Smoke and Mirrors: The Role of World Bank and IMF in Shaping Social Security Policy in the MENA Region*. Working Paper 4. Inclusive Social Security Policy Forum.

Knox-Vydmanov, C., Soni, N., Satriana, S. and Attenborough, J. (2023). *From Historical Trends to Investment Pathways: Social Protection Expenditure in Pacific Island Countries and Timor-Leste*. Canberra: Australian AID (AusAID).

Korpi, W. and Palme, J. (1998). *The Paradox of Redistribution and Strategies of Equality: Welfare State Institutions, Inequality, and Poverty in the Western Countries*. American Sociological Review 63 (5): 661–87.

Kovski, N., Pilkauskas, N. V., Michelmore, K. and Luke Shaefer, H. (2023). *Unconditional Cash Transfers and Mental Health Symptoms among Parents with Low Incomes: Evidence from the 2021 Child Tax Credit*. SSM – Population Health 22: 101420.

Kwame Sundaram, J. (2020). *Thandika Mkandawire, Pan-Africanist Par Excellence.* International Development Economic Associates Ltd Blog. 17 April 2020. London: International Development Associates Ltd.

Le, T.-H., Bui, M.-T. and Uddin, G. S. (2022). *Economic and Social Impacts of Conflict: A Cross-country Analysis. Economic Modelling* 115: 105980.

Leisering, L. (2019). *The Global Rise of Cash Transfers: How States and International Organisations Constructed a New Instrument for Combating Poverty.* Oxford: Oxford University Press.

Leite, P. (2014). *Effective Targeting for the Poor and Vulnerable.* Social Protection and Labor Technical Note 6. Washington DC: World Bank.

Leite, P., Karippacheril, T. G., Sun, C., Jones, T. and Lindert, K. (2017). *Social Registries for Social Assistance and Beyond: A Guidance Note & Assessment Tool.* Social Protection and Labor Discussion Paper 1704. Washington DC: World Bank.

Leon Solano, R., Alaref, J., Dorfman, M., Majoka, Z., Amir Sabbih, M. and Mata Lorenzo, E. (2024). *Rethinking Social Protection in South Asia: Toward Progressive Universalism.* Washington DC: World Bank.

Lindert, K., Karippacheril, T. G., Rodríguez Caillava, I. and Nishikawa Chávez, K., eds. (2020). *Sourcebook on the Foundations of Social Protection Delivery Systems.* Washington DC: World Bank.

Lindert, K., Leite, P., George Karippacheril, T. and Rodriguez Caillava, I. (2017). *For Social Programs, Social Registries Serve as a Tool for Inclusion.* World Bank Blog. 21 November 2017. Washington DC: World Bank.

Lindert, P. H. (2004). *Growing Public: Social Spending and Economic Growth Since the Eighteenth Century.* Cambridge: Cambridge University Press.

Loeser, J., Özler, B. and Premand, P. (2021). *What Have We Learned about Cash Transfers?* World Bank Blog. 10 May 2021. World Bank: Washington DC.

Luis Fiori, J. (2019). *The Myths about Pinochet's Chile that Persist in Brazil Today.* 26 August 2019. London: Open Democracy.

Madhav Thakur, S., Cerra, V., Horváth, B. and Keen, M. (2003). *Sweden's Welfare State: Can the Bumblebee Keep Flying?* Washington DC: International Monetary Fund.

Mandon, P. and Tesfaye Woldemichael, M. (2023). *Has Chinese aid benefited recipient countries?* Brookings Institution commentary. 6 April 2023. Washington DC: Brookings Institution.

Manuel, M. (2022). *Financing Social Protection: Domestic and External Options in Low-income Countries.* Bonn and Berlin: Friedrich Ebert Stiftung.

McCord, A. (2008). *A typology for Public Works Programming.* Natural Resource Perspectives 121. London: Overseas Development Institute (ODI).

McCord, A. and Slater, R. (2009). *Overview of Public Works Programmes in Sub-Saharan Africa.* London: Overseas Development Institute (ODI).

McCord, A., Lieuw-Kie-Song, M., Tsukamoto, M., Tessem, T. and Donnges, C. (2021). *100 Years of Public Works in the ILO.* Geneva: International Labour Organisation.

McGregor, K. E. (2009). *The Indonesian Killings of 1965–1966.* 4 August 2009. SciencesPo.

Meade, J. (1961). *The Economics and Social Structure of Mauritius – Report to the Government of Mauritius.* Malton: Methuen.

Microsave Consulting (2019). *Report on Findings of Impact Evaluation of Program Keluarga Harapan (PKH).* Lucknow: Microsave Consulting.

Milanovic, B. (2019). *Chile: The Poster Boy of Neoliberalism who Fell from Grace.* Global Policy Blog. 30 October 2019. Durham UK: Global Policy, Durham University.

Miller, C., Tsoka, M. and Reichert, K. (2008). *Impact Evaluation Report: External Evaluation of the Mchinji Social Cash Transfer Pilot*. Boston: Centre for International Health and Development, Boston University.

Ministry of Economic Planning and Development, Government of Malawi (2022). *Mid-Term Review of the Malawi National Social Support Programme II: 2018-2021*. Lilongwe: Ministry of Economic Planning and Development, Government of Malawi.

Ministry of Gender, Children, Disability and Social Welfare, Government of Malawi (2016). *Realising Income Security in Old Age: A Study Into the Feasibility of a Universal Old Age Pension in Malawi*. Lilongwe: Ministry of gender, Childre, Disability and Social Welfare, Government of Malawi.

Ministry of Gender, Labour and Social Development, Government of Uganda (2015). *The National Social Protection Policy: Income Security and Dignified Lives for All*. Kampala: Ministry of Gender, Labour and Social Development, Government of Malawi.

Ministry of Gender, Labour and Social Development, Government of Uganda (2019). *Uganda Social Protection Sector Review 2019*. Kampala: Ministry of Gender, Labour and Social Development, Government of Malawi.

Ministry of Labour and Employment, Government of Nepal and International Labour Organisation (2017). *An Analytical Briefing on the Social Security Sector in Nepal*. Kathmandu: Ministry of Labour and Employment, Government of Nepal. Geneva: International Labour Organisation.

Ministry of Labour, Employment and Youth Development, Government of Tanzania in Collaboration with HelpAge International (2010). *Achieving Income Security in Old Age for All Tanzanians: A Study Into the Feasibility of a Universal Social Pension*. Dar es Salaam: Ministry of Labour, Employment and Youth Development. London: HelpAge International.

Ministry of Labour and Social Protection, Government of Kenya (2017). *Kenya Social Protection Sector Review*. Nairobi: Ministry of Labour and Social Protection, Government of Kenya.

Ministry of Social Welfare, Women and Poverty Alleviation, Government of Fiji (2011). *Fiji National Policy on Ageing 2011–2015*. Suva: Ministry of Social Welfare, Women and Poverty Alleviation, Government of Fiji. Suva: United Nations Population Fund (UNFPA) Pacific Sub-Regional Office.

Mkandawire, T. (2005). *Targeting and Universalism in Poverty Reduction*. Geneva: United Nations Research Institute for Social Development (UNRISD).

Mulyani Indrawati, S., Nazara, S., Anas, T., Fajri Ananda, C. and Verico, K., eds. (2022). *Keeping Indonesia Safe from the COVID-19 Pandemic: Lessons Learnt from the National Economic Recovery Programme*. Singapore: ISEAS – Yusof Ishak Institute.

Munoz Boudet, A. M., Buitrago, P., Leroy de la Briere, B., Newhouse, D., Rubiano Matulevich, E., Scott, K. and Suarez-Becerra, P. (2018). *Gender Differences in Poverty and Household Composition through the Life-cycle: A Global Perspective*. Policy Research Working Paper 8360. Washington DC: World Bank.

Mvukiyehe, E. (2018). *What Are We Learning About the Impacts of Public Works Programs on Employment and Violence? Early Findings from Ongoing Evaluations in Fragile States*. World Bank Blog. 16 April 2018. Washington DC: World Bank.

Nally, D. P. (2008). *That Coming Storm: The Irish Poor Law, Colonial Biopolitics, and the Great Famine*. Annals of the Association of American Geographers 98 (3): 714–41.

Narsey Lal, P., Rita, R. and Khatri, N. (2009). *Economic Costs of the 2009 Floods in the Fiji Sugar Belt and Policy Implications*. Gland Switzerland: International Union for Conservation of Nature and Natural Resources (IUCN).

National Treasury and Economic Planning, Government of Kenya (2024). *Budget Statement Financial Year 2024/25*. Nairobi: National Treasury and Economic Planning, Government of Kenya.

Office of the United Nations High Commissioner for Human Rights (OHCHR). (n.d.). *OHCHR's Overview on the Right to Social Security/Social Protection*. Geneva: Office of the United Nations High Commissioner for Human Rights (OHCHR).

Office of the United Nations High Commissioner for Human Rights (OHCHR) (2023). *Women and Girls Deserve Full Access to Social Security*. 21 July 2023. Geneva: Office of the United Nations High Commissioner for Human Rights (OHCHR).

Office of the Vice President of the Government of Indonesia. (2015). *Indonesia's Unified Database for Social Protection Programmes: Management Standards*. Jakarta: Office of the Vice President of the Government of Indonesia.

Office of the Vice President of the Government of Indonesia. (2018). *The Future of the Social Protection System in Indonesia: Social Protection For All*. Jakarta: Office of the Vice President of the Government of Indonesia.

Organisation for Economic Cooperation and Development (OECD). (2009). *Social Protection, Poverty Reduction and Pro-Poor Growth*. Policy Guidance Note. Paris: Organisation for Economic Cooperation and Development (OECD).

Organisation for Economic Cooperation and Development (OECD) (2023). *Development Cooperation Report 2023: Debating the Aid System*. Paris: Organisation for Economic Cooperation and Development (OECD).

Ortiz, I., Chowdhury, A., Durán-Valverde, F., Muzaffar, T. and Urban, S. (2019). *Handbook on Fiscal Space for Social Protection: Assessing Financing Options*. Geneva: International Labour Organisation.

Ortiz, I., Cummins, M. and Karunanethy, K. (2017). *Fiscal Space for Social Protection: Options to Expand Social Investments in 187 Countries*. Geneva: International Labour Organisation. New York: UNICEF. New York: UN Women.

Ortiz, I., Durán-Valverde, F., Urban, S. and Wodsak, V., eds. (2018). *Reversing Pension Privatizations: Rebuilding public pension systems in Eastern Europe and Latin America*. Geneva: International Labour Organisation.

Orton, I. (2014). *Conditional Cash Transfers and the Human Right to Social Security*. 27 May 2014. Social Protection and Human Rights Commentary.

Ouma, M. and Adesina, J. (2018). *Solutions, Exclusion and Influence: Exploring Power Relations in the Adoption of Social Protection Policies in Kenya*. Critical Social Policy 39 (3): 376–395.

Overseas Development Institute (ODI), (2016). *Understanding the Impact of Cash Transfers: The Evidence*. London: Overseas Development Institute (ODI).

Özler, B. and Ferreira, F. (2011a). *Conditions Work! But Are They a Good Thing? (Part I)*. World Bank Blog. 28 October 2011. Washington DC: World Bank.

Özler, B. and Ferreira, F. (2011b). *Conditions Work! But Are They a Good Thing? (Part II)*. World Bank Blog. 1 November 2011. World Bank: Washington DC.

Özler, B., Mcintosh, C. and Baird, S. (2010). *Cash Or Condition? Evidence From A Randomized Cash Transfer Program*. Washington DC: World Bank.

Palacios, R. J. (2016). *Universal Social protection: Universal Old-Age and Disability Pensions, and other Universal Allowances in Nepal*. Washington DC: World Bank. Geneva: International Labour Organisation. Addis Ababa: African Union. Paris: Expertise France. Room: Food and Agriculture Organisation. New York: UNICEF. Brussels: EU Social Protection Systems Programme. Brasilia: International Policy Centre for Inclusive Growth. New York: United Nations Development Programme

(UNDP). Bonn: Deutsche Gesellschaft für Internationale Zusammenarbeit (GIZ). Washington DC: Inter-Americanm Development Bank. London: HelpAge International. London: Save the Children.

Peck, J. and Theodore, N. (2015). *Fast Policy: Experimental Statecraft at the Thresholds of Neoliberalism*. Minneapolis USA: University of Minnesota Press.

Porisky, A., Shariff Mohamed, T. and Mutinda Muthui, P. (2023). *Kenya's 'Universal' Social Pension: The Politics of Registration in Marsabit County*. World Development 164: 106164.

Prasad Adhikari, T., Bahadur Thapa, F., Tamrakar, S., Buda Magar, P., Hagen-Zanker, J. and Babajanian, B. (2014). *How Does Social Protection Contribute to Social Inclusion in Nepal? Evidence from the Child Grant in the Karnali Region*. London: Overseas Development Institute (ODI).

Prencipe, L., Houweling, T. A. J., van Lenthe, F. J. and Palermo, T. (2021). *Do Conditional Cash Transfers Improve Mental Health? Evidence From Tanzania's Governmental Social Protection Program*. Journal of Adolescent Health 69 (5): 797–805.

Pritchett, L. (2005). *The Political Economy of Targeted Safety Nets*. World Bank. Social Protection Discussion Paper 0501. Washington DC: World Bank.

Pruce, K. (2019). *Investigating the Politics of Global Policy Transfer: The Case of Social Protection in Zambia*. PhD thesis. Manchester UK: University of Manchester.

Ravallion, M. (2016). *The World Bank: Why It Is Still Needed and Why It Still Disappoints*. Journal of Economic Perspectives 30 (1): 77–94.

Raworth, K. (2017). *Doughnut Economics*. London: Random House.

Razavi, S., Behrendt, C., Nesterenko, V., Orton, I., Peyron Bista, C., Ramos Chavez, A., Schwarzer, H., Stern-Plaza, M. and Wodsak, V. (2022). *Building Universal Social Protection Systems for All: What Role for Targeting?* Socialprotection.org Blog. 2 June 2022. Socialprotection.org.

Richterman, A., Millien, C., Bair, E. F., Jerome, G., Dimitri Suffrin, J. C., Behrman, J. B. and Thirumurthy, H. (2023). *The effects of cash transfers on adult and child mortality in low- and middle-income countries*. Nature 618: 575–82.

Ridao-Cano, C., Moosa, D., Pallares-Miralles, M. and Pinxten, J. (2023). *Built to Include: Reimagining Social Protection in the Middle East and North Africa*. Washington DC: World Bank.

Sabates-Wheeler, R., Lind, J., and Hoddinott, J. (2020). *Graduation after 10 Years of Ethiopia's Productive Safety Net Programme: Surviving but Still not Thriving*. Development Policy Review 39 (4): 511–31.

Seekings, J. (2016). *The Introduction of Old Age Pensions in Zanzibar*. Cape Town South Africa: University of Cape Town.

Sengupta, A. (2019). *All Work and No Pay: The Invisibilisation of Women's Labour in Public Works Programmes*. Development Pathways Blog. 8 March 2019. London: Development Pathways.

Sepúlveda Carmona, M. (2009). *Promotion and Protection of all Human Rights, Civil, Political, Economic, Social and Cultural Rights, including the Right to Development*. Geneva: United Nations Human Rights Council.

Shamil: Technical Assistance for Inclusive Social Protection (2024). *Multi-tiered, Comprehensive, Social Security Systems: A Brief Description*. Shamil Briefs: Paper 2. London: Foreign, Commonwealth and Development Office, Government of UK.

Sibun, D. (2022a). *Can Leopards Change Their Spots? A Critical Analysis of the World Bank's and ILO's Approach to Universality*. London: Development Pathways. Uppsala: Act Church of Sweden. London: Action Against Hunger.

Sibun, D. (2022b). *Inclusive Social Security and the Social Contract: Overcoming Instability and Building Trust in the MENA Region.* Working Paper Series: Shifting the Paradigm 5. Inclusive Social Security Policy Forum.

Sibun, D. and Seglah, H. (2024). *Taking Stock of Progress A Compilation of Universal Social Security Schemes in Low- and Middle-income Countries.* London: Development Pathways.

Singh, R. K. (2017). MGNREGA: The History of an Idea. *Proceedings of the Indian History Congress* 78: 1070–7.

Slim, H. (2020). *We Need a New Way to Think About Aid.* Blavatnik School of Government, Oxford University Blog. 2 September 2020. Oxford: Oxford University.

Subbarao, K., del Ninno, C., Andrews, C. and Rodriguez-Alas, C. (2013). *Public Works as a Safety Net: Design, Evidence and Implementation.* Washington DC: World Bank.

Subramanian, A. and Roy, D. (2001). *Who Can Explain The Mauritian Miracle: Meade, Romer, Sachs or Rodrik?* International Monetary Fund Working Paper 2001/116. Washington DC: International Monetary Fund.

Tafere, Y. and Woldehanna, E. (2012). *Beyond Food Security: Transforming the Productive Safety Net Programme in Ethiopia for the Well-being of Children.* Working Paper No. 83. Young Lives, Oxford Department of International Development, University of Oxford. Oxford: Oxford University.

Tanzania Social Action Fund (2019). *Evaluating Tanzania's Productive Social Safety Net: Findings from the Midline Survey.* Dar es Salaam: Tanzania Social Action Fund.

Townsend, P. ed. (2009). *Building Decent Societies: Rethinking the Role of Social Security in Development.* Geneva: International Labour Office. London: Palgrave Macmillan.

Ulriksen, M. S. (2016). *The Development of Social Protection Policies in Tanzania, 2000–2015.* Working Paper 377. Centre for Social Science Research, University of Cape Town. Cape Town South Africa: University of Cape Town.

UN Women (2021). *Women and Girls Left Behind: Glaring Gaps in Pandemic Responses.* New York: UN Women.

UNICEF (2019a). *Universal Child Benefit Case Studies: The Experience of Iran.* New York: UNICEF.

UNICEF (2019b). *Universal Child Benefit Case Studies: The Experience of Mongolia.* New York: UNICEF.

UNICEF (2019c). *Universal Child Grant Benefit Studies: The Experience of the Kyrgyz Republic.* New York: UNICEF.

UNICEF (2021). *Social Protection & Gender Equality Outcomes Across the Life-Course: A Synthesis of Recent Findings.* New York: UNICEF.

United Nations (1967). *International Covenant on Economic, Social and Cultural Rights.* New York: United Nations.

United Nations (2015). *Universal Declaration of Human Rights.* New York: United Nations.

United Nations (2020). *Secretary-General's Nelson Mandela Lecture: Tackling the Inequality Pandemic: A New Social Contract for a New Era.* 18 July 2020. New York: United Nations.

United Nations (2021a). *Secretary-General's Policy Brief Investing in Jobs and Social Protection for Poverty Eradication and a Sustainable Recovery.* New York: United Nations.

United Nations (2021b). *UN Secretary-General Calls for Accelerated Action on Jobs and Social Protection.* United Nations Press Release. International Labour Organisation newsroom. 28 September 2021. Geneva: International Labour Organisation.

United Nations (2022). *Global Impact of the War in Ukraine: Billions of People Face the Greatest Cost-of-living Crisis in a Generation.* Brief 2. UN Global Crisis Response Group on Food, Energy and Finance. New York: United Nations.

United Nations Department of Economic and Social Affairs (UNDESA) and the International Labour Organisation (ILO). *Global Research on Governance and Social Protection: Case Studies on Mauritius and Fiji.* New York: United Nations Department of Economic and Social Affairs (UNDESA). Geneva: International Labour Organisation.

United Nations Development Programme (UNDP) (2020). *Gender-Based Violence and COVID-19.* United Nations Development Programme Brief. New York: United Nations Development Programme (UNDP).

United Nations Economic and Social Commission for Asia and the Pacific (ESCAP) and Development Pathways (2022). *Towards Universal Social Protection.* Bangkok: United Nations Economic and Social Commission for Asia and the Pacific (ESCAP).

United Nations Office of the High Representative for the Least Developed Countries, Landlocked Developing Countries and Small Island Developing States (UN-OHRLLS) (2022). *United Nations Doha Programme of Action for the Least Developed Countries 2022-2031.* New York: United Nations Office of the High Representative for the Least Developed Countrues, Landlocked Developing Countries and Small Island Developing States (UN-OHRLLS).

United Nations Permanent Forum on Indigenous Issues (2009). *Mission to Paraguay: Report and Recommendations.* New York: United Nations Permanent Forum on Indigenous Issues.

United Nations Research Institute for Social Development (UNRISD) (2010). *Why Care Matters for Social Development.* Research and Policy Brief 9. Geneva: United Nations Research Institute for Social Development (UNRISD).

University of Sussex (2018). *The Mahatma Gandhi National Rural Employment Guarantee Scheme (MGNREGS): Boosting Productivity and Agricultural Wages in India.* Falmer: University of Sussex.

van Stolk, C. and Tesliuc, E. D. (2010). *Toolkit on Tackling Error, Fraud and Corruption in Social Protection Programs.* Social Protection Discussion Paper 1002. Washington DC: World Bank.

Walker, H. (2015). Joy within Tranquility: Amazonian Urarina Styles of Happiness. *Hau: Journal of Ethnographic Theory* 5 (3): 177–96.

White, P., Hodges, A. and Greenslade, M. (2013). *Guidance on Measuring and Maximising Value for Money in Social Transfer Programmes – Second Edition.* London: Department for International Development (DFID), Government of UK.

White, P., Hodges, A. and Greenslade, M. (2015). *Measuring and Maximising the Value for Money of Social Protection Systems.* London: Department for International Development (DFID), Government of UK.

Widjaja,, M. (2009). *An Economic and Social Review on Indonesian Direct Cash Transfer Program to Poor Families Year 2005.* Department of Economics and Institute of Economic and Social Research, University of Indonesia. Jakarta: University of Indonesia.

William Senior, N. and Chadwick, E. (1834). *Poor Law Commissioners' Report of 1834.* Royal Commission into the Operation of the Poor Laws, UK. London: His Majesty's Stationery Office.

Willmore, L. (2003). *Universal Pensions in Mauritius: Lessons for the Rest of Us.* Discussion Paper 32. New York: United Nations Department of Economic and Social Affairs (UNDESA).

Willmore, L. (2007). *Universal Pensions for Developing Countries.* World Development 35 (1): 24–51.

Wolf, E. R. (2010). *Europe and the People Without History.* Berkeley USA: University of California Press.

Wollburg, C., Steinert, J. I., Reeves, A. and Nye, E. (2023). *Do cash transfers alleviate common mental disorders in low- and middle-income countries? A systematic review and meta-analysis.* PloS ONE 18 (2): article e0281283.

World Bank (2004). *Mauritius: Modernizing an Advanced Pension System.* Washington DC: World Bank.

World Bank (2006). *World Bank and the Government of Turkey Organize 3rd International Conference on Conditional Cash Transfers.* Press Release. 26 June 2006. Washington DC: World Bank.

World Bank (2010). *Nepal Public Expenditure Review.* Washington DC: World Bank.

World Bank (2011a). *Assessment of the Social Protection System in Fiji and Recommendations for Policy Changes.* Washington DC: World Bank.

World Bank (2011b). *Republic of Fiji Poverty Trends, Profiles and Small Area Estimation (Poverty Maps) in Republic of Fiji (2003–2009).* Washington DC: World Bank.

World Bank (2011c). *Program Keluarga Harapan: Main Findings from the Impact Evaluation of Indonesia's Pilot Household Conditional Cash Transfer Program.* Jakarta: World Bank.

World Bank (2012a). *BLT Temporary Unconditional Cash Transfer.* Jakarta: World Bank.

World Bank (2012b). *Project Appraisal Document on a Proposed Credit in the Amount of SDR 141.9 Million (US$220 Million Equivalent) to the United Republic of Tanzania for a Productive Social Safety Net Project.* Washington DC: World Bank.

World Bank (2012c). *Resilience, Equity and Opportunity: Social Protection and Labor Strategy.* Washington DC: World Bank.

World Bank (2014). *World Bank and Education in Indonesia.* World Bank Brief. 1 September 2014. Washington DC: World Bank.

World Bank (2016). *Project Appraisal Document on a Proposed Credit in the Amount of SDR 107.6 Million (US$150 Million Equivalent) to Nepal for a Strengthening Systems for Social protection and Civil Registration Project.* Washington DC: World Bank.

World Bank (2017a). *Indonesia Social Assistance Reform Program: Technical Assessment.* Washington DC: World Bank.

World Bank (2017b). *Kenya - National Safety Net Program for Results: Additional Financing and Restructuring Project Paper.* Washington DC: World Bank.

World Bank (2017c). *Program Appraisal Document on a Proposed Loan in the Amount of US$200 Millions to the Republic of Indonesia for a Social Assistance Reform Program.* Washington DC: World Bank.

World Bank (2017d). *World Bank Approves Financing to Expand Indonesia's Social Assistance Program.* Press Release. 9 May 2017. Washington DC: World Bank.

World Bank (2017e). *Zanzibar Poverty Assessment.* Washington DC: World Bank.

World Bank (2018a). *Country Partnership Framework for Nepal for the Period FY2019-FY2023.* Washington DC: World Bank.

World Bank (2018b). *The State of Social Safety Nets 2018.* Washington DC: World Bank.

World Bank (2019a). *Implementation Completion and Results Report on Three Credits to the Republic of Rwanda for a Social Protection System.* Washington DC: World Bank.

World Bank (2019b). *Project Appraisal Document on a Proposed Credit in the Amount of Euro 215.9 Million (US$250 Million Equivalent) to the Republic of Kenya for the Kenya Social and Economic Inclusion Project*. Washington DC: World Bank.

World Bank (2019c). *Project Appraisal Document on a Proposed Credit in the Amount of SDR 323.7 Million (US$450.0 Million Equivalent) to the United Republic of Tanzania for the Productive Social Safety Net Project II*. Washington DC: World Bank.

World Bank (2019d). *Project Appraisal Document on a Proposed Grant in the Amount of SDT 97.1 Million (US$125 Million Equivalent) and a Trust Fund Grant in the Amount of US$17 Million from the Global Risk Financing Facility to the Republic of Malawi*. Washington DC: World Bank.

World Bank (2019e). *World Bank Approves $142 Million to Support Resilient Livelihoods in Malawi*. Press release. 12 December 2019. Washington DC: World Bank.

World Bank (2019f). *World Development Report: The Changing Nature of Work*. World Bank: Washington DC.

World Bank (2020a). *Implementation Completion and Results Report: Tanzania Productive Social Safety Net*. Washington DC: World Bank.

World Bank (2020b). *Investing in People: Social Protection for Indonesia's 2045 Vision*. Jakarta: World Bank Indonesia.

World Bank (2021a). *Mauritius: Through the Eye of a Perfect Storm – Coming Back Stronger from the COVID Crisis*. Country Economic Memorandum. Washington DC: World Bank.

World Bank (2021b). *Nepal Social Protection: Review of Public Expenditure and Assessment of Social Assistance Programs*. Washington DC: World Bank. Foreign, Commonwealth and Development Office, Government of UK.

World Bank (2021c). *World Bank Approves Support to Strengthen Health Insurance, Improve Quality of Health Care in Indonesia*. Press release. 16 December 2021. Washington DC: World Bank.

World Bank (2022a). *Charting a Course Towards Universal Social Protection: Equity, Resilience and Opportunity for All*. Washington DC: World Bank.

World Bank (2022b). *Project Appraisal Document on a proposed credit in the amount of SDR 57.4 million (US$80 equivalent) and a Grant from Papua New Guinea and Pacific Islands Umbrella Facility in the Amount of US$10 Million to the Independent State of Papua New Guinea for a Child Nutrition and Social Protection Project*. Washington DC: World Bank.

World Bank (2022c). *Project Paper on a Proposed Second Additional Loan in the Amount of US $350 Million to the Hashemite Kingdom of Jordan for a Jordan Emergency Cash Transfer COVID-19 Response Project*. Washington DC: World Bank.

World Bank (2023a). *Developing Countries Paid Record $443.5 Billion on Public Debt in 2022*. Press release. 13 December 2023. Washington DC: World Bank.

World Bank (2023b). *Frequently Asked Questions about the World Bank's Support for Countries Towards Universal Social Protection*. World Bank Brief. 13 October 2023. Washington DC: World Bank.

World Bank (2023c). *Kenya Social Protection and Jobs Public Expenditure Review*. Washington DC: World Bank.

World Bank (2023d). *National Uganda Social Action Fund: Project Information Document*. Washington DC: World Bank.

World Bank (2024a). *A Better Bank for a Better World: Annual Report 2024*. Washington DC: World Bank.

World Bank (2024b) *Rethinking Social Protection in South Asia: Toward Progressive Universalism*. World Bank: Washington DC.

World Bank (2025). *State of Social Protection Report 2025: The 2-Billion Person Challenge*. Washington DC: World Bank.

World Bank and Asian Development Bank (2021). *Climate Risk Country Profile: Indonesia*. Washington DC: World Bank.

Yoshino, C. A., Sidney-Annerstedt, K., Wingfield, T., Kirubi, B., Viney, K., Boccia, D. and Atkins, S. (2023). *Experiences of Conditional and Unconditional Cash Transfers Intended for Improving Health Outcomes and Health Service Use: A Qualitative Evidence Synthesis*. Cochrane Database of Systematic Reviews. Hoboken: John Wiley and Sons.

ACKNOWLEDGEMENTS

I thank Stephen Kidd for his participation in this book amidst his very busy schedule, including in interviews and comments on drafts, and his partner Sandra for all of her warmth and support. I thank all I have interviewed – and been inspired by – particularly the sadly missed Michael Cichon and Philip White, whose warmth, reliability and commitment to universal social protection ran to the end of their lives. Some interviewees wished to remain anonymous. Others include Tareq Abuelhaj, Steve Barrett, Smart Daniel, Dr Dilli Raj Khanal, Sri Kusumastuti Rahayu, Mary Nyagato, Isabel Ortiz, Posh Raj Pandey, Daisy Sibun, David Tumwesigye and Bernie Wyler. I thank my partner Sarah for her daily advice and endless suggestions, and for tolerating me all of those times I rejected an idea only to quietly implement it the next day. For giving encouragement when confidence flagged I thank Patricia Hand, the first to read draft text and say 'Keep going'; Gunnel Axelsson Nycander from Act Church of Sweden, who was the first to read a complete draft and who encouraged me and secured funding from Act Church of Sweden for the book to be open access, and her colleague Karin Hugsen; and Holly Seglah, who also provided great encouragement on the first draft. But of course any errors in the text are mine alone. I also thank Luiz Vieira and Amy McShane from the Bretton Woods Project, who published the book's main messages on their excellent website, funded me to present them in person at the 2024 World Bank and IMF Spring Meetings in Washington DC and who provided funding for the book launch. I thank Lena Simet from Human Rights Watch, for all of her unwavering support throughout. And I thank the wonderful group of over ninety economic justice, human rights and faith-based organizations from all over the world who have joined forces to advocate for the right to social security, which has encouraged me greatly in the regular meetings which Lena chairs. For help on pitching and marketing, I thank, apart from Sarah, Isabel Alvarez, Chhani Bungsut, Laura Ulanowski, Rachel Dunachie and Oliver Greenslade. I particularly thank the book's endorsers, whose names you will see, for their vital help of reading the book and providing a supportive quote amidst their no doubt very busy lives. And a special thank you to Charles Knox-Vydmanov, who has supplied much information and data for the book and is always so responsive to emails. The book may not have been published at all if Nick Wolterman, senior commissioning editor at Bloomsbury, had not agreed to meet me in London to provide advice, despite being sceptical of my initial pitch. I am grateful for his support, warmth in communications, and for his later reconsideration of the manuscript. I thank Nick's assistant editors Nadine Staes-Polet and especially Anna Eggers for all their patience and support, Tia Ali for advice on marketing, production editor Sophie Campbell and, on the editing side, Winslet Jebasheeli and her team. More widely, I thank people I have worked with on social protection in DFID, especially those in the Social Protection Team who helped me through difficult times in my life and from whom I have learned a lot, though I know they won't agree with everything I have said in this book. I thank Bernadette Cichon, for her very kind encouragement and support after her beloved father Michael's death. And I thank staff at Development Pathways that have not already been mentioned, plus Dhanisha Raj, as well as Tim Burdon at Christian Aid, Anjela Taneja at Oxfam, Navin Dahal and Danny Greenslade, all of whom have given pointers and advice. I also thank Armando Barrientos, for meeting and advising, no doubt knowing he wouldn't agree with everything I said, and for giving me his last copy of the highly influential book that he co-authored, *Just Give Money To The Poor*. I thank my mother Sheila, whose positive response a long time ago to a blog I had written encouraged me to write this book, and Joseph and Ella, for their general support and help, including choosing the cover. And I thank another father, my own, who sadly died before this book was published. He gave us so much and his warmth and reliability, above all, will always be with me.

INDEX

Abuelhaj, Tareq 146–8
adaptive social protection 168
affordability of social protection 98, 113–15
   and COVID-19 58, 81, 128, 147
   Kenya 128
   national debt impact 173
   Nepal 111–12
   Uganda 78
Afghanistan 144–5
Angola 180
artificial intelligence (AI), *see* technology and social protection
Asian Development Bank (ADB) 139–40
AusAID/Australian government 29, 40, 53, 57

Bangladesh 133
   Food for Work 46
Barrett, Steve 79–80, 82, 86
benefit incidence analysis, *see* targeting error
Brazil
   Bolsa Familia 62, 64–5, 67
   Cadastro Unico 130
   Previdencia Social 65

capacity of government
   building 170–1
   and programme design 14, 154
   Uganda 81
categorical targeting, *see* universal social protection programmes
child labour 12
Chile
   Boric, Gabriel 52
   near-universal pension 52
   proxy means test (*see* proxy means testing, origin)
Chirchir, Richard 73

Cichon, Michael 12, 92–5, 101–3
climate crisis
   adaptation and mitigation 1–2
   adaptive social protection (*see* adaptive social protection)
   just transition 102, 173
   shock-responsive social protection (*see* shock-responsive social protection)
cognitive development 12
community-based targeting 42
comprehensive social protection system, *see* universal social protection system
conditional cash transfers
   definition 13
   and gender (*see* gender)
   and human rights (*see* human rights)
   negative side effects 66–7
   origin 61–2
   prevalence 68
   rationale 62
   scalability 67
   value for money (*see* value for money and programme design)
conflict, *see* social conflict
contributory benefits, *see* social insurance
cost-effectiveness, *see* value for money and programme design
COVID-19
   lessons for programme design 167–8
   programme response and global dialogue 59, 140, 167
   and World Bank commitments 38

Daniel, Smart 117–8, 120–2
debt, *see* affordability of social protection
demographic targeting, *see* universal social protection programmes

Department for International Development (DFID) (Government of UK)
  paper on social transfers 2005   9
  rise in spending on social protection after 2004   10
dignity, *see* human rights and dignity

economic empowerment   12, *see also* gender
  Uganda   78
economic growth
  and inequality   13
  and social protection   12, 78, 112, 118–19, 157, 175
education   12, 65, 79
entitlement, *see* human rights
Ethiopia, Productive Safety Net Programme (PSNP)   86–8
expenditure on social protection   163–4
  Bangladesh, Ethiopia, Nigeria   164
  Fiji   35
  Indonesia   59
  Kenya   126
  Nepal   106
  Uganda   75

Fiji
  Family Assistance Programme   31–2, 34
  Poverty Benefit Scheme   34–5
  Social Pension Scheme   34–5
financing social protection
  affordability (*see* affordability of social protection)
  expenditure (*see* expenditure on social protection)
Finland and universality   143
fiscal space, *see* affordability of social protection
fuel subsidy reform, *see* subsidy reform

gender   32–3
  childhood development   56
  economic activity   56
  fertility and early marriage   33
  legal entitlement to social protection   33
  public works programmes   87
  stereotyping and conditional cash transfers   66
  violence, domestic and sexual   12
Global Accelerator on Jobs and Social Protection   101–2
Global Coalition for Social Protection Floors   101, 161, 181
Global Partnership for Universal Social Protection to Achieve the Sustainable Development Goals   97, 165
Grosh, Margaret   38–9, 69, 133, 141–2
Guterres, António (UN Secretary-General)   102, 162

health   12, 66
HelpAge International   12, 29, 74, 117, 121
human rights
  and conditional cash transfers   66–7
  dignity   42, 85, 95, 155, 175
  entitlement to social protection   93, 99, 176
  and proxy means testing   42, 147, 155
  and social registries   134, 137
  stigma   41–2, 155
  Universal Declaration of Human Rights   92
  and World Bank   42, 176
Human Rights Watch   101

India
  Below Poverty Line (BPL) Card   130
  Mahatma Gandhi National Rural Employment Guarantee Scheme (MGNREGS)   46, 85
Indonesia
  Bantuan Langsung Tunai (BLT) Temporary Unconditional Cash Transfer   53
  National Team for the Acceleration of Poverty Reduction   53, 54
  Program Keluarga Harapan (PKH)   54, 55, 57
  Program Sembako   59
  Raskin   55
  Unified Database   54–5, 57
  Widianto, Bambang   57–8

Index

inequality
    civil war in Nepal   107
    combined impact of tax and benefits (*see* paradox of redistribution)
    reform in Chile   51–2
    reform in Mauritius   118–19
    social protection in Brazil   64–5
International Labour Organisation (ILO), *see* Social Protection Floor
International Monetary Fund (IMF)
    Lagarde, Christine   141
    New policy 2022   165
Irish Aid (Government of Ireland)   75, 78

Jordan, National Aid Fund (NAF)   147

Kenya   123–8
    Cash Transfer for Orphans and Vulnerable Children (CT-OVC)   125
    Hunger Safety Net Programme (HSNP)   6, 125, 127, 153
    Inua Jamii Senior Citizens' Scheme   126
    Kamau David   125, 127
    Kenya Social and Economic Inclusion Project   127–8, 168
    Mbaka, Cecilia   123, 125
    Mochache, Susan   125–6
    Older Persons Cash Transfer (OPCT)   125
Knox-Vydmanov, Charles   35, 160
Kyrgyzstan, Monthly Benefit for Poor Families (MBPF)   140–2

lifecycle social protection   32

Malawi, Social Cash Transfer Programme (SCTP)   122–3
Mauritius   118–19
    Basic Retirement Pension (BRP)   119
    CSG Child Allowance   119
Mexico
    López Obrador, Andrés Manuel   49
    Oportunidades/PROGRESA/PROSPERA   44, 45, 49, 62
migration   165

Mkandawire, Thandika   13–15, 32, 152, 154, 175
Mongolia, Child Money Programme (CMP)   139–40, 142

Nepal
    Bhattarai, Baburam   106–7
    Child Grant   106
    Full Disability Allowance/Partial Disability Allowance   105–6
    Senior Citizen Allowance   105–6
    Single Women and Widows Allowance   105–6

Oman   146–8
Ortiz, Isabel   26, 96–8, 103, 151–2, 181

paradox of redistribution   14–15, 50, 112
Paris Declaration on Aid Effectiveness   174
Philippines, Pantawid Pamilyang Pilipino Programme (4Ps)   45, 66
political economy of social protection
    donor depoliticization of decision-making   152–5
    (low) government financing of productive safety nets   88, 122–3
    political support for poverty targeting and universal schemes   44–50
    social contract   59, 109–10
poverty targeting
    history in World Bank   156
    in a universal system   44–5, 96
productive safety net, *see* public works programmes
protests, *see* social conflict
proxy means testing
    administrative cost   43
    definition   30
    errors in targeting (*see* targeting error)
    history in World Bank   38–40
    origin   38
    prevalence   51
    and results and value for money agenda   160
    value for money (*see* value for money and programme design)

public works programmes
   and children   87
   donor support for workfare   89
   history   83–4
   labour intensive infrastructure   84
   productive safety net   79, 86–7, 121
   value for money (*see* value for money and programme design)
   and women (*see* gender)
   workfare prevalence   84

Raj Pandey, Posh   111–12
Ravallion, Martin   40–1, 151, 158
Rwanda, Vision 2020 Umurenge Programme (VUP)   86–7

Samson, Michael   15, 63
shock-responsive social protection   168
single registries   129
social conflict
   and proxy means testing   43–4, 53, 55, 142, 144–6
   and universal schemes   118–19, 143–4, 146
social contract, *see* political economy of social protection
social insurance   7, 61, 100
Social Protection Floor
   development   91–6
   impact   101–4
   and World Bank   96–100
social protection system, *see* universal social protection system
social registries
   administrative cost   132–3
   coverage   134–5
   and COVID-19   137
   definition and rationale   129–30
   dynamic inclusion   131–2
   errors in targeting (*see* targeting error)
   history in World Bank   130–1
   prevalence   131, 133
   and universal programmes   135
   value for money (*see* value for money and programme design)
Sri Kusumastuti Rahayu   58–60
stigma, *see* human rights and stigma

subsidy reform
   Indonesia   53–4
   Iran   146
   Sudan   166
   Syria   145–6
Sudan, Sudan Family Support Programme (SFSP)   166
Sweden and universality   13
Syria
   Abdel Razzaq Al Dardarian, Abdallah   144–5
   National Social Assistance Fund (NSAF)   145–6

Tanzania, Productive Social Safety Net (PSSN)   121–2
targeting error
   benefit incidence analysis   183–4
   proxy means testing   30, 40–1, 131
   social registries   131
   universal schemes   41
technology and social protection   154–5
Tumwesigye, David   77–8, 80–2

Uganda
   Bbumba, Syda   74
   Kabahenda Rwabuhoro, Flavia   77
   Kasaija, Stephen   75
   Northern Uganda Social Action Fund (NUSAF)   79
   Senior Citizens' Grant (SCG)   75–9, 81–2
United Nations Children's Fund (UNICEF)   91, 96, 98, 110, 123, 139
universal basic income (UBI)   166
Universal Social Protection Initiative (ILO and World Bank)   97
universal social protection programmes
   affordability (*see* affordability of social protection)
   categorical targeting   100
   cost relative to poverty-targeted schemes   6, 43, 49–50
   demographic targeting   40, 42
   donor support   48
   errors in targeting (*see* targeting error)
   prevalence   44, 46–8
   value for money (*see* value for money and programme design)

universal social protection system   6–7, 32, 45, 95–6

value for money and programme design   14, 42, 50–1, 80, 160
   conditional cash transfers   57, 65–6, 68
   proxy means testing   36, 40–1
   public works   86, 88

White, Philip   39–40, 50–1
women and girls, *see* gender
work incentives   78–9
workfare, *see* public works programmes
World Bank
   financing of social protection   38
   lesson learning   158–9
   loan culture   150–2
   Performance-Based Conditions (previously Disbursement Linked Indicators)   135
   progressive universalism   99
   resources   38
   Social Risk Management   61–2
World Food Programme (WFP)   125
   Food Assistance for Assets   89
Wyler, Bernie   77, 166

Zambia, Social Cash Transfer (SCT)   49
Zanzibar
   Salum Mohamed, Khalid   118, 120
   Veerasamy, Anbanaden   120
   Zanzibar Universal Pension Scheme (ZUPS)   120